EQUAL PAY IN EUROPE?

ILO Studies
Series Standing Order ISBN 0–333–71118–1
(*outside North America only*)

You can receive future titles in this series as they are published by placing a standing order. Please contact your bookseller or, in case of difficulty, write to us at the address below with your name and address, the title of the series and the ISBN quoted above.

Customer Services Department, Macmillan Distribution Ltd
Houndmills, Basingstoke, Hampshire RG21 6XS, England

Equal Pay in Europe?

Closing the Gender Wage Gap

Jill Rubery
Professor of Comparative Employment Systems
Manchester School of Management
University of Manchester
Institute of Science and Technology

with Francesca Bettio, Marilyn Carroll, Colette Fagan, Damian Grimshaw, Friederike Maier, Sigrid Quack and Paola Villa

A study prepared for the
International Labour Office

First published in Great Britain 1998 by
MACMILLAN PRESS LTD
Houndmills, Basingstoke, Hampshire RG21 6XS and London
Companies and representatives throughout the world

A catalogue record for this book is available from the British Library.

ISBN 0–333–71604–3

First published in the United States of America 1998 by
ST. MARTIN'S PRESS, INC.,
Scholarly and Reference Division,
175 Fifth Avenue, New York, N.Y. 10010

ISBN 0–312–21129–5

Library of Congress Cataloging-in-Publication Data
Rubery, Jill.
Equal pay in Europe? : closing the gender wage gap / Jill Rubery
with Francesca Bettio ... [et al.].
p. cm.
"A study prepared for the International Labour Office."
Includes bibliographical references and index.
ISBN 0–312–21129–5 (cloth)
1. Wages—Women—Europe. 2. Pay equity—Europe. 3. Wages—Women–
–Europe—Case studies. I. International Labour Office. II. Title.
HD6061.2.E85R8 1998
331.2'150'094—dc21 97–37275
CIP

---

10 9 8 7 6 5 4 3 2 1
07 06 05 04 03 02 01 00 99 98

Printed and bound in Great Britain by
Antony Rowe Ltd, Chippenham, Wiltshire

Contents

List of Tables

List of Figures and Charts

Preface

Since its establishment the ILO has been pursuing the objective of ensuring respect for the principle of equal remuneration, as an important aspect of its mandate of promoting social justice. The preamble of the ILO Constitution, dating from 1919, retained among those conditions 'urgently requiring improvement' the one according to which men and women should receive 'equal remuneration for work of equal value'.

International Labour Convention No. 100 on equal remuneration between men and women for work of equal value, adopted in 1951, showed the path for achieving such an objective. It has been ratified by 123 countries, including the three countries included in this study, namely Germany, Italy and the United Kingdom. The ratification of the Equal Remuneration Convention, 1951 (No. 100) constitutes one step forward. However, such a step remains insufficient. As the study shows, equality in wages between men and women is far from having been reached. The gender wage gap is different in the three countries, as are the reasons, to varying extents, which explain such a gap. It is important to understand the reasons for this gap, if we are to progress toward reducing it.

Most of the studies undertaken in the field of gender pay inequality have tended to focus either on an analysis of the position of women in the labour market as a determinant of this inequality, or on the quantitative effect of pay policies on the gender pay gap. The approach chosen in this study is rather different. It explores a new line of investigation in analysing how the determination of the payment system and the pay structure may interact with the structure of employment to generate gender pay inequalities. It also explores how changes in different aspects of pay determination procedures and pay administration practices may help to overcome such inequalities. For example, it shows how changes in pay differentials over the years have acted to the disadvantage of female-based industries. Such a phenomenon seems to have been strengthened by the fact that women tend to be concentrated in sectors where the scope of collective bargaining has been shrinking.

At the same time, the study shows how some wage regulation practices may have a positive effect on the reduction of the wage differential between men and women. In Italy, for example, it seems that a price-related wage indexation system associated with an overall decline in the range of wage differentials between sectors led to a narrowing of the gender pay gap in the 1970s and early 1980s. However, the abolition of the wage indexation system at the beginning of the 1990s, combined with other factors, has reversed this trend, leading to a widening of the gender wage gap.

Wage determination in Germany has often been considered as favouring a narrowing of the gender wage gap because of the high level of coordination of the wage bargaining process. However, the existence of separate pay scales for manual workers and non-manual workers, on the one hand, and the concentration of women in low-paid occupations and organizations, on the other hand, seem to throw doubts on such a generally positive assessment.

In the United Kingdom, the long-term trend towards uncoordinated enterprise-level bargaining, in conjunction with a withdrawal of minimum-wage protection in low-paid employment, has had a negative effect on gender pay equality. At the level of the enterprise, the recourse to individual merit pay in many instances, including the public sector, to replace seniority-based incremental systems does not seem favourable to overcoming gender wage differentials.

This study, made up of an overview chapter and nine case-studies, provides the reader with a picture of the situation prevailing in three selected sectors, namely banking, the health sector and chemicals (telecommunications in Italy) in the three countries regarding the position of women in the pay and employment structures. Despite the fact that the three countries studied can be classified as advanced economies, the situation of women in terms of implementing the principle of equal remuneration is far from being similar in the countries and sectors under review. As such, the study illustrates how different pay systems and wage structures, when linked to specific patterns of employment, can lead to different outcomes in terms of wage inequality between men and women.

In terms of lessons for equal pay policy, the overview chapter singles out three areas for particular attention: centralized or universal minimum pay standards; narrowing of pay differentials; and transparency in the design and administration of payment systems. However, it is clear that given the differences across countries, as well as the ability of discrimination to creep into any aspect of pay determination, policies to promote equal pay should be flexible and should take into account the features of each national context. Furthermore, it should be emphasized that changes made to pay determination procedures at different levels, ranging from the national or branch level to the enterprise level, may have implications for the prospects of achieving equal pay at other levels, as illustrated by the examples of Italy and the UK. Therefore, all three social partners need to bear the possible effects in mind when considering pay determination and pay system reforms, if they wish to give real effect to equal pay policy.

The ILO would like to thank all the national collaborators for their contribution to this book, in particular Professor Jill Rubery who agreed to coordinate the group.

Among those who worked hard to make this publication possible, mention should be made of my colleagues, François Eyraud, who was involved in the initial conceptualization of this project, and Youcef Ghellab, who enthusiastically followed up the project in its final phases. He was ably assisted by David Grayston, an independent editor, who helped to edit the country case-studies published in this volume.

Zafar Shaheed
Head
Remuneration Section
Labour Law and Labour Relations Branch

Acknowledgements

This book arises out of a project funded by the ILO, co-ordinated by Jill Rubery and organized in Germany by Friederike Maier and Sigrid Quack, in Italy by Francesca Bettio and Paola Villa and in the UK by Colette Fagan and Jill Rubery. All the organizers of the project were members of the European Commission's network of experts on the situation of women in the labour market and drew on the work undertaken for this network in wage determination and sex segregation in employment. We would like to acknowledge the support of both the ILO, particularly Zafar Shaheed and Youcef Ghellab, and the European Commission, particularly Els Van Winckel, in the development of our research in this area. We would also like to thank the companies who agreed to participate in this research.

1 Payment Systems and Gender Pay Differentials: Some Societal Effects

Jill Rubery, Francesca Bettio, Colette Fagan Friederike Maier, Sigrid Quack and Paola Villa

1.1. INTRODUCTION

Comparative studies of women's labour market position tend to be limited to analyses of women's employment patterns (OECD, 1987; Hakim, 1992; Meulders *et al.*, 1993; Dex and Shaw, 1986; Dex and Walters, 1989). They indicate the degree of occupational and industrial segregation or the relative concentration of women in atypical employment. Employment segregation is the foundation of gender discrimination, since it is through segregation that women receive differentiated pay and benefits and have differentiated promotion opportunities. Yet what is often lacking in these comparative studies is information on the consequences of segregation for women (Rubery and Fagan 1994); similar measured levels of segregation will not necessarily generate the same degree of inequality in different labour markets.

There are several reasons for differences in the consequences of segregation. The first derives from the difficulties of making comparisons by employment categories. Industrial and occupational categories are standardized to international scales, but this standardization does not ensure that like is being compared with like. Similar occupational titles may encompass very different levels of skill and forms of work organization from one society to another, as comparative studies of apparently technologically and organizationally matched plants have revealed (Maurice *et al.*, 1986). Even industrial categories do not provide homogeneous employment divisions; it matters, for example, rather a lot whether employees in the health sector are private or public sector employees. Atypical work categories also have different statuses; in some labour markets part-time work may be used to retain skilled female labour during a period of domestic responsibility (O'Reilly, 1992), while in others it may be found primarily in low-skilled occupations, designed to employ either young people or women returning to the labour market after breaks for child rearing.

The second reason is that countries have different pay structures and payment systems, so that the penalty attached to a particular pattern of segregation will be less in some labour markets than others. These differences in 'penalties' arise along several dimensions. First, there is the size of differentials between different job categories; second, there is the type of payment system, resulting in different forms of penalty (for example, seniority pay systems penalize women who interrupt careers, while pay according to training and qualifications will penalize women who fail to acquire recognized credentials); and third, there are the opportunities associated with specific job categories for pay progression over the life cycle (for example, differences in access to higher-level jobs, or differences in the extent to which pay within the same job category increases with experience or skill).

Finally, the consequences of patterns of segregation for women have to be assessed against differences in the extent and form of female participation in the labour market, for example in the level and continuity of employment careers. These differences may be regarded as a factor influencing women's access to wage income, and also in part as a consequence of differences in employment and pay opportunities.

Studies of the gender segregation of employment thus reveal only one side of the picture; equally important is the analysis of how employment patterns and payment systems interact to create gender inequalities in pay. Comparisons of women's position in different labour markets require consideration along three main dimensions: participation patterns, employment segregation and pay structures.

This study attempts to add the pay structure dimension to the comparative study of women's employment position in three European countries: Germany, Italy and the United Kingdom. It arose out of a small-scale research project designed to look at the implications of payment systems and practices for gender equality. The project was conducted in two stages. During the first stage, secondary source material was drawn upon to analyse the different types of payment practices, and their association with systems of work, employment organization and participation in the three countries. The purpose of this analysis was to consider both the overall impact of these systems on gender pay differentials, and the problems they pose for comparative research. During the second stage, some primary research was done on specific organizations in the three countries.[1] The case-studies were aimed at identifying how different payment practices lead to different outcomes in terms of gender discrimination within similar sectors. However, the first stage of the research raised so many conceptual and methodological issues that needed to be resolved before undertaking a detailed sector- and plant-specific comparison that the focus of this introductory chapter is directed at exploring the differences at country-system or societal-system level to provide a framework for interpreting the case-study findings in the other chapters of the book.

1.2. DIFFERENCES AND SIMILARITIES IN WOMEN'S LABOUR MARKET POSITION IN THE THREE COUNTRIES

The three countries studied can all be classified as relatively developed, advanced economies. Italy has a greater tendency towards a dual economy than the others, with a large share of informal work and strong interregional income differences. Nevertheless, all three countries still belong firmly in the category of the more developed European Member States. Within this context the differences that emerge between them cannot be regarded as resulting primarily from different stages of economic development.[2]

The first difference to emerge is in the size of the overall pay gap between men and women in the three countries. Unfortunately, there are no harmonized earnings data for earnings covering the whole economy, and thus the differences between the countries have to be pieced together using Eurostat and national data sources, which often cover only parts of the employment system. Table 1.1 shows that for all categories of employees for which we have data women's pay is highest in Italy, next highest in Germany and lowest in the UK. Information from national data sources and from the case studies suggests that if complete data sets were available, covering all groups in the formal sector, the position of the UK at the bottom and Italy at the top of the gender pay hierarchy would be confirmed. Some of the significant groups excluded from Eurostat earnings data include part-timers (in Germany and the UK), most private service sector and all public service sector workers. These groups constitute the majority of female employment, but their impact on the gender pay gap is not necessarily the same in each country. For example, part-timers in the UK account for 44 per cent of female employment in that country but earn only 75 per cent on average of female full-timers' pay. In Germany part-timers also earn lower wages, but such data as are available indicate a smaller wage gap (Büchtemann and Quack, 1989); and in Italy

Table 1.1. Trends in the gender pay gap in Germany, Italy and the UK for selected categories of workers

Gender pay gap	1980	1985	1991
Manual industry			
Germany	72.4	72.8	73.4
Italy	83.2	82.7	*79.3
UK	69.8	67.1	67.2
Non-manual industry			
Germany	66.0	66.0	67.1
Italy	..	69.2	*66.3
UK	54.5	56.3	58.3
Non-manual Retail			
Germany	64.6	67.1	70.0
Italy	..	..	*73.1
UK	..	..	63.8

*1988/9 data: National sources.
Source: Eurostat (1992).

part-timers constitute a relatively small but also protected group within the employment system.

With regard to the public sector, case-study evidence from Italy points to a very high relative level of pay for women in that sector when compared with the position in Germany or the UK. For example, women's average earnings in the hospital studied for this project were over 90 per cent of men's, even when annual and not hourly wages were considered. Previous research has also indicated that if, within the industrial sector, data for non-manual and manual workers were combined, the effect would be to confirm the existence of a wide differential between women's position in Germany and the UK (Rubery, 1991; 1992b). Comparisons of manual workers imply a gap of only six per cent, but for non-manual workers – the most important group, particularly in the UK – the difference in ratios is much wider at over nine per cent.

The above information relates to average pay. Another dimension to the issue of gender inequality is the risk of low pay. A European study of low pay (CERC, 1991) confirmed the existence of differences between European States in the extent of low pay among women even though the tendency for women to have a higher risk than men is common to all countries. In Table 1.2 the twin effects of the overall share of low-paid workers in the economy and the higher risk of being low paid that women face are combined to generate estimates of the different shares of the

Table 1.2. Gender and low pay in Germany, Italy and the UK

	% women full-timers who are low paid	% low-paid full-timers who are women
Germany	33	82
Italy	23	62
UK	41	63

Source: CERC (1991).

female labour force that are low paid within the formal and full-time employment sector. Again Italy has the smallest share of low-paid female full-time employees (earning, that is, less than two-thirds of the median wage), Germany the next highest ratio and the UK the highest of all at 41 per cent. These estimates exclude part-timers, who in national data for the UK constitute almost half of all employees paid below two-thirds of the median hourly wage for full-timers.

However, the table reveals that Germany has, according to the full-time data, the most 'feminized' low-paid labour force, with no less than 82 per cent of the low paid being female (even if only a third of all female full-timers are low paid compared with 41 per cent in the UK). It is also the case that the data refer only to the formal sector and that this seriously understates the extent of the low paid among women in Italy. These differences between countries are indicated in Table 1.3 in two respects: Italy has a lower female participation rate (although some activity may be unmeasured in the informal sector) and a much higher share of self-employment.

Table 1.3. Women's activity and employment patterns in Germany, Italy and the UK in 1991

	Women aged 15–64			Employed women	
	Activity rate	Unemployment rate	Employment rate	Part-time rate	Self-employment*
Germany	55.1	4.8	52.3	34.3	5.6
Italy	37.8	15.8	30.7	10.4	16.8
UK	61.9	7.4	57.0	43.7	7.3

*1989 data.
Source: *European Labour Force Survey*.

Differences between Germany, Italy and the UK in women's employment position do not in fact apply solely or mainly to pay structures. Table 1.3 shows that women in Italy not only have a lower participation rate but also a much higher unemployment rate, so that the overall employment rate of women aged 15 to 64 is under 60 per cent of the UK and German employment rates. Germany and the UK show greater similarities both in their participation and employment rates and in the shares of part-time and self-employment. These apparent similarities in employment patterns nevertheless disguise major differences in systems of work organization and pay determination. Moreover, it may not be possible to determine the degree of similarity or difference between these three States, taking labour market criteria in turn; instead we need to understand how within a particular society the system of employment organization, payment systems and female participation patterns interact to determine the particular form of gender inequality. This societal system approach, which we develop further below, has been followed in other studies, aimed at, for example, understanding differences between countries in women's participation and employment patterns. Yet while these studies address a range of differences in institutional arrangements within countries, for example child care, employment law and training systems (Gregory, 1991; O'Reilly, 1992; Dex and Walters, 1989), the differences in the institutional systems of wage determination and forms of payment systems between societal systems have not been systematically explored.

1.3. SOME METHODOLOGICAL CONSIDERATIONS

Interest in issues of pay structures and payment systems and their impact on gender pay equality has increased over recent years, but generally within country-specific studies and policy analyses. It has coincided with a redefinition of what is meant by equal opportunities. Equality is now often regarded as better measured with reference to equality of labour market outcomes, measured in terms of economic rewards and power, and not by progress towards homogeneity of employment patterns between men and women. This position is consistent with the view that it is possible to be different but equal. Furthermore, there is evidence that pay differentials for particular occupations are affected by the sex composition of the labour force; that is, female-dominated jobs tend to be lower paid relative to their worth (Acker, 1989; Evans and Nelson, 1989; Kahn and Meehan, 1992). Even when women are apparently making progress towards greater equality by entering male-dominated jobs, this is often because these jobs are slipping down the pay hierarchy and becoming less attractive to men (Reskin and Roos, 1990).

Research within individual countries has thus revealed the importance of the pay structure in explaining the gender pay gap (Rubery, 1992a). However, possibly because gender pay gaps are found in all countries, less consideration has been given to the issue of whether differences in the form and nature of the pay structure between countries contribute to differences in the degree and form of gender discrimination in pay. This relative neglect of the issue of pay structures is in part a consequence of the greater difficulty in acquiring information on pay compared with information on employment. Standardized data sets on employment patterns can be used, but data sets which match occupational or industrial employment patterns to relative pay levels are hard to come by. Moreover, as we have outlined above, assessment of the reward attached to particular jobs is more complex than can be grasped simply by comparing average current wage levels, although that would still be a useful complement to information on occupational and industrial segregation.

A recent study which did use data on pay structures as well as employment patterns found that differences in the pay structures between industrialized countries were important in explaining the gender earnings gap at the aggregate level.[3] Relatively small gender pay gaps in Scandinavia were found to be the result primarily of a narrow dispersion of pay, and not the result of greater equality in the position of men and women within the pay hierarchy (Blau and Kahn, 1992; Blau, 1992). In contrast, in the United States women were relatively well positioned within the pay hierarchy by international standards, but the wide overall dispersion in pay resulted in a relatively large average gender pay gap. The similarly large gender pay gap in the UK was found to be a consequence of both factors: wide pay dispersion and a relatively high concentration of women towards the bottom of the pay hierarchy. Other studies have provided recent information on the significance of differences in pay structures between countries (Rowthorn, 1992) and on the role of different forms of wage determination in reducing the gender pay gap (Whitehouse, 1992).

These macro- or country-level studies are significant in pointing to the existence of sizeable differentials between countries. However, they stop at the macro level of average wage levels and structures and do not consider the basis for the differences in wage levels. More detailed analysis at the country level of the pay determination institutions is necessary in order to understand the processes by which these differences in wage structures, and women's position within those structures, are produced.

The present study aims to contribute to that endeavour. The framework adopted for this comparative research is close to the societal system approach developed by the LEST school (Maurice *et al.*, 1986). The significance of this approach is that it treats all elements of a societal system as interpretable and understandable only within the coherence of the specific society that is being studied. Applying this logic to the issue of payment systems, we find that we can analyse the impact of seniority or qualification-based pay only within a specific societal context, in which women's participation patterns and their position in the education or training system can be defined and analysed. In pursuing this approach we will be concerned both to identify differences in payment systems and forms between Germany, Italy and the UK, and to highlight their implications for gender equality. Some systems will be identified as being more likely than others to reduce gender pay gaps, but the merits or demerits of particular payment systems, whether seniority, merit or job evaluation, for example, will also be shown to depend upon the particular context in which they are introduced.

The causes of women's labour market inequality can be found in their weaker bargaining power in society and in the labour market, and not in the application of specific rules or regulations. Thus the type of payment system used will not in itself guarantee higher gender pay levels; what matters is the context in which it is used and implemented, including for example the commitment, or otherwise, to changing differentials or reducing pay inequality. Nevertheless, payment systems are devised for multiple functions and objectives, and not only with the establishment of gender inequalities in mind. Thus women may benefit or indeed suffer from trends towards particular forms of pay determination or types of payment systems, where the incentive for this development is not primarily the restructuring of gender relations (although gender relations are still likely to have an underlying impact on the types of policies and developments that are pursued).

In assessing trends in payment systems, we need not only discuss their implications for, and their relationship to, the pattern of gender relations. We need also to address the issue of whether there is evidence within the three countries we are studying of an evolution towards a common system of pay, such that the differences we describe here may disappear over time. A related question is whether in fact it is possible or appropriate to talk of societal pay systems, or whether the main factors shaping pay can be found at the industry or sector level. International integration is increasing and may be requiring similar firms in different countries to make similar adaptations to their payment practices (Quack *et al.*, 1993). This issue can only be explored briefly here but will be returned to in more detail when in later work we analyse the case studies associated with this project.

The discussion is organized as follows. First, we identify the main contours of difference in the payment structures and payment systems between the three countries. Second, we discuss the dynamics of change in payment structures and the validity of the societal versus the sectoral approach. Third, we discuss the impact and the interpretation of these differences in payment systems with regard to gender equality.

1.4. PAYMENT STRUCTURES AND SYSTEMS: CONTOURS OF DIFFERENCE

Three dimensions to the structure of pay and payment systems will be discussed: the structure of inter-industry and inter-firm pay levels; the system of job grading; and the payment systems in use.

1.4.1 Inter-industry and inter-firm pay levels

Inter-industry and inter-firm differentials take on importance for the gender pay gap because of the prevalence of industrial and organizational sex segregation of employment. Women tend to be concentrated in service sectors and in particular branches of manufacturing industry, and also to be overrepresented in small firms. These segregation patterns are common to the three countries studied, but the structure and dynamics of change in the pay structure are quite different.

In the 1970s and early 1980s the gender pay gap in Italy narrowed significantly. Research suggests that the main factor in this narrowing was an overall decline in the range of inter-industry and inter-organizational wage differentials, associated with the system of flat-rate wage increases as compensation for inflation (Bettio, 1988; Rubery, 1992b; Rowthorn, 1992; Bettio and Villa, 1993a). These wage indexation supplements were first reduced in the 1980s and then abolished in 1992, leading to a renewed widening of the pay dispersion by industry and by firm. All firms outside the informal sector are still subject to industry-level collective agreements, although there is wide scope for firm-level supplements. This scope is used more in some male-dominated sectors such as engineering, with female-dominated sectors such as textiles offering few opportunities for increasing pay above the industry level. Moreover, the ending of the wage indexation system has left a vacuum in the system of minimum pay protection, as most industry agreements are renegotiated only every three or four years.

In Germany pay differentials between sectors have been remarkably stable (OECD, 1987, 1993; Rowthorn, 1992).[4] This reflects the highly coordinated system of pay bargaining based on a notion of consensus about both the size and the ordering of pay differentials. However, this stability and this high level of coordination do not imply narrow dispersion of earnings. The German system permits both quite wide differentials between sectors in minimum wage rates and significant inter-firm differentials within the same industry. Unlike in the UK, these inter-firm differentials are negotiated within a framework laid down by and coordinated by social partners at the sectoral level (firm-level supplements may be negotiated by the works councils but under 'opening clauses' specified at the industry level). Industry-level agreements are generally observed by most firms, at least as regards minimum rates; there exists, however, a small but growing segment of the labour market which is not covered by the collective bargaining system because there are some service industries in which no agreements have been established.

In the UK, inter-industry wage differentials are now primarily determined by the outcome of enterprise-specific pay agreements. Industry-wide agreements setting minimum rates and minimum wage increases which enterprises are free to improve upon have now largely disappeared, giving way either to enterprise-specific bargains or more frequently to pay determination by management decision (Millward *et al.*, 1992). Trends in the United Kingdom in the 1980s were towards widening pay dispersion (OECD, 1993), although these have not necessarily resulted in systematic widening of inter-industry differentials, as this depends upon the different agreements made at enterprise level. There is at present no system of minimum wage protection in Britain at a national or an industry level. The only organizations that set legally enforceable minimum wages – that is, the Wages Councils covering many service sectors such as retail and catering – have now been abolished. Compliance with industry-level agreements has always been strictly voluntary (in comparison with Italy, where industry-level agreements are legally binding, and Germany, where compliance with industry agreements is brought about by strong organization and by strong expectations that firms will comply). However, in the UK many of these agreements have now disappeared, and a large number of firms thus have no guidance about pay levels.

These differences between the countries in pay structures within the private sector are mirrored to some extent in their public sector pay structures. Germany has the most coordinated pay structure across the public sector, and has maintained relatively stable differentials between public and private sectors. Italy and the UK, in contrast, have experienced changing differentials between public and private sectors but in quite opposite directions in recent years. In the 1980s public sector pay determination in Italy became more centralized, and public sector earnings rose relative to private sector earnings (Treu, 1989; Rubery, 1991). In the UK, public sector pay decreased relative to private sector pay at the same time as in principle the system of pay determination was further decentralized – although many would argue that in practice centralized control over pay settlements increased (Brown and Rowthorn, 1990).

A further difference between the countries is found in their 'atypical' workforces. This difference relates both to the size and form of the atypical workforce and to the system of pay regulation. The most important atypical workforce in Italy is in the informal sector. Here either pay regulations do not apply, or where they exist, for example for homeworkers, they are in practice not enforced. Taking into account the informal sector tends to widen pay differentials between men and women, as men often work in the informal sector to increase their earnings above what can be obtained in the formal sector, whereas women are more likely to work part time and for low pay in the informal sector, particularly since part-time work is very rare in the formal sector. In Germany and the UK, by contrast, the main form of atypical work, at least for women, is part-time work. In Germany part-timers on short hours are still often excluded from collective agreements, although in practice firms may observe the agreements in fixing basic pay. Thus the formal exclusion of part-timers does not necessarily lead to wide pay differentials (Büchtemann and Quack, 1989). In the UK part-timers are relatively low paid compared with full-timers, but this is due as much to the concentration of part-timers in firms and industries without collective regulation as to differential treatment within organizations (MacGregor and Sproull, 1992).

The implications for gender pay differentials of these different systems for setting pay at the industry and firm level can be summarized as follows. First, there is a greater likelihood in the UK than in Italy or Germany that women employed in the formal sector will be outside the scope of collective regulation. The diminishing scope of collective bargaining has particularly affected women, since they are concentrated in sectors with limited collective bargaining. However, in Italy there is an increasing danger that low-paid workers will suffer pay erosion over the period between revisions of industrial pay agreements now that the indexation system has been abolished. Moreover, only looking at the formal sector may be misleading because of the larger size of the informal sector in Italy.

A second difference between countries is in the rate of change of differentials between sectors and organizations; this seems to be lowest in Germany and higher in both Italy and the UK. In the latter two countries changes in pay differentials over recent years have acted to the disadvantage of several female-based industries. For example, in Italy textile and clothing sectors have benefited much less than engineering from the move to local pay bargaining, and in the UK sectors such as catering have slipped down the pay hierarchy compared with manufacturing (although banking – a sector which also employs a large number of women – has experienced even faster rates of earnings growth (Wilkinson, 1992)). Where pay differentials between firms and sectors are changing, progress towards closing the gender pay gap requires not only that progress is made for women within organizations, but also that female-dominated firms or industries do not slip down the pay hierarchy.

For public sector workers in Italy and Germany the main threat of a deterioration in relative pay levels comes from a general squeeze on public sector pay. In the UK, however, pay levels vary for different public sector groups, and in recent years many female-dominated groups have slipped down the pay hierarchy, while others such as nurses have improved their relative pay. The effect of this can be seen in the outcome of the attempt to implement the principle of equal value within the collective agreement covering local authority manual worker jobs in the UK. This resulted in an improvement in the grading of several female-dominated jobs such as care assistants. However, the expected improved pay for women did not materialize, despite these favourable job evaluations, for at least three reasons. First, the evaluations affected only basic pay, and not total pay (and male workers continued to receive bonuses and other pay supplements (IRS, 1991)); secondly, the group as a whole slipped down the public sector pay hierarchy; and thirdly, public sector pay declined relative to private sector pay.

One common feature in the three countries is the existence of quite wide differentials between industries and organizations, such that there is no presumption in the pay system in the economy as a whole that pay levels reflect relative skill or job content (even where these factors are considered to influence pay within industries or organizations). Specific organizations' and firms' sectoral characteristics and their ability to pay are expected to – and do – influence pay. However, the structure of these inter-sectoral and inter-organizational pay differentials still varies by country. For example, pay levels in the banking sector in Italy are relatively high compared with those in Germany and the UK (CERC, 1993 for data on labour costs). Pay levels in the food processing industry in Germany are relatively low compared with those found in other countries, particularly Italy, while in Italy motor vehicles and office machinery are relatively low-paying industries for female manual workers compared with their ranking in Germany and the UK (Rubery, 1991). Thus there are differences between countries in the wage 'penalty' for being employed in particular female-dominated industries, or in the wage 'bonus' earned by escaping to male-dominated employment areas. These differences do not depend just on the overall size of wage differentials and degree of wage dispersion but also on the particular structure of differentials by sector and organization. This issue of the structure of pay differentials applies not only to industrial but also to occupational pay differentials, an issue to which we now turn.

1.4.2 Job grading

Very different systems and principles of job grading prevail in the three countries under consideration. Italy provides the most straightforward case: there are four legally recognized categories of employees (blue-collar workers, white-collar workers, senior white-collar workers, and managers), but a single unified grading system applies to the first three categories of workers in almost all industries. The allocation of jobs to grades is specifically not established through job evaluation. Job grading is not regarded as reflecting any objective measure of job content or qualifications, but instead is recognized as the result of collective bargaining.

In Germany there is also a formal distinction between white-collar workers and blue-collar workers, linked to differences in social security arrangements. In practice, these groups tend to be covered by separate collective agreements. However, there are further important divisions or cleavages within these occupational groups – between those jobs that require and those jobs that do not require a vocational training qualification. The existence of apprenticeships in both blue- and white-collar sectors provides in fact a form of linkage between the two groups, such that a job requiring apprenticeship training for white-collar workers would not normally be graded below a blue-collar job not requiring such training, or vice versa. The importance of vocational training for job grading in Germany is illustrated by the tendency to use vocational qualifications as job titles (Méhaut, 1992). Thus although job grading in Germany is also the result of collective bargaining and not job evaluation, there is a general perception that the job grading system does reflect skill and job content, a perception that is not shared in the Italian case. In Germany the measure of skill is strongly tied to vocational training requirements, and the collective bargaining process is constrained by these strongly held perceptions.

Nevertheless, the emphasis on vocational qualifications is greater among blue-collar workers. This is also the area where women are less likely to be qualified, and thus this form of grading serves to establish gender differentials. Among white-collar workers there is little difference in the share of qualified male and female workers. Here the emphasis for job grading is on job content, and many female skills and responsibilities are not recognized in the traditional grading structures. Thus possession of qualifications is not sufficient to guarantee women a favourable place in the grading scheme. It can be argued that where qualifications do not adequately differentiate between men and women, other criteria may be added.

Practices in the UK diverge from both the German and the Italian system, and in fact can be characterized as demonstrating the absence of any national system of job grading. There is no formal or legal distinction between blue- and white-collar work, although both groups of workers have tended to be covered by different wage agreements or systems of pay determination (with white-collar workers much less likely to be covered by collective bargaining arrangements). In practice, organizations tend to divide their jobs into a number of job clusters for grading purposes, and research has found no coherent pattern to this division other than that job clusters tend to consist of either male-dominated or female-dominated jobs (IRS, 1991). As comparisons tend not to be made across job clusters, female- and male-dominated job groups are often graded and paid according to completely separate systems. There is no national system of vocational qualifications spanning occupational groups to provide some basis for comparing jobs in, for example, blue- and white-collar areas, unlike in Germany. There is thus much greater freedom in the UK for firms to create job grading systems which vary between and within firms and which certainly do not conform to any national system of conventional hierarchies. Analytical job evaluation is made greater use of in the UK than in Germany and Italy but is often used only for specific groups of jobs, or different systems are applied to different job clusters. It does not normally result in integrated job grading systems.

One example of how this fragmented system can lead to different outcomes in the grading of clerical work between the UK and Germany can be found in the equal value claim lodged by secretaries in the Midland

Bank (Arthurs, 1992). Their case was based on the fact that the primarily male manual workers were paid on a separate and higher pay scale under a different collective agreement. The employers argued unsuccessfully that the difference in that collective agreement, coupled with the previously active support by the union for paying these men higher wages, was sufficient justification for paying semi-skilled and non-qualified men more than female secretaries. The result of this claim was that banks in the UK took action to integrate manual and secretarial jobs in the same grading structure before the issue was finally decided in the courts. Such differences in basic pay would have been unlikely to emerge in the first place in the German context, where pay differentials would not be compatible with the system of paying vocationally trained workers more than those who are not in jobs requiring qualifications. Interestingly, the recently integrated agreement for manual and non-manual workers in the chemicals industry would allow in principle the employment of clerical workers in the lowest grades (whereas previously all clerical workers would have been paid above those grades). This has not happened in the chemical company studied for this project because only qualified clerical workers are employed. In contrast, many agreements in the UK allow for clerical workers to be paid less than, for example, semi-skilled manual workers, and these are applied in practice (IDS, 1992).

Grading in the public sector also conforms to these national systems, with Germany retaining the emphasis on vocational qualifications and distinctions between blue- and white-collar work, while Italy has an integrated single grading system. In the UK the situation is somewhat different because of the continued influence of national-level agreements in the public sector, compared with the private sector where they have largely disappeared. However, most national agreements cover only specific occupational groups, and as a result there is no integrated grading structure covering all groups at the organizational level. One of the incentives for decentralization in the public sector is in fact to provide the opportunity to establish integrated grading and pay structures at the organizational level.

Many different issues are raised by these grading practices for the establishment of equal pay for work of equal value. There is perhaps a paradoxical situation in which the UK makes most use of analytical job evaluation, the often preferred method for the application of the principle of equal value, but has probably the least integrated grading structure, such that the comparisons between jobs tend to be made across a relatively narrow field. Italy probably pays the least attention to actual job content but has the most integrated system of job grading whereby white-collar and manual jobs are placed in grades alongside each other, while in Germany the common system of vocational training provides at least some form of integration between the structures. However, there is still no strong tendency in Germany within the trade union movement, let alone within the employers' associations, to question whether the traditional job gradings reflect principles of equal value (Jochmann-Döll, 1990). Nevertheless, as we have already argued, in Italy as well as in Germany it would be difficult for a skilled clerical worker, for example, to have a lower salary than a semi-skilled production worker in the same factory, but this is a normal and possible outcome in the UK.

Grading systems in Germany and Italy still cannot be regarded as based on gender-neutral principles. In Germany which jobs are deemed to require vocational training and at what level is an important area of potential and actual discrimination, and the focus on vocational training, while providing a source of integration, also diverts attention from actual skills and job content. In Italy job grading is seen as the outcome of a process of collective negotiation, and this raises the issue of the relative power of women to negotiate their grading within the collective negotiation process. The significance of this problem has, however, been diminished in recent years by the egalitarian pay policy which reduced differentials between grades. Moreover, the benefits of the integrated grading structure for women have been revealed in recent years; because female-dominated jobs such as clerical jobs are situated in the intermediate rungs of an integrated hierarchy they have benefited in part from changes in pay structures towards wider differentials, while manual workers, situated at the bottom of hierarchies, have suffered most from the widening of pay differentials within organizations.

1.4.3 Payment systems

Comparisons of pay structures across countries are complicated by the existence of different types of payment systems, which in turn reflect different social attitudes towards work and rewards, and indeed different systems of labour market organization. At the simplest level payment systems are often regarded as primarily additions to basic pay levels, factors to be taken into account when comparing total remuneration instead of basic pay. Closer examination of payment systems reveals complex interrelationships between payment systems, job grading systems and systems of work organization. They do not simply result in additional payments with little impact on basic pay and job grading. The three countries selected here for comparison illustrate this point.

Take, for example Italy, where much greater importance is attached to seniority pay than in the other two countries. This means that pay is related to age and experience as much as to job category. In many cases movement through the job grades depends mainly or only on seniority. Pay comparisons for a particular occupational group, say bank clerks or nurses, across the three countries would present major conceptual problems. While in Germany and the UK some promotion with seniority or experience is likely, it is not so automatic as in Italy. Thus to take the pay level for an occupational group, even if a given number of years of experience were specified, would not provide a comparative picture of rewards from this occupation, as the prospects of moving on to higher-level rewards are greater in some countries than in others. Overall the system of seniority pay and promotion through the grades by seniority on the one hand, and the use of an integrated grading structure on the other, reduce the significance of specific job grading factors in Italy. The emphasis on seniority is both a cause and a reflection of different social attitudes towards employment; job tenure is much longer in Italy and it is considered 'normal' to stay with a particular employer.

Seniority is less important in both the German and the UK payment systems, and this reflects the greater job mobility in both countries and the reduced emphasis on internal labour markets outside the very large firms (Eyraud *et al.*, 1990). As already stressed, pay in Germany tends to be related to job grades, which in turn reflect recognized vocational qualifications or transferable skills. The importance of occupational labour markets in Germany probably restricts the importance of factors other than job grade in determining pay, although it should be stressed that there is much more extensive use of output- and merit-related pay through the grading structure in Germany than there has been traditionally in Italy, where unions maintained strict opposition to this type of pay in the 1970s and 1980s. In the UK, however, such occupational labour markets as previously existed, largely found in male craft production jobs, have broken down through the demise of the apprenticeship system, and organizations are thus freer than in Germany to experiment with more organization-specific pay structures and systems. The current trend in the UK is to reduce the importance of job grade in overall pay by creating flatter grading structures, yet at the same time to increase differentiation in pay levels through the use of performance-related pay. Thus the UK is moving away from job-based pay towards more individualized pay. In contrast to the systems described for Italy and Germany, these are relatively new arrangements and cannot be portrayed as necessarily reflecting deeply embedded social values. Indeed, it is still an open question whether these systems will survive or whether they will be found to have major demotivating effects or be too costly to establish and maintain. However, the opportunity to experiment with very different payment systems derives in fact from the relative chaos of the UK employment system and indeed the absence of strongly established national-level pay practices. United Kingdom payment systems have historically involved a mixture of job-based pay, output- and merit-related pay and seniority pay (with merit pay often also acting in practice like seniority pay). The absence of either strong occupational or internal labour markets provides greater scope for innovation in payment systems, as has occurred over recent years.

The chaotic and piecemeal nature of the United Kingdom payment systems was indicated by the research into pay structures which found that there was no specific coherence to or rationale for the division of jobs into job clusters; this has evolved largely out of gender divisions in the workplace (IRS, 1991). Some moves are now apparent to introduce single pay spines, associated with moves towards single table bargaining arrangements, but in many cases the new integrated job grading structures will be combined with increased emphasis on performance-related pay. These changes will thus not result in the development of pay systems which systematically reflect job content.

The different types of payment systems found in the three countries have complex implications for the application of equal value principles. Job-related pay is in principle closer to the notion that pay should reflect the value of work done than are other forms of payment, but seniority pay in Italy has been an important factor in both equalizing women's pay with men's and providing prospects of pay promotion over the life cycle. If women have restricted job promotion prospects, and perhaps, for example in Germany, find it difficult to acquire further vocational qualifications, a job-related pay system is likely to generate a very flat earnings curve for women over their life cycle, thus increasing pay inequality at older age levels. Similar arguments can be made in favour of payment systems of the performance-related type, for these provide the opportunity to reward women who have not been promoted to higher grades for their superior performance in their current job. But the problem is that performance-related pay also introduces factors that are likely to widen gender pay gaps. First, it is often used to widen differentials between grades, with higher grades having greater opportunities for higher bonuses or increments (IRS, 1991; Casey *et al.*, 1992). Secondly, it is often used as a thinly veiled disguise for paying higher rates of pay to workers who are more difficult to recruit or retain, and this introduces market-based factors into pay structures and not job-content-related factors. Thirdly, there is inherent subjectivity and thus the potential for discrimination in the application of the system.

However, it cannot be assumed that payment systems which purport to relate to objectively measured aspects of jobs do not contribute to gender pay discrimination. Job-related supplements appear to compensate for unpleasant working conditions, but in the German public sector among the 41 occupations receiving supplements for unhealthy conditions only four were found in female-dominated areas. Supplements are more common for working outside than for dealing with soiled dressings in hospitals, and for lifting objects rather than people. Even working-time supplements may contribute to gender discrimination: supplements for weekend work tend to be more common in the male-dominated manufacturing areas than in the female-dominated service sectors (Horrell and Rubery, 1991; Maier and Quack, 1993). These provide further support for the proposition that it is the context and method of implementation, and not the form of payment system itself, which determine the impact on gender pay differentials. Nevertheless, the discriminatory effects of job or working-time related supplements may be easier to research and monitor than systems of individualized and performance-related pay.

1.5. TOWARDS CONVERGENCE OR DIVERGENCE: SOCIETAL OR SECTORAL PAYMENT STRUCTURES?

Major differences in the three countries' systems of pay determination have been described. However, to assess the significance of these differences two questions need to be addressed. First, to what extent is there evidence that the societal systems we have described are moving towards more homogeneous systems of employment and pay? Second, and this is related to the first question, to what extent are payment structures determined as much by industrial or sectoral requirements as by country-specific systems; and to what extent are changes in these structures being driven by the same industrial changes at the sectoral level in each country?

These questions are extremely wide, and only partial answers can be given here, drawing upon both the general background material and the specific case studies of pay structures.

There is some evidence which would support the thesis that country-specific payment structures are moving in the same direction. Italy has moved a long way along the same path towards decentralized pay determination as has been followed in the UK. This decentralization has involved individualized and merit pay as well as collectively negotiated pay differentials. In Germany some doubt is now being cast on the future of industry-level collective agreements, with small firms in particular pressing for more scope for local differences, downwards as well as upwards, in the level of pay that is set. Thus there can be said to be a general trend towards more decentralized, firm-based pay. There is also some evidence of a breakdown in the German system of occupational labour markets; in some sectors training is becoming more firm-specific and the increase in the number of young people going on to higher education is threatening the universality of the vocational training system. Privatization is now underway in the Italian and the German public sector following the UK example. This has already led to changes in the employment status of Italian public sector workers, and a move back to more decentralized systems of pay determination in the Italian public sector is also threatened.

However, similarity in the direction of trends does not necessarily imply convergence. Differences in starting points and in the intensity of trends need also to be considered. Thus the UK has moved rapidly towards a highly decentralized system, but from the starting point of an already highly fragmented bargaining system. The moves towards decentralization within Italy and Germany are taking place within a context in which there is still a widespread system of collective regulation (although the abolition of the wage indexation mechanism in Italy threatens the effective regulation of minimum wages). Moreover, there is little evidence of widespread moves towards replacing the established job grading and payment systems by individual performance-related pay systems. Where individual merit pay has been introduced in Italy it has been largely paid alongside and in addition to seniority pay, unlike in the UK where it has been used to replace existing incremental scales in many cases, including large parts of the public sector.

Turning next to the issue of sectoral factors, we must first recognize that characterizations of societal systems at best provide a simplified description of payment structures at the sectoral level. Some similarities in payment systems can be detected across countries at the sectoral level from the case studies carried out. For example, if we take the banking sector, we find that in each of the three countries there is a relatively well established internal labour market system. Thus pay structures in all three countries are oriented towards providing internal career ladders and rewards, and not so concerned with the recruitment of external staff and specialists. In the chemical companies there is a trend towards integrated pay structures, reflecting the breakdown of distinctions between blue- and white-collar work in this area. In the hospitals there has been a general upgrading of pay for nurses in all three countries. The pressure for the upgrading of nurses' pay also probably had a common cause: as the range of professional and skilled jobs open to women expands, so it may be more difficult for the health sector to recruit able and committed women for relatively low-paid nursing jobs.

However, further investigation suggests that there are marked societal differences in the form of adjustment made to perhaps common trends and incentives. Within the internal labour market framework in banking there are substantial differences in the form of payment systems. In Italy the main source of differentiation is seniority, with promotion and pay rises dependent mainly upon seniority until a certain position is reached, after which promotion is by merit. In Germany pay is largely related to job title, but with some seniority increases within the job grade, and with access to job title linked to qualification and internal promotion on 'merit'. In the United Kingdom job-based grading structures are becoming less important as a source of differentiation, and pay is becoming more linked to performance assessment of both the individual and the unit in which the individual is employed (although distinctions between clerical and managerial staff are being widened by the differential application of performance pay to the two groups). Seniority pay rises have been replaced by 'all merit' reviews.

When we consider the moves towards the development of integrated grading systems for manual and non-manual workers in the German and UK chemical company case studies we find that although the blurring of the distinction between these work categories provides a similar background to this development, the specific motivation was quite different. While the move in the UK company towards an integrated pay and grading structure was to increase flexibility in working arrangements in the manual areas, in the German company it was to increase promotion opportunities for manual workers. Thus similar policies have entirely different objectives. Moreover, in Germany the application of the new integrated agreement is still strongly influenced both by the traditions of separate pay scales for manual and non-manual workers, and by the system of vocational training. It is this latter system which has protected clerical workers' pay in Germany. In the UK the relative improvement in pay for clerical workers achieved through the job-based grading scheme is more open to challenge, and already the manual workers who have lost out because of the agreement have called for a new review of the structure.

If we turn to the case of nurses' pay we find that very different systems were used to deal with a common problem — the need to improve relative pay for nurses. In Italy, in keeping with the general tendency to find solutions other than job evaluation to problems of pay differentials, the pay for nurses was boosted through adjustments to working-time supplements rather than through changes to grades. In Germany and the UK the issue was resolved through the development of new grading structures. In Germany the stability of differentials allowed this issue to be resolved by a new agreement which effectively established nurses' pay grades at a higher position within the overall public sector grading system (although the nurses' pay agreement is separate from the general public sector agreement). However, in the UK the development of new pay scales for nurses and the establishment of a Pay Review Body have by no means provided a stable 'solution' to the issue of nurses' pay. Not only did the new grading structure lead to a massive number of appeals by nurses against grading, but also the value of the new pay levels is constantly subject to erosion because there is no integrated system of pay determination for the public sector, and no commitment by the Government to maintain the relative value of public sector pay. Even within hospitals the greater flexibility which they now have to determine pay rates for non-clinical staff means that internal differentials between nurses and managers, and between clerical and ancillary workers, are subject to variation over time and between hospitals.

Thus the case studies we have carried out, while revealing some similarities across sectors in both the types of employment systems and the economic conditions under which organizations are operating, have tended to confirm that country-specific solutions will be sought to resolve internationally comparable problems.

1.6. INTERPRETING THE IMPACT OF PAY STRUCTURES ON GENDER INEQUALITY

The pay structures and payment systems, as described above, create different problems and forms of inequality between men and women, and also have different effects on groups or types of female employees. Moreover, the impact of different systems must also be interpreted within a societal context.

The first problematic area for interpretation relates to the system of job grading and the associated issue of how access to particular job grades is obtained. The pattern of gender pay and employment inequality has to be interpreted within a general understanding of how the labour market system functions in the three countries studied. In the UK there is a relatively weak relationship between educational or vocational qualifications and position in the labour market. Educational qualifications have been primarily important in obtaining access to employment at the top end of the labour market. Studies have even found that extra education, below the level of higher education, has a negative association with labour market position (Clarke, 1991). In part this trend may have a gender dimension to it. It has been primarily female jobs such as clerical jobs where vocational qualifications have been obtained outside the labour market, and male job skills that have been acquired through work experience; and it is the latter that have been more highly valued. The UK is in a process of change, associated with a much higher rate of entry into higher education, which will probably affect labour market patterns in the future. The pattern that has prevailed up until now is that of much greater flexibility for employers to determine the relative pay and grading of jobs, irrespective of qualifications, than is the case in either Italy or Germany. This has made women as well as men mainly reliant on employer-based employment practices. Interpretation of the pay and grading of clerical jobs, for example, must thus be understood within a social context in which formal training or educational requirements are not the dominant legitimating factor in pay differentials. This contrasts with the German situation where pay, grading and vocational qualifications are closely and hierarchically related.

However, the dominance of vocational training in Germany leads to some similarities with the UK, for example with regard to the importance of employing organizations in providing access to skills and higher-paid jobs. Success within the education system in Germany is not sufficient for acquiring access to intermediate-level jobs; employers have an important role to play in providing access to the initial dual training system and to further education. This role includes not only the allocation of training places (and there is evidence of informal gender quotas in some areas) but also, together with trade unions, deciding which jobs require vocational training or further qualifications.

In Italy the important determinant of employment career path is initial access to a job ladder, given the subsequent tendency for employees to remain within the same organization and to move up a job ladder, often by seniority. Women in Italy are increasingly using educational qualifications and competition through examinations to gain access to more favourable employment positions. However, it is primarily in the public sector that access is strictly regulated by competition and qualifications; where employers have more discretion, educational qualifications may not be sufficient to secure access. Nevertheless, it is the initial entry point that has greater significance in Italy than in Germany or the UK. The problem of gaining access to employment in Italy is indicated by the higher unemployment rate, and also by the higher share of women out of the labour market and in self-employment. A large part of the differences in participation rates between women in Italy and their counterparts in Germany and the UK may be the result of their failing to enter the formal labour market and then dropping out from unemployment into informal or non-employment (Bettio and Villa, 1993b); it is not due to their leaving formal sector jobs, unlike in Germany and the UK where women still quit formal sector jobs to have children.

The second difference which affects interpretation is in fact the impact of labour market participation patterns. This affects, for example, the interpretation of the impact of seniority pay. In the case-studies carried out for this project women in Italy were found to have the same seniority as men in the same plants, or even higher seniority. This micro-level evidence complements macro-level evidence showing a tendency for women in Italy to have relatively continuous employment careers. As we discuss below, this continuous employment path may have certain costs for Italian women, but we must nevertheless recognize the importance of cultural difference in the organization of labour market participation. It is not only women but also men in Italy who tend not to quit their jobs when they have found work with a formal sector employer. These institutionalized internal labour markets tend to provide guaranteed but relatively slow access up a career path for both men and women; the major source of inequality is thus found in the initial career paths that are entered upon by men and women (including segregation by industrial sector and between public and private sectors) and in the problems that women face in breaking through the glass ceiling at the end of the seniority-based promotion ladder. In Germany and the UK there is perhaps more scope for differential advancement for men at earlier stages within particular organizations and career paths.

The final difference between the countries studied is the extent of the female labour force covered by formal pay systems. Here the share is probably lower in Italy than in either Germany or the UK because of the importance of the informal sector. Moreover, men employed in the informal sector may often have high earnings at least in net terms, while women's earnings are likely to be much lower than in the formal sector. Thus in comparing the position of women in the formal sector in the three countries we are not comparing like with like. Women in the UK, for example, tend to be relatively lower paid than women in Italy, particularly if we take into account part-timers' earnings, but this comparison covers a larger share of the female population in the UK than in Italy.

These differences between the countries suggest that when policies and strategies to improve women's position within the pay and employment systems are being formulated, attention needs to be paid to the particular points or areas where discrimination occurs within individual countries.

1.7. CONCLUSIONS

The payment structures and payment systems that we have described as characterizing the three countries result in different levels and forms of gender pay inequality and generate different obstacles to the closure of the gender earnings gap. Comparisons of the size of the gender pay gap between the three countries are hampered by lack of data (see Rubery, 1992b), but such data as do exist suggest that women in the UK face the largest gender pay gap, even when only full-timers are considered, and that this difference is not primarily explained by differences in occupational distribution. The more regulated pay structures in Germany and Italy, with protection for minimum pay rates, have provided a framework in which women have fared better than in the UK context. The importance of the regulated framework is indicated by the tendency for differentials in Italy in the second half of the 1980s to widen again with the collapse of the indexation system and the increase in local pay bargaining. However, these comparisons are somewhat distorted by the absence of good data on atypical workers, both inside and outside the formal sector. Taking into account the informal sector would certainly reduce the advantages that Italy offers over the other two countries, but would not diminish the fact that, within formal full-time work, women in Italy fare better than either their German or UK counterparts.

The other dimensions to payment systems that are linked to improvements in women's pay include low degrees of pay dispersion and high degrees of transparency, which improve the scope for effective monitoring and analysis. Three criteria — centralized or universal minimum standards, narrow pay dispersion and transparency — provide some guidance as to the type of payment systems which should be pressed for in policy debates about how to improve or protect women's pay. These criteria refer as much to the effects of payment systems as to the processes of pay determination, since it is clear from the analysis above that no pay system is unambiguously beneficial for women's pay; what matters above all is the context in which the payment system is introduced. Some systems which have beneficial consequences for one dimension or one group of women have negative consequences for others. For example, the centralized system of pay bargaining in Germany, while perhaps providing protection against absolutely low pay, has also been the mechanism which has generated the high share of women among low-paid workers. Within the manual employment area in particular the emphasis on vocational training on the one hand, and the scope for wide inter-industry differentials on the other, have resulted in a highly segmented pay structure for men and women.

In other cases payment systems may both not transfer easily to different contexts, in addition to having negative as well as positive benefits for women. An example of this is seniority pay in Italy. For it to work to the advantage of women there has to be a labour market system in which women opt for continuous full-time careers. In other contexts seniority pay would add to, and not reduce, gender differentials. However, seniority pay is also closely linked in the Italian case to the closure of labour markets, which has negative employment consequences for women as they have difficulty in securing initial entry into the formal sector. Another example is analytical job evaluation. While in the UK context the introduction of integrated job evaluation systems may provide a basis for improving the relative pay for women's work, in other contexts these systems may be introduced in order to reduce the influence of collective bargaining on the pay and grading structure, with potential long-term negative consequences for labour standards. Moreover, while other systems of job grading such as vocational qualifications may tend to discriminate against women in some contexts such as manual work, they may provide greater pay protection than job evaluation systems in other contexts — for example, for clerical workers in Germany.

It is thus essential to recognize that what constitutes 'female-friendly' pay policies can be determined only within a specific national or societal context. This conclusion applies equally to labour market policies designed to reduce the discriminatory aspects of existing pay arrangements. For example, in Germany and the UK it might be beneficial for women to have more opportunities to switch from full- to part-time work as this would enable them to stay in continuous employment, and thereby reduce the extent to which they tend to be concentrated in low paid occupations and organizations. In other contexts this may be interpreted as reintroducing into employment the assumption that women alone have domestic responsibilities.

Nevertheless, there may be a need to step outside the societal system and recognize that women's preferences and behaviour are being shaped by specific societal conditions or constraints. Thus while it would be foolhardy to consider, for example, that Italian women seek the same work and family trade-offs or arrangements as German or British women, it is nevertheless important to recognize the costs as well as the benefits to Italian women of pursuing continuous careers. The main 'cost' can be seen in terms of reduced fertility (Bettio and Villa, 1993b), a variable not necessarily included in comparisons of payment structures. The argument here is not that there is a universal 'normal' level of fertility, but recent rapid reductions in fertility in Italy and other southern countries do suggest that these countries, under current arrangements, may be requiring women to make a choice between work or children, and that societal systems make it difficult to opt for both (or at least for more than one child and a career). Societal systems where combinations of formal wage work and motherhood are the norm, for example in the UK, do not necessarily provide more favourable conditions for women. In this case women are often confined to low-paid part-time work and even those women who choose the full-time employment path, with or without children, are likely to fare worse that their Italian counterparts.

Thus there are tensions within any societal system and the apparently internal coherence of the relationship between the production system and the social reproduction system should not be allowed to obscure these underlying conflicts, nor the costs of particular systems to individuals and groups. Nevertheless, because each labour market system does appear to have its own specific pattern of organization and path of development, it is important that policy to further women's pay position should reflect the particular tensions and the particular priorities within each labour market. In the UK for example, policy to improve women's pay probably has to focus mainly on two issues: the absence of any minimum wage standards, and the impact of trends towards performance-related pay on gender pay differentials. Emphasis on job grading and job evaluation will have little effect under these conditions, while in Germany the priority appears to be more to highlight the potentially discriminatory nature of the traditional job grading system, which pays too much attention to training and too little attention to female job characteristics.[5] In Italy the relatively minor importance of job grading in determining pay outcomes suggests that more attention needs to be paid to desegregation, to changing the types of job area or career area that women enter, and to breaking the glass ceiling at the point at which promotion by seniority ends. This approach now has to be combined with finding a new method of protection against low pay, following the ending of wage indexation.

Policies to promote equal pay need to reflect the overall system of pay and employment organization and to identify the appropriate areas for action within a specific national context. This flexibility of approach is perhaps required simply because of the flexibility and pervasiveness of discrimination. Regulations, legal rights and monitoring systems are not in themselves sufficient to ensure smooth progress towards equal pay, although each is likely to make a contribution in this direction. What is perhaps remarkable is how the very wide differences in payment practices in European countries still give rise in all contexts to sizeable gender pay gaps. Thus potential for discrimination exists under all systems. In the future even greater attention may need to be paid to the details of how pay structures and payment systems cause gender pay differentials, if the trends in pay determination are towards more individualized, decentralized and consequently more opaque and subjective payment systems.

Notes

1. The case-studies carried out for this project comprise investigations of a bank in Germany, Italy and the UK, a hospital in Germany, Italy, and the UK, a chemical company in Germany, and the UK and a telecommunications company in Italy.
2. It is true that Italy continues to have a lower share of service sector employment than Germany or the UK, but these differences can be seen as resulting from a different path of economic development in Italy (Bettio and Villa 1993b).
3. The method adopted was to rank all individuals by level of pay; comparison could thus be made between the relative importance of the ranking of women in the pay hierarchy and the overall dispersions of pay within the hierarchy in determining the earnings gap.
4. For example, the pay dispersion between manufacturing industries hardly narrowed at all between 1973 and 1985 (14.5 and 13.7 per cent respectively), while in Italy it fell by 50 per cent (19.9 to 9.9 per cent) and in the UK it fell only slightly (from 21.6 to 18.3 per cent), primarily as a result of narrowing differentials by gender offsetting trends towards ever wider inter-industry differentials (Rowthorn 1992).
5. The need to stimulate a debate on these issues is indicated by the research by Jochman-Döll (1990), which found that most trade unions believed the job grading systems to be gender neutral.

References

J. Acker, *Doing comparable work: Gender, class and pay equity* (Philadelphia: Temple University Press 1989).

A. Arthurs, 'Equal value in British banks: The Midland Bank case', in P. Kahn and E. Meehan (eds): *Equal value/comparable worth in the UK and the USA* (London: Macmillan 1992).

F. Bettio, *The sexual division of wage labour: The Italian case* (Oxford: Oxford University Press 1988).

F. Bettio, and P. Villa, *Wage determination and sex segregation in employment in Italy*, Report for the European Commission Network on the Situation of Women in the Labour Market, Working Paper (Manchester: University of Manchester Institute of Science and Technology 1993a).

——, 1993b. 'Strutture familiari e mercati del lavoro nei paesi sviluppati: l'emergere di un percorso mediterraneo per l'integrazione delle donne nel mercato del lavoro', in *Economia e Lavoro*.

F. Blau, 'Gender and economic outcomes: The role of wage structure', keynote speech, Fourth Conference of the European Association of Labour Economists, University of Warwick (September 1992).

F. Blau, and L. Kahn, 'The gender earnings gap: Learning from international comparisons', in *American Economic Review*, Papers and Proceedings (May 1992), pp. 533–8.

W. Brown, and R. Rowthorn, *A public services pay policy*, Fabian Pamphlet No. 542 (London: Fabian Society 1990).

C. Büchtemann, and S. Quack, '"Bridges" or "Traps"? Non-standard employment in the Federal Republic of Germany', in G. and J. Rodgers (eds): *Precarious jobs in labour market regulation* (Geneva: International Institute for Labour Studies 1989).

B. Casey, J. Lakey, and M. White, *Payment systems: A look at current practice*, Research Series No. 5 (London, Department of Employment 1992).

CERC (Centre d'Etudes des Revenus et des Coûts). *Les bas salaires en Europe*, Report No. 101 (Paris: CERC 1991).

——, *Wages and labour costs in the main industrial countries*, Report No. 106 (Paris: CERC 1993).

K. Clarke, *Women and training: A review of recent research and policy*, Equal Opportunities Commission Research Series (Manchester: Equal Opportunities Commission 1991).

S. Dex, and L. Shaw, *British and American women at work* (London: Macmillan 1986).

S. Dex, and P. Walters, 'Women's occupational status in Britain, France and USA: Explaining the difference', in *Industrial Relations Journal*, Vol. 20, No. 3 (1989) pp. 203–212.

S. Evans, and B. Nelson, *Wage justice: Comparable worth and the paradox of technocratic reform* (Chicago and London: University of Chicago Press 1989).

Eurostat, *Earnings: Industry and Services* (Luxemburg: Office for Official Publications of the European Community 1992).

F. Eyraud, D. Marsden, and J.-J. Silvestre, 'Occupational and internal labour markets in Britain and France', in *International Labour Review* (Geneva: ILO (1990) pp. 501–17).

A. Gregory, 'Patterns of working hours in large-scale grocery retailing in Britain and France: Convergence after 1992?' in *Work, Employment and Society*, Vol. 5, No. 4 (1991) pp. 497–514.

C. Hakim, 'Explaining trends in occupational segregation: The measurement, causes and consequences of the sexual division of labour', in *European Sociological Review*, Vol. 8, No. 2 (1992) pp. 127–52.

S. Horrell, and J. Rubery, *Employers' working-time policies and women's employment*, Equal Opportunities Commission Research Series (London: Her Majesty's Stationery Office 1991).

IDS (Incomes Data Services). *Integrated pay structures*, Study No. 509, July 1992.

IRS (Industrial Relations Services). *Pay and gender in Britain* (London: Equal Opportunities Commission and IRS 1991).

A. Jochmann-Döll, 'Gleicher Lohn für gleichwertige Arbeit: ausländische und deutsche Konzepte und Erfahrungen', doctoral dissertation, University of Trier (1990).

P. Kahn, and E. Meehan (eds) *Equal value/comparable worth in the UK and the USA* (London: Macmillan 1992).

A. MacGregor, and A. Sproull, 'Employers and the flexible workforce', in *Employment Gazette*, September 1992.

F. Maier, and S. Quack, *Wage determination and sex segregation in employment in Germany*, Report for the European Commission Network on the Situation of Women in the Labour Market, Working Paper (Manchester: University of Manchester Institute of Science and Technology 1993).

M. Maurice, F. Sellier, and J.-J. Silvestre, *The social foundations of industrial power* (Cambridge, Mass: MIT Press 1986).

P. Méhaut, 'Further education, vocational training and the labour market: The French and German systems compared', in A. Castro, P. Méhaut and J. Rubery (eds): *International integration and labour market organization* (London: Academic Press 1992).

D. Meulders, R. Plasman, and V. Van der Stricht, *Position of women on the labour market in the European Community* (Aldershot, UK: Dartmouth 1993).

N. Millward, M. Stevens, D. Smart, and W. R. Hawes, *Workplace industrial relations in transition* (Aldershot, UK: Dartmouth 1992).

OECD (Organization for Economic Cooperation and Development), 'Occupational differentials in earnings and labour demand', in *Employment Outlook* (Paris: OECD 1987).

——, 'Earnings inequality: Changes in the 1980s', in *Employment Outlook* (Paris: OECD 1993).

J. O'Reilly, 'Where do you draw the line? Functional flexibility, training and skill in Britain and France', in *Work, Employment and Society*, September 1992.

S. Quack, J. O'Reilly, and S. Hildebrandt, 'From national to sectoral pattern? Training in the German, United Kingdom and French banking system', paper presented to conference on 'Production regimes in an integrating Europe' (Wissenschaftszentrum: Berlin 1993).

B. Reskin, and P. Roos, *Job queues, gender queues: Explaining women's inroads into male occupations* (Philadelphia: Temple University Press 1990).

R. Rowthorn, 'Centralization, employment and wage dispersion', in *Economic Journal*, May 1992.

J. Rubery, *Equal pay and institutional systems of pay determination: A comparative study*, Directorate-General for Employment, Industrial Relations and Social Affairs (Luxembourg: Commission of the European Communities 1991).

——, *The economics of equal value*, Equal Opportunities Commission Discussion Paper (Manchester: Equal Opportunities Commission 1992a).

——, 'Pay, gender and the social dimension to Europe', in *British Journal of Industrial Relations*, Vol. 30, No. 4 (1992b) pp. 605–22.

J. Rubery, and C. Fagan, *Occupational segregation of men and women in the European Community, Social Europe* (Luxembourg 1993a) Commission of the European Communities.

J. Rubery and C. Fagan (1994) *Wage Determination and Sex Segregation in Employment in the European Community, Social Europe, Commission of the European Communitties*, Luxembourg.

T. Treu, 'Labour relations in the public sector in Italy', in T. Treu *et al.*: *Public service labour relations: Recent trends and future conflicts* (Geneva: ILO 1989).

G. Whitehouse, 'Legislation and labour market gender inequality: An analysis of OECD countries', in *Work, Employment and Society*, Vol. 6, No. 1 (1992) pp. 65–88.

F. Wilkinson, *Why Britain needs a Minimum Wage* (London: IPPR 1992).

Part 1

Equal Pay in Germany

2 Case Study of a German Hospital

Friederike Maier

2.1. EMPLOYMENT STRUCTURE IN THE GERMAN PUBLIC HEALTH SECTOR

There exists in Germany at all levels (federal, *Länd,* municipality) a public health administration which is responsible for implementing legal regulations. Health insurance and pension insurance are part of the social services, and some departments have functions within the public health administration. The health insurance administration negotiates the funds available for hospitals and private doctors. The health care system is divided into the in-patient system, comprising hospitals and homes for the elderly, and the out-patient system, comprising physicians in private practices and out-patient care services for the elderly, the handicapped and so on (see Table 2.1).

In 1989 about 1.3 million people were employed in the public health system, an area of rapid employment growth. The relevant employment data are not very exact, the only reliable data being on hospital staff (for data problems, see Alber, 1991). Approximately 44 per cent of all public health employees work in the out-patient system (mainly in private practices), and 56 per cent work in the in-patient system; 75 per cent of all employees are female. The health system has a high degree of gender-specific segregation: the largest group of employees comprises skilled nurses and midwives (442 000 – 85 per cent female), followed by skilled medical assistants (296 000 – 99 per cent female), physicians (188 225 – 28 per cent female) and unskilled or semi-skilled care workers (72 000 – 63 per cent female). The number of skilled medical or technical assistants (encompassing a variety of different occupations) is growing: 71 000 in 1989, 91 per cent of whom were female.

Table 2.2 provides an overview of the different health sector occupations according to female employee distribution. As will be seen, more than 95 per cent of all skilled medical assistants work in private practices, whereas approximately 55 per cent of skilled nurses and midwives,

Table 2.1. Current organizational and employment structure of the public health sector

Institution	Type of employment	Type of wage regulation	Number of employees	Women (%)
Public health administration	Civil servants, salaried employees, workers	Law, BAT, MTB/MTL/BMT-G	Physicians 21 705	44
Health and old-age insurance	Civil servants, salaried employees, workers	Single-employer agreements (with reference to law, BAT,MTB, etc.)		
Health care system: Hospitals run by:			878 012	75
– municipalities, federal *Länder*, universities	Civil servants, salaried employees, workers	Law, BAT, KR for nurses, MTB, etc.	507 603	n.a.
– non-profit organizations (Red Cross, churches)	Salaried employees, workers	Single-employer agreements (with reference to BAT/KR, MTB, etc.)	298 707	n.a.
– private enterprises	Salaried employees, workers	Single- or multi-employer agreements (not in all regions/firms)	65 041	n.a.
Homes for the elderly (see hospitals)	See hospitals	See hospitals		n.a.
Physicians in private practice	Physicians: self-employed, salaried employees	Single- or multi-employer agreement	74 040	22
Dentists in private practice	Dentists: self-employed, salaried employees	Single- or multi-employer agreement	38 176	23
Pharmacists	Pharmacists: self-employed, salaried employees	Single- or multi-employer agreement	35 181	56
Out-patient care for the elderly	Salaried employees, self-employed, freelancers	Multi-employer agreement, single-employer agreement, no agreement	n.a.	

n.a. = not available.
Sources: Statistisches Bundesamt, Fachserie 12, Reihe 1 (Gesundheitswesen), 1989; own calculations.
© Maier/Quack 1993.

Table 2.2. Health sector occupations, 1989

	Total number	Women (%)	Total not in hospitals (%)	Public hospitals (%)	Non-profit hospitals (%)	Private hospitals (%)
Skilled nurses and midwives	442 000	85	50	61	35	4
Unskilled/semi-skilled care workers	72 000	63	21	46	44	10
Skilled medical assistants	296 000	99	95	56	34	10
Medical/technical assistants	71 000	91	30	65	30	5
Physicians	188 225	28	56	63	31	6
Dentists	40 805	23	94	–	–	–
All employees	1 329 000	75	44	60	35	5

Sources: Statistisches Bundesamt, Fachserie 12, Reihe 1 (Gesundheitswesen), 1989; own calculations.
© Maier/Quack 1993.

30 per cent of medical or technical assistants and 21 per cent of unskilled or semi-skilled workers are in private practices or other parts of the outpatient system.

Two main areas of employment for women can be identified: hospitals and private practices run by physicians and dentists. In this paper we shall deal only with hospitals, as the case study was conducted in a public hospital.

The employment situation in the public health sector is characterized not only by its highly segregated occupational structure but also by a series of specific problems. For example, although the number of physicians is growing, it is difficult to find qualified medical personnel in hospitals and private practices. According to our assessment, the situation in hospitals is quite serious because they have problems in recruiting new trainees (nurses' vocational training takes place in schools attached to hospitals, lasts three years and is not a real school-based education because students work in hospitals for two-thirds of their working time); the turnover among nurses is quite high; there is an extremely high rate of absenteeism; and the health risks are considered to be the greatest among typical female jobs (see Löser and Priester, 1992).

The word 'emergency' is commonly used to describe the situation in the care sector (Alber, 1991) which is due to the complex and difficult working conditions of hospital care workers. These conditions are characterized by severe physical and psychological stress, unsociable working hours (long night-shifts and a great deal of overtime, and growing care requirements resulting from both the different type of clients (more elderly people in need of permanent care) and technical and diagnostic developments. The organization of work in most hospitals is fragmented: unskilled or semi-skilled care workers at the bottom of the hierarchy are used as 'cleaners and lifters', but even skilled nurses provide only part of the medical care because the work is fragmented, with one nurse giving medicine, one writing reports, one helping when the physicians come to see the patients, and so on. (Demmer and Kupper, 1984).

Hospitals have a diversified hierarchical structure, with the doctors the only group at the top of the hierarchy. Although nursing and midwifery are skilled occupations, there is no equivalent in the skilled manual occupations: in the latter further training may lead to a trade qualification ('Keister'), whereas nurses and midwives do not have this kind of certificated training. However, a career in nursing demands further training, and any such training that qualifies nurses for higher-paid positions is strictly regulated by the *Länder* (Ulshoefer, 1992). Combined with low status and income (compared with physicians and other administrative employees in the health care system), this situation leads to a high drop-out rate: the average nurse works only four to six years after completing vocational training, and two out of three of all care workers are under the age of 35 (Rosenbrock *et al.*, 1992).

2.2. WAGE AGREEMENTS IN PUBLIC HOSPITALS

As the health sector in Germany is quite diversified, wages and working conditions are subject to a variety of regulations, dependent first of all on the status of the employer. Public health administration is part of the civil service and therefore has three groups of employees (civil servants, salaried employees and workers), each with its own wage agreement. Civil servants are paid in accordance with a law known as the *Beamtengesetz*; salaried employees in accordance with a collective agreement known as the BAT; and workers in accordance with agreements known as the MTB (federal level), MTL (*Länd* level) and BMT-G (municipality level).

Hospitals and homes run by public authorities (federal, *Länd,* municipalities, universities) have the same three groups of employees and the same regulations with one exception: there is a special agreement – the KR – for medical care personnel. Hospitals and homes may also be run by non-profit organizations such as the Red Cross, in which case salaried employees and workers are paid in accordance with single-employer agreements, reference being made to the BAT, KR and MTB. Hospitals run by churches are counted as non-profit organizations; their wage system, however, is not based on a collective agreement but on a special arrangement similar to the agreements already mentioned. Since public authorities and non-profit organizations employ nearly 95 per cent of all those who work in hospitals, most hospital employees are paid in accordance with public sector agreements.[1]

Examination of the health care system in Berlin revealed that there are agreements like the BAT, KR and BMT-G in the whole of the public sector, eight single or multi-employer agreements covering Berlin or Germany as a whole, and another 15 single-employer agreements covering, for example, the German Red Cross and the Association of Private Homes and Social Welfare. It appears that most female health care employees are covered by collective agreements based on the BAT, KR or BMT-G; a minority, however, working in private practices and so forth, are not covered. Their pay and working conditions are subject to individual work contracts, and may be worse than those of others.

2.3. CASE STUDY: HOSPITAL M IN BERLIN

Hospital M is one of the 102 public hospitals in Berlin, and specializes in geriatrics, psychogeriatrics, and psychotherapy for handicapped children and teenagers. With 729 beds, it is one of the larger public hospitals in Berlin. It employed 1141 staff in 1993, and is a teaching hospital; that is, it trains young physicians for the first two years after the completion of their university education (this training is obligatory for all physicians). The hospital is run by the municipality (Berlin has 24 municipalities)[2] but is not part of the local administration; it is economically independent without however being a legal entity. Its annual budget is negotiated with the regional branch of the public health insurance administration and (for investments) with the municipality and the Berlin Senate. In its economic decisions it is required to conform with the budget. It is not required, however, to follow the rules of public finance and administration; instead it has its own profit and loss accounting system. The supervisory board of the hospital consists of three appointed members of the municipal council, three elected employees of the hospital and the head of the local administration. The hospital is run by the hospital management, which consists of three members: the medical manager, the administrative manager and the head nurse. The medical manager and the head nurse are appointed by the supervisory board for five years and the administrator for eight years.

Hospitals are organized into three units: medical, care and administration. The first comprises all physicians, the second all care personnel and the third the whole of the administration. Schools of nursing are separate units. (Hospital M has its own school, which is capable of training 60 nurses in the three-year period of vocational training for skilled nurses, and 20 nurses in a one-year period for semi-skilled nurses.)

Since Hospital M is a specialized hospital, it has no surgical unit and no anaesthesia unit, but units for psychotherapy, ergotherapy, logopaedics and so forth. The main parts of the hospital are the wards for the patients.

2.3.1 Employment structure

The following figures were provided by Hospital M's management and show the employment structure at the end of 1991 (see Table 2.3). The hospital employed a total of 975 people (72.2 per cent female), 39 nursing students and two clerical trainees. As in the German public service in general, there are three different groups of employees. One hundred and sixty-three of them were workers, employed mainly in transport, catering,

Table 2.3. Employment structure in Hospital M, December 1991

Employment status	Total	Proportion of total (%)	Proportion of women (%)
Workers	163	16.7	59.5
Salaried employees	792	81.2	75.1
– medical care personnel	404	41.4	79.2
– medical/technical	109	11.2	82.6
– physicians	49	5.1	40.8
– civil servants	20	2.5	60.0
Skill level of care personnel			
– 3 years' vocational training	124	30.7	85.5
– 1 year's vocational training	179	44.3	76.5
– no job-specific training	125	30.9	76.8
Working time			
– full-time	765	78.4	69.7
– part-time	210	21.6	81.4
Contract status			
– fixed term contract	139	14.2	71.9
– regular contract	836	75.8	72.2
New entrants	168	17.2	n.a.
– exits from job	152	15.6	n.a.
Trainees			
– 3 years' nursing course	26	–	69.2
– 1 year's nursing course	13	–	76.9
– clerical trainees	2	–	50.0

n.a. = not available; – nil or negligible.
Source: Case study hospital.

cleaning the wards and technical supply; 20 were civil servants, working mainly in the administrative areas of the hospital; and 792 were salaried employees, 404 of whom worked in medical care (nurses with all levels of qualifications), a further 109 were medical or technical employees (medical technical assistants, ergotherapists, and so on) and 49 were physicians. Of the medical care employees, only 124 (30.7 per cent) were skilled nurses with three years' vocational training, 179 (44.3 per cent) were semi-skilled nurses with one year's training and 125 (30.9 per cent) had no specific training in care. In 1991, the school of nursing was training 26 students on the three-year course and 13 on the one-year course.

Eighteen different nationalities were represented among the hospital's staff, and approximately 20 per cent of all employees were not of German nationality.

2.3.1.1 Labour turnover

As in other hospitals, the turnover of care personnel at Hospital M is high. More than a quarter of all nurses leave within a year, and thus within four years the composition of the care personnel has changed almost completely. Only among the care section's top positions (leading nurses in wards and units) is the labour force more stable. Older nurses in particular have low turnover rates and the hospital even recruits nurses aged over 50. The high general turnover of staff enables the hospital to offer regular employment to all nurses who have finished their training, but not all such nurses are interested in staying.

Although the hospital has no problems in recruiting trainees for the nursing school (the school has a good reputation in Berlin), it is difficult to develop stable employment patterns for care personnel. The management explains the high turnover in terms of the special conditions in the medical care occupations and in geriatric care in particular. Hospital M competes in geriatric care with non-profit or private institutions which provide ambulant care. In ambulant care wages are often no higher than in the public hospitals, but it offers a higher degree of working-time flexibility (especially part-time work and individual working-time arrangements), a higher degree of independent work and a less hierarchical work organization. Some private institutions providing ambulant care offer higher wages and compete with the public and non-profit hospitals in terms of remuneration. In the case of Hospital M, the management's strategy for stabilizing employment is to offer further training and career planning (see section 2.3.3).

2.3.2 Analysis of the payment systems

2.3.2.1 Basic pay regulation

Public hospital employees are paid in accordance with the BAT. Administrative employees' pay and grading are regulated by the general part of the BAT, while the pay and grading of employees in medical occupations are regulated by Part D of the BAT. On the other hand, nurses, midwives and so forth are paid and graded in accordance with the KR. The BMT-G applies to persons employed as workers (for example cleaners, ambulance drivers, housekeepers and electricians). Physicians are salaried employees and are covered by the BAT; physicians in important positions may be civil servants (that is, their pay and conditions are regulated by law) or may receive a salary above the highest BAT group. Administrative managers are paid above the BAT scale.

Table 2.4 provides an overview of the distribution and remuneration of nurses in Hospital M and compares their remuneration with that of administrative and clerical employees.

Table 2.4. Nurses' distribution in wage groups, Hospital M, 1991

KR groups	All employees	% female	Average monthly earnings – gross salary (DM)[1]	In % of comparable BAT group[2]
I	53	73	3670	105
II	108	79	4150	117
III	55	73	3940	101
IV	92	76	4650	117
V	32	87	4360	110
Va	37	84	4740	118
VI general	17	76	5050	118
in managerial position	2	100		127
VII	22	91	5400	117
VIII	12	100	5530	115
in managerial position	3	66	n.a.	
IX	–	–	5510	102
X (head nurse)	1	0	7260	123
XI	–	–	–	–
XII	–	–	–	
XIII	–	–	–	
Total	428	79		

n.a. = not available; – = nil.

[1] Gross salary calculated by the employer: includes holiday payments, Christmas bonus, allowances for shift work and weekend work, special allowance for geriatric care and employer's contribution to social security (unemployment insurance, health insurance and pension payments); employees' net income is therefore 25 per cent lower. The gross salary is calculated for a married, middle-aged employee with one child and some years of occupational experience. Individual employees may receive a lower salary (if they are single, childless or new entrants) or a higher one (if they have more than one child and longer experience).

[2] The comparable wage groups are defined in the BAT, Section 11. No account is taken of the fact that the necessary skill levels and years of experience are equal, for example; a nursing position in KRV requires three years' vocational training, whereas a clerical position in BAT VIb does not require comparable training. Most of the difference between KR and BAT earnings is due to the special allowances and the shift or weekend work allowances that are paid.

Source: Case Study hospital.

The wage groups in the KR range from KR I to KR XIII. The KR is different from the general BAT in that it does not refer to general job descriptions and grading or ranking criteria but clearly defines the position in which a person must be employed to be paid according to a certain wage group. A clear distinction is made between unskilled (KR I and II), semi-skilled (KR III) and skilled nurses, midwives, and so on (KR IV and above). For example, care personnel without vocational training are classified as KR I, while nurses with a year's vocational training are classified as KR III. KR IV is the entry level for skilled nurses. Skilled nurses, midwives and the like are generally classified as KR V (basic pay entry level in 1991: DM1989.07)[3] after two years' employment, and KR Va is the highest level for skilled nurses without any special responsibilities. That level is reached after six years' satisfactory work. After 20 years' continuous employment nurses at that level reach their highest basic salary (DM2823.29 in 1991). To advance beyond KR Va, skilled nurses must have a special task or position. In each wage group the basic salary increases every two years on the basis of seniority, rising to a maximum.

The criterion for entry into the higher paid wage groups is the supervision of other nurses' performance of tasks requiring further training or the training of student nurses. Appointment as a managerial nurse also leads to entry into the higher wage groups. The highest possible wage group, KR XIII, is for head nurses in hospitals employing more than 900 care personnel (in Germany as a whole less than one per cent of all hospitals are of that size, and in Berlin there is only one such hospital).

In Hospital M most of the medical care personnel have less than three years' vocational training and are therefore graded from KR I to KR III. After four years in KR III automatic promotion to KR IV is possible, and this is the highest grade for a semi-skilled nurse. In 1991 37.6 per cent of all nurses were graded in KR I and KR II, and 12.8 per cent in KR III. The high proportion of unskilled or semi-skilled nurses is a problem at Hospital M: since geriatric care is difficult work involving a great deal of stress, it is difficult to recruit skilled nurses.

As Hospital M has no special departments/units such as surgery, most skilled nurses are in groups KR IV to KR Va;[4] the deputy managerial nurse of a ward (there are 19 wards) is in KR VI or VII; and the managerial nurse of a ward is in KR VII or VIII, as is the deputy managerial nurse of a unit (Hospital M has seven units). The managerial nurse of each unit is in KR VIII or IX, and the head nurse is in KR X (in 1991 that person was male). Hospital M is not large enough to grade nurses' positions higher than KR X. Head nurses, who are part of a hospital's management, are poorly paid in relation to the requirements of their job: they are responsible for the whole of the medical care section, including personnel management, work organization and training on a scale similar to that of a medium-sized firm, and are required to have considerable experience and to have undertaken internal further training, etc. The highest possible basic salary for a head nurse is DM5218 (this includes a special allowance for managerial tasks performed as part of the hospital management). In general, the basic salary of a top-level physician will be twice as high, and that of an administrative manager 50 per cent higher.

The gross salary figures in Table 2.4 are those calculated by the employer, Hospital M. The figures show that higher wage groups do not necessarily have higher earnings. For example, nurses in KR II and KR III earn DM4150 and DM3940 respectively, this being due to the fact that KR II is the highest wage group for an unskilled nurse, whereas KR III is the entry wage group for a semi-skilled nurse. Other differences are due to the fact that teaching nurses (in KR V) do no weekend work or night shifts.

When the job requirements of the BAT for administrative and clerical employees are compared with those of the KR, it becomes obvious that the latter are more exactly defined in terms of necessary skills, certificates and further training requirements. The KR covers only three groups of unskilled or semi-skilled employees, whereas the BAT covers four groups (BAT X to BAT VII) and is less precise in defining the skills required and the special tasks to be performed within a particular wage group. The entry level pay of unskilled employees under the KR is slightly higher than under the BAT. In Table 2.4 a comparison of average earnings under the KR and BAT reveals that most KR employees have higher earnings than employees in the comparable BAT groups. The comparability of the wage groups, however, is not fully indicated: whereas a nurse in KR IV, for example, needs to have completed three years' vocational training, a clerical employee in BAT VI does not need a similar qualification. The BAT provides more flexibility in grading and remuneration as it defines wage groups more according to task than to skill level. Therefore, the remuneration of skilled nurses is relatively lower than that of skilled administrative employees.

As all groups in the public sector are divided into four main career levels – ordinary, intermediate, upper intermediate and higher – we can compare nurses' wages with those of other public employees. All nurses' pay groups are located in the ordinary, intermediate and upper intermediate levels since nurses do not have a university education, which is the main requirement for the higher level. Whereas physicians start at BAT II (the entry level for university-trained staff) and top-level hospital managers (both physicians and administrators) are paid more than the highest BAT group (BAT I), a nurse cannot be paid more than a KR XIII wage.

The absence of any general description of requirements (such as responsibility for patients or material, possession of all-round knowledge, ability to work independently) for job promotion within the general BAT is obvious. In the tradition of the German health care system, nurses do not have any responsibility for medical care matters; their work is subordinate to that of the physicians and if they do possess any of the above requirements, this is not mentioned and they are therefore not paid extra. In fact, such requirements are regarded as basic skills which every nurse must possess. The definition of special tasks includes an unwritten (or hidden) definition of different requirements. These precise definitions have advantages and disadvantages for nurses. For example, since the job hierarchy is transparent, every nurse knows what skills are necessary for certain occupations. When a higher-paid position becomes vacant every candidate has to meet the same requirements; consequently, a high percentage of nurses do further training in order to qualify for better paid positions.

Compared with that of other public service employees and employees in the administrative units of Hospital M, medical care work in general is under-evaluated because additional requirements allowing higher wages are not remunerated but included automatically in the relevant tasks. The administrative manager of Hospital M said that 'medical care is medical care'; the KR regulations define minimum and maximum wage groups. Promotion is always related to a clearly defined new position and the management has no room for manoeuvre concerning nurses' pay.

The situation is different for administrative or clerical employees. Since it is possible to define job requirements more explicitly, the management can promote employees by giving them jobs which require more independent work or more responsibility. If the management wants to promote a person within the range of his or her formal skills (that is within the main career level), it can do so by redefining tasks, grouping them differently and giving them a higher degree of responsibility. To upgrade certain care occupations, the management of Hospital M defined new positions: one nurse is responsible for the quality control of medical care, another is responsible for the management of further training, and another is responsible for environmental matters and occupational safety. Since there are no wage groups in the KR for such positions, these nurses are paid according to the general BAT.

The notions of skill and position feature quite prominently in the special section of the BAT (Part D) regulating the basic pay of other medical and medical or technical employees. But this special section does not include a group for unskilled employees, since admission to even the lowest group (IX) requires at least two years' training as a medical assistant (traineeship in a private practice). Skill-related entry levels depend on the length and status of the vocational training; for example, a medical or technical assistant (training period: three years in a school) starts in wage group VII and after six months enters group VIb, while an audiometrist (training: two years in a university hospital) starts in Vc. From the bottom up, each wage group requires a certain period of occupational experience, additional tasks or special training. The highest group is BAT IVa, which is comparable to the entry group in the general BAT for the higher intermediate service (occupations requiring a polytechnic education).

2.3.2.2 *Other allowances and supplements*

As in the public sector in general, remuneration, regional allowances and other allowances and supplements are fixed in collective agreements. There are no performance-related allowances in the public sector or in any hospitals.

The BAT for salaried employees, the BMT-G for workers and the KR for medical care employees contain detailed regulations on night work, work on call, overtime, emergency work and so forth. Employees doing regular shift work receive an allowance of DM200 per month,[5] employees working weekends, public holidays and periodic night shifts receive hour supplements of between 15 and 35 per cent, and physicians working on call receive supplements of 20 per cent. As 90 per cent of nurses do regular shift work, most of them are paid shift work allowances, which increase their gross income compared with that of administrative employees. A head nurse receives a supplementary allowance of 15 per cent, while other leading nurses are upgraded but are not paid a supplementary allowance. Since they do not do regular shift work, a deputy leading nurse of a ward (KR VI or VII) sometimes earns less than a nurse in KR Va doing regular shift work. Most of the differences in earnings between the BAT and the KR are due to the allowances for night, shift and weekend work and the special allowance for geriatric care.

In response to the scarcity of nurses in special branches of the health care sector, a DM90 monthly allowance was introduced in 1989 for nurses in psychiatric hospitals/units and geriatric hospitals/units, and for those working with AIDS patients. Since all Hospital M units/wards are in the first two categories, all nursing staff receive this allowance.

The management of Hospital M points out that since such allowances are always introduced in response to the public sector's labour market problems, it is difficult to abolish them later. Trade unions would never accept a downward adjustment in the event of a change in labour market conditions. As the whole system of special allowances and of automatic promotion for certain occupations did not develop systematically, that is as part of a concept of job grading and job evaluation, it creates some unfair imbalances. This is most obvious in the case of physicians: although their entry level is defined as BAT IIa, they are automatically promoted to BAT Ib after five years' service, whereas other university-trained public sector employees receive automatic promotion only after 15 years' service.

2.3.3 Further training and career planning

As noted earlier, Hospital M has a high labour turnover and it therefore recruits approximately 150 care personnel a year. Vacancies are not advertised: the hospital recruits from its own school of nursing and from jobseekers who send in applications (most of these are women wishing to re-enter the labour market after child-rearing). The hospital invites them for an interview whenever a position is vacant. Although the grading of positions is fixed by the internal job grading system and by the budget, it is possible to recruit care personnel with qualifications different from those formally required. For example, if there are not enough skilled nurses among the applicants, the hospital recruits semi-skilled or unskilled nurses for positions formally graded in wage group KR IV and places (and pays) them in wage groups KR I, II or III. They are recruited on a six-month fixed term contract,[6] the procedure being known as a 'below value' recruitment. Approximately 14.2 per cent of Hospital M's staff have fixed term contracts, a proportion higher than the average for the economy as a whole (5.1 per cent) and for care occupations in Germany (8.9 per cent) (Rudolph, 1994).

If these nurses and semi-skilled and unskilled nurses with regular contracts are interested in pursuing a career in the hospital and in the upgrading of their jobs, they have to attend the nursing school. As mentioned before, Hospital M has a high proportion of unskilled and semi-skilled nurses, and the temporary recruitment of 'below value' nurses contributes to the high labour turnover. To offer training in the nursing school to unskilled and semi-skilled nurses is not particularly attractive. Nursing school students receive a training wage which is regulated in a separate collective agreement; first year DM955; second year DM1048; and third year DM1197 (1992 figures). Attending the school means a loss in monthly income of about one-third – a high investment for staff who will have only slightly better remuneration and career prospects after training.

Higher-paid positions, such as deputy nurses and leading nurses in wards and units, are rare; when a vacancy occurs, it is filled by an internal or external candidate. To qualify for such a position it is necessary to be a fully trained nurse (three years' training) and to have completed further training for leading positions (one day's training a week for one year). Hospital M offers 20 further training places; the training is internal and takes place during working time.

As training hours have to be filled by recruiting additional employees, the number of training places and additional recruitments has to be negotiated with the health insurance administration within the annual budget negotiations. The representatives of the health insurance administration are aware of the problem of further training, and Hospital M has therefore had no problems in negotiating 20 training places and additional recruiting. The head nurse selects the nurses who will receive further training. One criterion is professional experience, taking into account such higher duties as a nurse may have performed (without being paid for them). Since Hospital M has developed a stable internal further training system and offers career planning possibilities, labour turnover in the higher positions is not as great as before. However, as the hospital's supervisory board is responsible for filling important medical care positions such as leading nurses in a unit or the head nurse, and political decisions influence its choice, the management cannot fully guarantee careers within the hospital.

Hospital M offers all other employees a broad range of further training not leading to a certificate or career advancement. For example, there are special seminars for ergotherapists to learn new methods, seminars on medical care for long-term or handicapped patients, general seminars on the principles of care of the elderly, and seminars for senior nurses in care management and communication training. Most of these are held during working time and attendance is counted as working time; only a small number take place at weekends or in the evenings, and these are not counted as working time.

2.3.4 Trends and developments

Since the mid-1980s the public health labour market has been characterized by a lack of skilled medically trained persons in the lower and middle levels of the occupational hierarchy. With a high rate of drop-outs, a high turnover of staff and public health care in a serious financial situation, many hospitals face severe problems in recruiting skilled medical employees. These problems are 'solved', as in the 1960s, by recruiting nurses from foreign countries. The countries of origin, however, have changed: in the 1960s the nurses recruited were from the Philippines and other Asian countries, whereas today they come from Eastern European countries.

Hospital M is not recruiting non-German nurses. Its foreign employees are mainly cleaners, drivers and so forth. As long as the regional labour market continues to provide enough applicants, it is unnecessary to start recruiting in other regions or countries of the world. At the moment, with the high unemployment rate (14 per cent) and the rapid increase in women's unemployment (women account for two-thirds of all the unemployed) there is an adequate labour supply, especially after the closure of the East Berlin polytechnic hospitals.

The other way of dealing with recruitment problems has been to increase the basic wages of all KR groups. Thus the pay rates quoted in the previous section represent the situation after the increase, which was demanded by the trade unions and supported by the nurses and other medical staff. The promotion regulations within the KR wage groups were redefined to make it possible for more nurses to be paid in a higher wage group.

Further wage increases are being demanded. The ÖTV (Gewezkschaft Öffentlicher Dienst, Transport und Verkehr) trade union has started discussing whether the internal hierarchy of the KR wage groups is still adequate for job requirements, and is demanding other forms of work organization and more responsibility for staff. Work organization, particularly in the care sector, should be changed to achieve more integrated care and more group work, and the demanding requirements of these occupations should be acknowledged. New ideas are being developed to improve nurses' status by opening up university-based education and to give nurses in managerial positions the same vocational status as their medical and administrative counterparts.

Notes

1. Only five per cent are employed in private hospitals, where wages and working conditions are regulated by single-employer or regional multi-employer agreements. These agreements are sometimes based on the BAT, KR and MTB, but it is hard to determine how many employees are covered by them.
2. The following description is valid for Berlin only. Since public health care is regulated by *Länder* laws, the situation may be different in other *Länder*.
3. A 'regional allowance', paid to all public sector employees, is added to basic pay. Unmarried employees in groups KR I to KR VI receive DM700 a

month; those in groups KR VII to KR XII DM743 a month; and those in KR XIII DM836 a month. Married employees receive an additional DM150 a month.

4. Both the BAT and the KR have a mixed system of grading. Skills and job requirements constitute the most important grading principle, followed by seniority. Promotion is linked to the number of years' experience in the lower groups.
5. Employees doing regular shift work are also granted additional leave.
6. We have doubts about whether employing such persons on a fixed term contract is in accordance with legal regulations governing that type of contract. However, since the hospital's Works Council accepts this policy, the management may continue it.

References

J. Alber, 'Ausmass und Ursachen des Pflegenotstandes in der Bundesrepublik', in K.-D. Henkel, J. J. Hesse and G. F. Schuppert (eds): *Die Zukunft der sozialen Sicherung in Deutschland* (Baden-Baden) (1991) pp. 73 ff.

H. Demmer, and B. Kupper, *Belastungen bei Arbeitsplätzen, die überwiegend mit Frauen besetzt werden* (Schriftenreihe der Bundesanstalt für Arbeitsschutz, Forschungsbericht 383, Dortmund 1984).

R. Rosenbrock, H. Noack, and M. Moers, 'Qualitative Bedarfsabschätzung gesundheitswissenschaftlicher und pflegewissenschaftlicher Qualifikationen im öffentlichen Gesundheitswesen in Nordrhein-Westfalen' (unpublished 1992).

H. Rudolph, 'Befristete Beschäftigung weitgehend stabil', in IAB Kurzbericht Nr. 3 (Nuremberg 1994).

H. Ulshoefer, 'Frauenerstausbildung in den Gesundheits- und Sozialberufen – mit Perspektive oder im Abseits?', in S. Damm-Rüger (ed.): *Frauen – Ausbildung – Beruf, Tagungen und Expertengespräche zur beruflichen Bildung*, No. 14 (Berlin: Bundesinstitut für Berufsbildung 1992), pp. 97 ff.

3 Gender-specific Pay Differentials in Banking: Case Study of A-Bank in Germany[1]

Sigrid Quack[2]

3.1. INTRODUCTION

In international comparisons the German wage system has often been regarded as advantageous for women because collective bargaining is highly coordinated and has a high coverage, which reduces company- and sector-specific wage differentials. Furthermore, the German training system covers a large proportion of male and female school leavers, which is not the case in all European countries. This study attempts to analyse to what extent these factors have a positive impact on equal wage grading and promotion for women and men. The banking sector is one of the service sectors that offer skilled jobs for women in Western Germany and has been a typical female sector in Eastern Germany. However, it still operates a strongly segregated internal labour market along horizontal and vertical lines.

This study also analyses the impact of the existing wage systems and occupational segregation on women's pay in banking. The first section describes the business and employment situation in the German banking sector before and after reunification. The second section outlines the sectoral collective agreements which set the framework for grading and career promotion systems at the company level. In the third section, an in-depth analysis of a large German bank provides insights into grading and promotion conditions and procedures at the company level. From this case study some preliminary conclusions are drawn as to the impact of German reunification on women's pay situation in the East German banking sector.

3.2. EMPLOYMENT IN THE GERMAN BANKING SECTOR

The banking industry in West Germany was an important employer for women throughout the 1950s and 1960s. Whereas in 1950 women accounted for only one in three bank employees, since 1970 every second bank employee has been a woman. Employment in the industry as a whole has continued to expand rapidly and since the mid-1970s women have also accounted for half of all trainee bank clerks. The proportion of women remained stable when employment growth slowed down in the 1980s. Even then, the banking industry continued to be one of the growth areas in the West German service sector.

Since the mid-1970s banks have increasingly made use of rationalization and job restructuring. The introduction of new technology focused largely on the automation of back-office jobs, which were compensated for by the expansion of front-office jobs in line with a continuously growing volume of business. In the 1980s, however, markets for standardized banking products became increasingly saturated and profit margins were squeezed. As a result, West German banks are now concerned with their economic performance and productivity. For the years ahead, they envisage a 'lean banking' strategy which encompasses more technology for customer self-service, reduction of the branch network and more service differentiation between various customer groups. Banks also want to implement stronger incentives for job performance by introducing new assessment methods and performance-related pay. As part of this development, private banks have continuously reduced their staff numbers since 1992 and announced further reductions for the near future. The unions expect a 15 per cent reduction in the number of jobs in the Frankfurt banking centre, which would be equal to 100 000 jobs over the next few years.

Overall, however, the total number of employees in German banking is still increasing because of the growth of the formerly underdeveloped banking sector in East Germany. Before the collapse of the GDR, employment in the East German banking industry was highly segregated by gender, with about 80 per cent of all employees being female. This was due to the marginal economic role of banking in the state planned economy and the low social status and pay of so-called unproductive jobs. The function of banks in the GDR was more or less restricted to collecting savings from private customers, which meant that most employees were working as cashiers. After unification, the West German type of universal banking was introduced into East Germany. To offer a wider and more sophisticated range of financial services, the East German banking sector went through a rapid process of technological and managerial restructuring. As part of this process, the gender profile of this sector has been reconstructed. The upgrading of job structure, pay and social prestige in financial services increasingly attracted male employees and banks willingly recruited male candidates for qualified and managerial jobs (Philipp *et al.*, 1994). Hüning (1996) estimates that the proportion of female employees in financial services dropped from 90 per cent before unification to 70 per cent in the mid 1990s.

In both parts of Germany, employment is spread through the three major banking groups: private, savings and mutual banks. In 1994, savings banks employed 44 per cent of all bank clerks in West Germany and 57 per cent of all bank clerks in East Germany; the private banks employed 33 and 22 per cent respectively; and 24 per cent of West German and 21 per cent of East German bank clerks worked in mutual banks.

3.3. COLLECTIVE BARGAINING IN BANKING

In Germany, wages, working time and employment security are negotiated between the social partners at the industry level. In banking, collective bargaining takes place at the federal level, separately for each banking group. The employers are represented by three associations for the private, savings and mutual banks.[3] On the employees' side three different unions (HBV, ÖTV and DAG)[4] are involved in the negotiations for each group. There are major differences between the agreement for the savings banks on the one hand and the agreement for the private banks on the other. The agreements for mutual and private banks are nearly identical. After unification, existing agreements were extended to East Germany, where senior bank staff started at 60 per cent of West German salaries, received 85 per cent in 1994, and should reach West German standards in mid 1997.

Despite the rather low level of unionization, most bank clerks are covered by these agreements. This is because most German banks are members of an employers' association and apply the agreements to all employees whether they are union members or not. However, in private and mutual banks there are three categories of employees that are not covered by collective bargaining: managers who earn more than the collectively negotiated wages, part-time workers who work less than one-third of the actual working time and cleaning staff. Collective agreements not only cover wage increases but also contain a definition of grading structures which minimize company-specific differences. Furthermore, collective agreements still determine the greater part of the income of those employees to which they apply (81 per cent plus collectively agreed supplements). Before looking at wage determination at the company level, a brief overview of the grading structure defined in existing wage agreements is provided.

3.3.1 The collective agreement for private banks[5]

The collective agreement for private banks differentiates between nine wage groups for salaried employees (TG1–TG9; for details see Table 3.1). Each of the groups is subdivided into between four and seven levels according to years of occupational experience. Groups are defined according to two different criteria: a list of job examples, and general knowledge and skill requirements. Grading according to the list of job examples has priority over grading according to the second criterion, although examples might sometimes be out of date. The two lowest levels (TGl and TG2) are for low-skill jobs not specifically related to banking, and TG3 is for low-skill clerical jobs. To differentiate the wage groups TG4 and TG5 from the lower grades, indirect reference is made to training requirements. TG5 has become the entry level for young bank clerks. Typical jobs in this wage group are cashiers, and bank clerks who advise private customers or perform simple tasks in specialized departments. Job experience becomes increasingly important from TG5 upwards, and expert knowledge and responsibility from TG6 upwards.

3.3.2 The collective agreement for savings banks

Employees in savings banks are covered by an amendment to the overall BAT agreement for the public sector. This agreement comprises 14 grades from BAT X up to BAT I, each of them subdivided according to age groups (for details see Table 3.2). Grades are defined by skill requirements of tasks and managerial functions. Groups X to VII cover simple and mechanical tasks. From VIb onwards thorough and broad banking knowledge is required. The next groups are characterized by a growing degree of independent working, responsibility and complexity. The highest groups (II and I) require a university degree or equivalent job experience. In contrast to the private sector agreement, managerial positions are explicitly classified according to the number and grades of subordinate employees. A separate paragraph in the agreement requires vocational training as a

Table 3.1. Wage grades in the collective agreement for private banking, West Germany 1992 (extended, with modifications, to East Germany)

Wage grade	Requirements	Examples
TG1	No skills at all	Cleaners; kitchen personnel
TG2	Knowledge/skills which can be obtained by means of brief on-the-job training	Clerks with simple tasks in back office; security; doorkeepers
TG3	Knowledge/skills which can be obtained by means of longer on-the-job training	Clerks in accounts/savings department; typists; data processors; telephonists; drivers
TG4	Knowledge/skills which assume a vocational training certificate or longer on-the-job training with additional job experience	Counter service personnel; cashiers (small cash desks); clerks in back office; shorthand typists; telephonists with complex tasks; craftsmen; drivers with complex tasks
TG5	Detailed and multi-purpose knowledge/skills based on the same preconditions as in TG4, supplemented by further job experience, training or expert knowledge	Bank clerks at counter giving advice; cashiers; clerks in back office with higher skills; bank clerks with simple tasks in the credit, securities, foreign and central division; secretaries, shorthand typists with foreign languages
TG6	Theoretical and detailed practical knowledge and some decision-making	Bank clerks (front office) giving final advice on specific lines of business; cashiers with particular job requirements; bank clerks in the credit, securities, foreign and headquarters division; secretaries with complex tasks; head of back-office departments
TG7	Comprehensive knowledge and mostly own decision-making combined with a corresponding degree of responsibility	Financial advisers; bank clerks with complex tasks in credit, securities, foreign and central division; computer programmers and specialists
TG8	Particularly high degree of technical skills and/or responsibility	Financial advisers with higher skills; heads of small branches; bank clerks with special tasks in credit, securities, foreign and central division; computer specialists with complex tasks
TG9	Higher skills than TG8 owing to the complexity and/or responsibility of the tasks	Financial advisers with particular skills; heads of branches; shift overseers

Source: Tarifverträge für das private Bankgewerbe und die öffentlichen Banken, 1992, summarised by the author.

Table 3.2. Wage grades in the BAT amendment for savings banks, West Germany 1993 (extended, with modifications, to East Germany)

Wage grade	Requirements	Managerial tasks
X–IXa	Simple, schematic and mechanical tasks	
VIII	More complicated tasks, involvement in ongoing business under someone else's direction	
VII	Thorough and broad banking knowledge for at least one-quarter of the tasks	
VIb	Thorough and broad banking knowledge, with at least one-fifth of tasks carried out independently (for customer advisers at least one-quarter). Cashiers at on-line cash desks	Group leaders with at least two subordinate employees graded at least BAT VII
Vc	Thorough and broad banking knowledge with at least one-third of tasks carried out independently (for customer advisers, one-quarter). Cashiers at larger cash desks	Group leaders with at least three subordinate employees graded at least BAT VII. Managers of one-person branches
Vb	Thorough and broad banking knowledge, working independently; examples: customer advisers, credit, bond or personnel officers	Group leaders with subordinate employees: one graded at least BAT Vb and one at least BAT VIb. Managers of small branches (mainly routine business). Heads of department with two employees graded at least BAT VIb
IVb	Tasks which, compared with Vb, are particularly responsible (at least one-third); example: credit and bond officers with complicated tasks	Group leaders with two employees graded at least BAT Vb/VIb. Managers of branches with private customers. Heads of department with employees graded at least BAT Vb/VIb
IVa	Tasks which include one-third very difficult and responsible tasks with substantial requirements; example: customer advisers for corporate and wealthy customers	Group and department leaders with two employees graded at least BAT IVb and VIb. Managers of larger branches

Table 3.2. (continued)

III	One-third more responsibility than IVa; very difficult tasks	Group and department leaders.* Managers of very large or difficult branches
II	University degree or tasks with equivalent responsibility	Group and department leaders.* Branch managers with very difficult tasks
Ib-Ia	University degree or tasks with equivalent responsibility	Heads of department.* Branch managers with very difficult tasks
I	University degree or tasks with equivalent responsibility	Heads of department*

* With increasing number or grading of subordinate employees.
Note: A separate paragraph on training requirements prescribes vocational training as a bank clerk for BAT VIb and Vc, and sometimes also for BAT VII. Furthermore, a specific further training course is required from BAT Vb onwards. Exempted are employees who are over 40 years and who have a university degree or a high degree of professional knowledge and experience in a special field.

Source: *Bundesangestelltentarifvertrag für Sparkassenangestellte,* 1993, summarized by the author.

bank clerk or an equivalent training certificate for tasks classified in groups from VIb onwards; in some cases this also applies to group VII. For those without a university degree, a specialized further training certificate (Specialized Banking Course, see Section 3.4.6) is necessary for certain tasks classified in groups from Vb onwards.

3.3.3 Major differences between the two agreements

The major differences between the two agreements are summarized in Table 3.3. Employers regard the BAT amendment as less flexible than the private banking agreement for two reasons:

1) Whereas the private banking agreement excludes most managers and some part-time workers, the BAT amendment covers all employees of savings banks.
2) Whereas the private banking agreement defines only minimum wages which individual banks can exceed, under the BAT amendment minimum standards are also maximum standards.

Thus, savings bank employers have little freedom to reward performance by wage increases beyond negotiated wages, especially for

Table 3.3. Major differences between the collective agreement for private banks and the BAT amendment for savings banks

	Private bank agreement	BAT agreement for savings banks
Coverage	Excludes managerial staff, part-timers (working less than one-third of usual working time), cleaning staff	All employees
Normative value	Minimum standard	Minimum and maximum standards (according to the statute of the public employers' association)
Criteria for wage grading	Skill requirements of the 'formative task'. 1. Job examples; 2. General definitions	Skill requirements of the dominant task; no job examples
Access to promotion	Task related evaluation by supervisor	Task-related evaluation by supervisor; further training certificates
Seniority (within wage groups)	Years of occupational experience; low spread	Age; large spread
Social pay components	None	Regional allowances according to marital status and number of children
Flexibility	+	–
Transparency with regard to		
Grading according to task/skill	–	+
Other components	+	–

Source: author's assessment based on Tables 1 and 2.

managerial staff. As a consequence, managers in savings banks earn only 70 per cent of the salaries of private bank managers.

As far as transparency for employees is concerned, the comparison is less clear:

1) Both agreements are based on job evaluation as the main criterion for wage grading. In contrast to the principle of a 'formative task'

(identified by job examples), the savings bank agreement provides that every single task has to be considered and the grading into a particular wage group is done according to the task absorbing most of the working time. It also defines the grading of managerial tasks more precisely and mentions further training explicitly as a precondition for promotion.

2) More transparency with regard to the grading criterion, however, is offset by the opacity of other wage components. Social elements in the BAT agreement are regional allowances which differ considerably according to marital status and number of children. Furthermore, differentiation within wage groups is on the basis of age (as opposed to years of occupational experience) and is spread more widely than in the private banking industry. Differences in age and marital status can lead to wage differences of several hundred Deutschemarks for the same job.
3) Another problem is that promotion to a higher wage group is often linked to downgrading into a lower age group. Therefore, promotion does not automatically result in a wage increase and may even entail a decrease in wages.

3.4. THE CASE-STUDY BANK

The case-study bank (A-Bank) is one of the larger regional banks within the savings banks group. It had a large private customer basis with high volumes of savings and money transfer products, and controlled a large proportion of the market for small and medium-sized enterprises and institutional (public) investors. A-Bank operated as a universal bank at the regional level with a dense network of branches. Approximately every second employee out of a total of 7700 was located in a branch, with the other half in central departments.

During the previous years, A-Bank had undergone considerable expansion and restructuring. In 1990, it merged first with a West German savings bank and then with a savings bank in East Germany. Owing to these mergers, A-Bank expanded very rapidly in terms of volume of business and number of employees. Compared with 1988, the volume of business quadrupled and the number of employees nearly doubled until 1992. In January 1994, A-Bank became part of a larger bank holding which then ranged among the top ten German banks. In this study, however, we will concentrate on the period from the 1980s up to 1994.We shall describe below the evolution of gender-specific wage grading before and during the first period of restructuring and analyse possible explanations.

3.4.1 Gender-specific grading in A-Bank during the 1980s

The growing need for highly skilled personnel as customer advisers and specialized bank clerks is reflected by the increasing proportion of employees in higher grades. This upgrading, however, has affected men and women differently. Whereas for male employees the very top grades gained importance at the expense of the lowest grades, for women the upgrading remained limited to the middle grades. Even in 1989, only 10 per cent of women were graded in BAT IV or higher, whereas the figure for male employees was 44 per cent (see Table 3.4). These inequalities persisted even though female recruits were as well educated as male recruits or better, and were represented among the bank's trainees in a proportion equal to that of men. In 1980 more women than men entered the bank with qualifications equivalent to the British General Certificate of Education at Advanced level (41 per cent compared with 35 per cent) and the proportion of women among trainees was 59 per cent.

Despite continuing inequalities at the top, women's representation in the middle-level categories grew considerably. In grade Vb, which is for qualified customer advisers and credit officers as well as managers of middle-sized branches, the proportion rose from 42 to 63 per cent. In grades IVb to III, which require a higher level of expertise and responsibility (advisers for corporate or wealthy customers and managers of larger branches), women's representation increased from 22 to 34 per cent. These changes are partly the result of a changing employment pattern for

Table 3.4. Employees of A-Bank according to wage groups and gender, 1980 1989

BAT	Men		Women		% women	
	1980	1989	1980	1989	1980	1989
I–II	9.7	13.9	0.2	0.7	2.9	7.2
III–IVb	28.9	29.9	4.9	9.5	21.6	33.7
Vb	16.2	18.1	7.4	18.8	42.2	62.6
Vc–VIb	29.2	30.1	53.0	57.9	74.5	75.5
VII–X	15.9	8.0	34.5	13.1	77.7	72.4
Total	100	100	100	100	61.7	61.6

Source: Personnel statistics provided by the case-study bank.

Table 3.5. Employees of A-Bank according to age and gender, 1980, 1989 and 1992

Age group	Men			Women		
	1980	1989	1992	1980	1989	1992
>20	9.0	5.0	6.6	10.5	3.3	4.5
20–29	26.7	34.6	39.0	33.0	30.7	32.4
30–39	27.6	19.5	18.1	29.9	21.5	25.0
40–49	20.8	22.6	19.0	16.9	28.6	20.8
50–59	13.7	16.8	15.7	8.9	15.5	16.7
60>	2.2	1.6	1.6	0.9	0.4	0.6
Total	100	100	100	100	100	100

Source: Personnel statistics provided by the case-study bank.

women. As can be seen in Table 3.5, in 1980 women were still underrepresented in the middle and higher age groups. This indicates that many women still interrupted their employment or left the bank when they became mothers. By 1989, as a result of women's more continuous employment participation the age structure of female employees had aligned with that of their male colleagues.[6] This is supported by the fact that the proportion of employees leaving the bank because of maternity decreased from 18 per cent in 1979 to 3 per cent in 1989. However, these figures may overemphasize the change because the proportion of employees leaving for private reasons increased over the same period, and this category may include many women who interrupted their employment for family reasons.

Continuous employment as such, however, is not a guarantee of career advancement. As we noted earlier, the collective agreement for savings banks mentions further training as one of the conditions for promotion to higher grades. Whereas in 1980, according to Figge and Quack (1991), only 15 per cent of the graduates of the *Bankfachwirt* (a formalized further training course for employees of private banks) were women, they accounted for 30 per cent of all graduates in 1987. As the equivalent course for savings banks is held during working time, women are more likely to participate. Nevertheless, women were also underrepresented for a long time and it is very likely that participation increased considerably during the 1980s before reaching 45 per cent in 1989. Women's employment careers and participation in further training should also be seen in relation to a growing awareness by A-Bank's management of women as a human resource and of equal opportunity (see below). Compared with private

Table 3.6. Employees of A-Bank according to wage groups, working time and gender, 1989

BAT	Full-time			Part-time		
	Men	Women	% women	Men	Women	% women
I–II	13.9	0.7	6.6	0.0	0.4	100.0
III–IVb	30.0	10.8	33.0	0.0	1.9	100.0
Vb	18.1	20.5	60.9	0.0	8.8	100.0
Vc–Vb	30.1	55.5	71.7	50.0	71.4	99.5
VII–X	8.0	12.4	68.1	50.0	17.6	97.8
Total	100	100	57.9	100	100	99.2

Source: Personnel statistics provided by the case-study bank.

banks, savings banks are often regarded as less attractive employers, particularly by A-level school leavers and university graduates. Consequently, savings banks have traditionally recruited a higher proportion of female school leavers than private banks. This might also explain the emphasis which A-Bank has recently been placing on the internal career development of women.

One reason for the continuing underrepresentation of women in higher grades could be that they change to part-time jobs when they have children. Like other German banks, A-Bank offered only low-skilled part-time jobs during the 1980s, thus entailing an underutilization of qualifications. A-Bank's part-time rate, however, is still quite low (3.6 per cent of all employees and 5.6 per cent of all female employees in 1989). Thus part-time work cannot explain the remaining differences in grading between full-time male employees and full-time female employees (see Table 3.6). Given the equal educational level of women and men entering the bank, the remaining differences in grading are likely to be the result of gender-specific job definitions and promotion ladders, factors which will be analysed in more detail (see Section 3.4.7).

3.4.2 The former East German savings bank: integration through segregation?

At the time of German unification, A-Bank was subject to the West German BAT wage agreement for savings banks. However, the former East German savings bank with which it merged operated a completely different work organization and grading system. In the former GDR, the functions of savings banks were restricted to simple saving products and payment services. As a result, 40 per cent of branch employees worked as cashiers, the degree of work division was low and employees would rotate between jobs. Women accounted for 90 per cent of employees and most branch managers. The grading structure was less differentiated and the distribution of wages less dispersed than in West Germany (Quack *et al.*, 1992). The East German BAT agreement was introduced in July 1991, guaranteeing a wage level of 60 per cent of West German wages. Because of its location near the former border, A-Bank decided to pay 75 per cent of West German wages from the beginning and increased the proportion to 100 per cent in January 1992. This meant a very significant increase in net wages and a revaluation of the work of the savings bank clerks in the East.

After the merger, female East German branch managers were replaced by (mainly male) West German managers whose task was to reorganize jobs and to reclassify employees according to the grading structure of the BAT agreement. Most of the former East German employees were classified in preliminary grades (one group below normal grading) until they completed further training courses and could move up after an assessment by their (West German) line manager. Only cashiers were graded immediately according to their task. The bank made a considerable effort to retrain personnel during working time and at weekends according to new needs. Very often, however, the consequences of new job definitions, further training and new grading structures remained unclear to employees (Maier, 1993). Former East German employees – most of them women – now had to compete with West German colleagues, newly hired male colleagues from other industries in East Germany and young trainees.

Unfortunately, A-Bank no longer differentiates between East and West Germany in its employee statistics. A study of East German savings banks in the Brandenburg area (Philipp *et al.*, 1994), however, found that in 1993 the proportion of women among employees had fallen to 83 per cent and the proportion of women among trainees to 57 per cent. In many cases, the proportion of male employees graded in wage groups from BAT Vb upwards already exceeded the proportion of female employees in these groups. This was the result of a growing gender segregation of jobs and the fact that women benefited less often than men from promotion-related further training courses – processes which are likely to have also occurred in A-Bank. Another factor which puts women at a disadvantage is that A-Bank classified the jobs in East German branches much lower than those in West German branches. In 1992, 90 per cent of all employees in Eastern branches were classified in wage groups below Vb compared with only 55 per cent in Western branches (see Table 3.7). Even if this gap reflects continuing differences in skills, it nevertheless illustrates the

Table 3.7. Employees of A-Bank in East and West German branches according to wage groups, 1991 and 1992

BAT	East German branches		West German branches	
	1991	1992	1991	1992
I–III	0.2	0.5	11.3	12.3
Vb–IVa	7.8	9.8	31.0	32.2
VII–Vc	55.0	71.8	50.3	49.1
X–VIII	37.0	17.9	7.4	6.4
Total	100	100	100	100

Source: Personnel statistics provided by the case-study bank.

disadvantaged starting point from which the majority of female employees in Eastern branches had to enter into competition with other personnel for more senior jobs.

3.4.3 Transition from the BAT to the private banking agreement

After a change in the ownership statute in 1992, A-Bank left the association of savings banks and became a member of the private banks' association in order to apply their collective agreements. The main aim of this move, which the management had planned for a long time, was to implement a more flexible and performance-oriented grading system. Employees, particularly the younger and better qualified ones, were discontented with the inflexibility and seniority rules of the old agreement (Maier, 1993). A-Bank and the public employees' union (ÖTV) agreed upon a company-specific agreement which established the rules according to which employees would be reclassified into the new grading structure. Existing entitlements were fully guaranteed to all employees. Existing wage grades were collectively transferred to the new grading structure without any individual reassessment (see Tables 3.8 and 3.9). To the TG9 group were added wage groups 9a–d in order to cover the existing managerial workforce. The transition did not have any immediate gender-specific effect because existing employees remained subject to the company-specific agreement. Newly recruited staff, however, became subject to the private banking agreement. The most important effect in the medium term was that managers and highly skilled specialists were no longer covered by collective bargaining. They had to negotiate individual contracts which included a performance- or profit-related component. To

Table 3.8. Transition of wage groups from BAT agreement to private banking agreement

BAT amendment	X	IX	VIII	VII	VIb	Vc	Vb	IVb	IVa	III	II	Ib	Ia	I
Private banking agreement	1	2	3	4	5	6	7	8	9	9a + 10%	9b + 22%	9c + 32%	9d + 45%	9c + 60%

Source: Collective agreement between the case-study bank and the public sector union concerning the transition from the BAT to the private banking agreement, 1992.

Table 3.9. Transition from age groups in BAT agreement to years of occupation experience in private banking agreement

Age group in BAT	20–21	22–23	24–25	26–27	28	29	30
Years of occupational experience in banking agreement	1–2	3–4	5–6	7–8	9	10	11

Source: Collective agreement between the case-study bank and the public sector union concerning the transition from the BAT to the private banking agreement, 1992.

the extent that women have a weaker bargaining position in such negotiations, this may have had a negative effect on female branch managers' income position compared with that of their male counterparts.

3.4.4 Job evaluation in A-Bank

The analysis of differences in wage grading between women and men for the period 1980–9 indicated that gender-specific job evaluation and promotion ladders might be one explanation for the continuing inequalities. As company-specific procedures have to implement the rather broad grading criteria set out in the collective bargaining agreements, it is interesting to see whether there are gender-specific biases at the company level. Since the early 1980s, A-Bank has been operating a job evaluation system similar to the Hay system[7] with two different forms of application: catalogue based job evaluation and structural job evaluation.

Catalogue-based job evaluation is the normal one and consists of three stages. First, the personnel department in cooperation with the supervisor produces a job description outlining functional assignment, decision-making and qualification requirements.[8] Second, the supervisor draws up a catalogue of tasks relating to the job, of which the employee is given notice and which will be checked by the personnel department. Third, the personnel department carries out job evaluation based on this catalogue and assigns the job to one of the wage groups of the collective agreement. Furthermore, the personnel department defines performance and task-related criteria for possible promotion to the next highest wage groups. For example:

- A junior financial adviser in a large branch with 'wealthy customers' would be graded as TG8 with promotion to TG9 on the basis of an excellent sales performance
- A senior financial adviser in a large branch with 'wealthy customers' would be graded as TG9 with promotion to TG9d after many years of experience and an excellent sales performance

Structural job evaluation is applied to most of the jobs in branches. In this case, evaluation is not based on detailed task catalogues for each job, but on structural data from the personnel department. Service jobs (savings and giro accounts) are graded:

- as TG4 with promotion to TG5 after one year's service (plus assessment) (40 per cent of all jobs in this area); or
- as TG5 with performance-related promotion (assessment) to TG6 (60 per cent of all jobs in this area).

Jobs in customer advice (credit and securities) are graded:

- as TG7 (40 per cent of all jobs in this area); or
- as TG7 with performance-related promotion (assessment) to TG8 (60 per cent of all jobs in this area).

Branch managers are graded according to the results of a profit-related personnel allocation system, which means that they are paid according to the size of their branch in terms of number of employees. Most of them are graded from TG9 onwards. The number of employees itself is influenced by a branch's yearly profits. They must remain in their job for at least two years to be promoted, and promotion depends on profit and management-related criteria and a positive assessment, particularly concerning managerial skills.

3.4.5 Entry levels

A-Bank operates as an internal labour market with the trainee system as the main point of entry. In addition, there is a trainee programme for university graduates but they still represent a minority of all appointments. The trainee system is used to train bank clerks, who represent the majority of trainees, as well as of clerical employees. Depending on the level of their education, trainees are trained for between two and three years. Training is organized according to the principles of the dual system, which involves theoretical instruction in public vocational schools and practical on-the-job training as well as specialized theoretical classes in the bank, leading to a state-recognized certificate.

Positions are offered to all trainees who pass their examination. Most of these start work in the branches, where they are placed in the service area or basic advisory positions. Another common starting position is in the flexible personnel reserve for branches. This reserve of staff replaces employees who are temporarily absent due to, for example, holidays or illness. On the basis of their performance during their traineeship, some graduates are classified as having high or good potential compared with other candidates. Such graduates are offered entry jobs which are linked to a fast development track or, if they wish to continue their higher education,[9] special assistance during their studies. The fast development track normally starts with a job in the 'all-round personnel reserve', which in contrast to the flexible reserve also includes rotation to more qualified advisory jobs in securities and credit departments. These candidates gain experience more rapidly and advance more quickly to other positions.

In 1992, women accounted for 56 per cent of the 674 trainees in A-bank. According to the personnel manager, women graduate from the training with better marks than men (approximately eight out of the ten best trainees are women) and are therefore more likely to be placed in the more promising entry jobs.[10]

A-Bank has been operating a trainee programme for university graduates since 1990. With the exception of 1992, when there was a great demand for qualified personnel, only a few graduates have been recruited each year. Table 3.10 shows that the proportion of female applicants invited to an oral presentation was equal to or even greater than their proportion of all applicants. Compared with the proportion of women among applicants, recruitment also favoured women (except in 1993, when more men were recruited). On completion of the trainee programme university graduates are graded according to their jobs in TG8 or TG9 or remunerated as so-called extra-contractual employees whose pay conditions are

Table 3.10. Applications for the trainee programme, 1990–3

Number of	1990		1991		1992		1993	
	M	W	M	W	M	W	M	W
Applications	15	10	13	22	69	52	7	8
Immediate refusals	14	9	12	17	52	35	2	4
Invitation to oral presentation	1	1	1	5	17	17	5	4
Rejection after oral presentation	1	0	1	1	7	10	1	3
Recruitments	0	1	0	4	10	7	1(2)*	0(1)*

* Values in brackets refer to recruitments still undecided.
Source: Personnel statistics provided by the case-study bank.

not subject to collective agreements. Trainees with a state-recognized certificate start in TG5.

As a result of unification, there was an increasing demand for personnel which resulted in additional recruitment from the external labour market. Table 3.11 indicates a 'glass ceiling' for recruitment from the external labour market from BAT IVa and TG9 onwards. This becomes particularly clear when we compare the proportion of women among recruits with their proportion among applicants for positions. Table 3.12, which includes applications for internally advertised positions, shows a higher proportion of women among applicants than among recruited candidates.

Table 3.11. Recruitment from the external labour market, 1989 and 1992

	1989			1992		
Grade (BAT/TG)	Men	Women	% women	Men	Women	% women
IX-VIII/1–3	12	14	53.8	22	110	83.3
VII/4	2	4	66.7	12	55	82.1
VIb–Vc/5–6	1	0	0	4	21	84.0
Vb/7	0	0	0	7	11	61.1
IVb/8	2	2	50.0	6	12	66.7
IVa–IV/9	2	1	33.3	4	2	33.3
III–Ia/9a–d	1	0	0	5	1	16.7
Extra-contractual	0	0	0	18	0	0

Source: Personnel statistics provided by the case-study bank.

Table 3.12. Proportion of women among applicants for positions, 1990 and 1992

Grade (BAT/TG)	1990 (%)	1992 (%)
VIb/5	71	–
Vc/6	72	98
Vb/7	60	67
IVb/8	46	41
IVa/9	30	55
III/9a	59	21
II/9b	17	30
Ib/9c	0	–
Ia/9d	0	13

Source: Personnel statistics provided by the case-study bank.

3.4.6 Promotion and further training

Promotion from entry jobs depends on merit and participation in formal further training. The performance of employees is assessed by their line manager at least every three years. Such an assessment is also required if an employee wants to change jobs within the bank. Promotion is either on the job or through changing to another job. In the latter case, employees can apply for vacancies which are advertised internally. In many cases, however, those who are seen as appropriate for promotion to certain jobs are chosen directly by the management. This selection takes place in 'personnel development discussions' which are scheduled with trainees who have taken their examination (particularly those deemed to be of high or good potential), those who have completed further training courses (see below) and university graduates after their trainee programme is finished. Although in theory a reassessment should take place on completion of all further training, the initial classification is likely to have a strong impact on the development track.

Besides requirements for knowledge and experience, most job definitions include requirements for formal qualifications obtained during initial or further training. In many cases, several qualification profiles are defined which would fit the position. The completion of certain further training courses can be a precondition for promotion to a particular position. In other cases, participation in further training is regarded as an additional criterion for promotion, or as distinguishing between applicants with the same merit. As most of the further training in savings banks takes place during working time, participation depends on the agreement of the line manager.

The most important further training courses are the customer adviser course *(Kundenberaterlehrgang)* and the specialized banking course *(Fachlehrgang)*. The first one is oriented towards sales training and is taken by 50–70 per cent of all those who have completed a traineeship. The course comprises 270 hours of teaching, takes place as a part-time course during working time and is organized by the savings banks' own academy. After completion, participants are likely to return to their jobs in the branches or be promoted to the next grade. The specialized banking course prepares participants for promotion to middle management, requires an entry test and leads to a recognized certificate. It also takes place during working time, but is organized as a six to seven-month full-time course for which participants leave their job. After completion they will be given a management or highly qualified task. In addition, there are more specialized courses for certain subjects which are regarded as important for promotion. Participation in such courses, however, does not automatically entitle a person to promotion.

Promotion of secretarial staff is more or less restricted to office work. The BAT agreement, however, provides an opportunity for those with sufficient experience in savings banks to participate in an introductory banking course which will allow them to carry out service and basic advisory tasks in branches. This was extensively used to adjust the qualifications of East German employees after unification (Schäfgen, 1993).

Table 3.13 shows that in 1992 the proportion of employees with clerical or other non-bank-specific training was much higher among women

Table 3.13. Employees of A-Bank according to training and educational qualifications, 1992 (%)

	All employees		Employees with a bank-specific starting qualification	
	Men	Women	Men	Women
Bank clerk traineeship	40.3	39.2	54.2	81.8
Customer adviser course	0.2	0.1	0.7	0.2
Specialized bank course	11.2	5.8	33.6	12.2
Management course	0.4	0.1	1.8	0.2
University/Polytechnic	7.8	2.7	9.7	5.7
Clerical or other traineeship	13.9	41.0	100	100
Other	6.0	12.0		
Total	100	100		

Source: Personnel statistics provided by the case-study bank.

Table 3.14. Participation in further training according to gender, 1989 and 1992

	1989			1992		
	Total	Men	Women	Total	Men	Women
Customer adviser course	93	n.a.	n.a.	264	87	177 (67%)
Specialized banking course	80	44	36 (45%)	76	22	54 (71%)

n.a. = not available
Source: Personnel statistics provided by the case-study bank.

(53 per cent) than among men (20 per cent). If we concentrate on those employees with a bank-specific starting qualification, it becomes clear that for the great majority of women (81 per cent) a bank clerk's training certificate is also the occupational final stage, whereas nearly half of the men have higher qualifications. The difference is particularly marked with regard to the specialized banking course, which only 12 per cent of women but 34 per cent of men have completed.

Data show that in former times participation in further training was much lower among women than men (Rogas *et al.*, 1994). Data for the 1980s indicate a considerable increase in women's participation. Nevertheless, in 1989 the proportion of women (45 per cent) was still lower than their proportion among all employees (62 per cent). Owing to the retraining of East German employees, who are mostly women, women accounted for 67 per cent of participants in the customer adviser course and 71 per cent in the specialized banking course in 1992 (see Table 3.14). With the exception of this particular period, participation in formal further training still seems to be one of those areas in which women are disadvantaged.

3.4.7 'Courage for success'

Although the personnel department regards the grading and promotion criteria as gender-neutral, it is nevertheless aware of the underrepresentation of women in higher grades and leading positions. Consequently, equal opportunity programmes focus on women in management – and not so much on reconciliation of family and professional life as is the case in other German banks (see also Claus 1995). A-Bank's equal opportunity policy proceeds from two assumptions:

1) Because of traditional gender roles women and men have different career planning, and women are less self-important and more realistic

than men in their self-evaluation and are more likely to choose a career on the basis of specialization than on the basis of management responsibilities.

2) Managers might unconsciously apply gender-specific evaluation and selection criteria.

In order to overcome these problems, the bank offers a series of training courses which are addressed to both women and the (mainly male) senior management. One of the seminars for women operates under the title 'Courage for success' and covers themes such as different types of communication, analysis and career plans and orientations. A second seminar deals in more depth with gender-specific communication styles and aims at increasing participants' ability to communicate and to deal with conflicts in their professional life. The reactions to these seminars were quite different. Female employees welcomed them and female supervisors were positive about them, but male supervisors did not support them. To increase the acceptance of equal opportunity policies, the personnel manager then initiated compulsory seminars to sensitize male senior managers which would discuss gender-specific perceptions and attitudes affecting personnel assessment and recruitment decisions. Furthermore, a sponsorship system was established in which senior managers sponsor the career of junior women managers. As a result of these programmes, sensitivity towards equal opportunity issues increased. However, at the time of the interview for this case study, in Spring 1994, the bank did not have an equal opportunity plan.

3.5. SUMMARY AND CONCLUSIONS

The analysis shows the importance of collective bargaining agreements as a framework for wage grading, job definitions and job evaluation in the German banking sector. Rather broad definitions of grades in the collective agreements are used at the company level. The case-study of a particular bank revealed that at both levels the skill requirements and responsibility of a given job are the most important criteria for grading. These requirements are defined indirectly by reference to formal training, job experience and/or further training. Although formal qualifications are important for entering skilled jobs, they cannot explain the continuing gender differences in higher wage grades. The case study analysis showed that women in general have the same or even better school-leaving and vocational training certificates. Segregation into 'good' and 'bad' jobs takes place after initial training.

At the levels of collective bargaining and company-specific grading, job evaluation proved to be closely correlated with job segregation. Jobs which are typically performed by women are in general regarded as less skilled and responsible than those which are in general performed by men. Dealing with private customers is seen as less demanding than dealing with corporate customers; negotiating many small consumer credits as involving less responsibility than negotiating a few but large credits with companies; selling savings products as less skill-intensive than selling bonds; and managing a small branch with many retail customers as less responsible than managing a larger branch with fewer but more wealthy customers. It is beyond the scope of this study to investigate whether this evaluation corresponds to the real requirements of the tasks. Given that different values are ascribed to different jobs, the main question is whether women have restricted access to the more 'valuable' jobs, and if so, how the barriers can be removed. Personnel recruitment and promotion criteria are therefore important factors for understanding gender-specific pay differences in the German banking sector.

In the case-study bank we observe improvements in the grading structure which resulted from a shortage of qualified staff, changes in women's employment and training careers, and a growing sensitivity on the part of the personnel department concerning equal opportunities. The bank's programme for confronting senior managers with their gender-specific evaluation criteria seems to come very close to the central problem. The experience throughout German unification, however, shows how easily growing competition in the labour market can lead to the re-establishment of traditional lines of segregation. It remains to be seen whether equal opportunity programmes which rely on the goodwill of more 'women-friendly' managers are sufficient to improve women's position, particularly in a period when job growth is slowing down and competition is increasing in the unified German labour market.

Notes

1. The case-study was undertaken in summer 1994 and the manuscript completed in December 1995. We would like to thank the personnel manager of A-Bank for his friendly support of this study.
2. Wissenschaftszentrum Berlin.
3. Some savings banks have become members of the private banks' association.
4. Union of Trade, Bank and Insurance Employees (Gewerkschaft Handel, Banken und Versicherungen; HBV), Union of Public Service and Transport Employees (Gewerkschaft Öffentlicher Dienst, Transport und Verkehr;

ÖTV) and Union of German Employees (Deutsche Angestellten Gewerkschaft; DAG).

5. The following applies also to mutual banks.
6. The lower percentage of women among younger employees, however, indicates a new problem: in 1989, the bank reduced the proportion of women trainees to 49 per cent, before it increased to 56 per cent in 1992.
7. The Hay system is one of the best known hybrid models of job evaluation, developed by the US firm, Hay consultants. It combines the features of a point rating and factor comparison methods and is used in some 30 countries, particularly for managerial, professional and technical jobs (ILO 1986).
8. Including vocational training certificates, occupational experience and performance-related criteria.
9. Each year approximately 12 per cent of graduates leave for university.
10. A study of saving banks in West Germany reports, however, that women are particularly dissatisfied with their starting jobs because they involve too much routine work and are not demanding enough.

References

M. Claus, 1995. 'Führungskräfte reflektieren Karrierechancen ambitionierter Frauen', in H. Hüning, H. M. Nickel *et al.* (eds): *Gestaltungschancen und Handlungsgrenzen. Zur Transformation des Finanzdienstleistungssektors in Ostdeutschland.* Graue Reihe – Informationsmaterialien der KSPW 95-01 (Berlin), pp. 80–87.

H. Hüning, 1996. 'Der Transformationsprozenß im Finanzdiensleistungssektor der neuen Bundesländer und die betriebliche Integration Ost-West', in H. Hüning and H. M. Nickel (eds): *Dienstleistungsbeschäftigung in den neuen Bundesländern 1989/90–1995. Eine Zwischenbilanz.* Freie Universität Berlin. Zentralinstitut für sozialwissenschaftliche Forschung (Berlin), pp. 46–53.

ILO, 1986. 'Job Evaluation', Geneva.

F. Maier, 'Betriebliche Personalpolitik: Entlohnung, Eingruppierung und interne Arbeitsmärkte', in H. Hüning, F. Maier and H. M. Nickel: *Berliner Sparkasse: Unternehmen in der Vereinigung* (Berlin 1993), pp. 75–87.

S. Quack, F. Maier, and K. Schuldt, 'Occupational segregation in the Federal Republic of Germany and the former German Democratic Republic 1980–1989', Discussion Paper of the Manchester School of Management (Manchester: University of Manchester Institute of Science and Technology 1992).

V. Philipp, F. Maier, and K. Rogas, *Anpassung an westliche Beschäftigungsstrukturen oder neue Wege betrieblicher Personalpolitkk? Die Beschäftigungssituation von Frauen bei den Sparkassen im Land Brandenburg – Stiftung Weiterbilbung* (Berlin 1994).

K. Schäfgen, 'Modifizierung des Aus- und Weiterbildungssystems im Zusammenhang mit der Integration der Sparkasse der Stadt Berlin', in H. Hüning, F. Maier, and H. M. Nickel: *Berliner Sparkasse: Unternehmen in der Vereinigung* (Berlin 1993), pp. 88–99.

4 The Chemical Industry in Germany: A Case-study of the S Company

Friederike Maier

4.1. INTRODUCTION

The number of employees in the chemical industry in West Germany grew by about seven per cent during the 1980s. This, however, was lower than the average increase in employment throughout the economy (10.8 per cent), and the increase in overall employment was less than in other manufacturing industries. Women's share of employment in the chemical industry rose slightly from 26.4 to 27.7 per cent during the same period, mainly because of the increase in their share of non-manual employment (from 33.3 to 36.3 per cent), whereas their share of manual work decreased (from 23.2 to 20.7 per cent). In 1991 approximately 1.8 per cent of all female employees and 3.4 per cent of all male employees worked in the chemical industry (see Table 4.1).

The German chemical industry is dominated by large multinational firms, with their headquarters in Germany and branches worldwide. Some 72 per cent of all employees work in firms employing more than 1000 people, with women being more likely than men to work in smaller firms (see Table 4.1).

Working conditions, remuneration and so forth in the chemical industry are highly regulated. The centralized bargaining process has resulted in a single national pay agreement (which defines and describes all the wage groups) and 21 regional pay agreements (which determine the regional level of remuneration). There is a greater degree of consent in the chemical industry's bargaining processes than in those of other manufacturing industries. The trade union IG Chemie, Papier, Keramik had 666 851 members in 1991 in the western part of Germany, 19.5 per cent of whom were women. Both the employers and the employees are well organized.

Since 1987 all workers and salaried employees have been covered by the national agreement, which sets out a uniform pay system for all groups

Table 4.1. Employment structures in the chemical industry, West Germany

	1980		1990	
	Total (1 000)	Women	Total (1 000)	Women
Self-employed	10	—	8	—
Dependent employees	700	26.4%	750	27.7%
(% in part-time[1] work)	4.9%	17.3%	6.3%	18.3%
Employees covered by				
social insurance (in June) total	556	27.8%	586	28.7%
manual workers	303	23.2%	285	20.7%
non-manual workers	253	33.3%	300	36.3%
Employment by firm size in %				
20–49 employees	2.2%	3.2%	2.1%	3.2%
50–99	3.2%	4.6%	3.0%	4.3%
100–199	13.3%	19.3%	5.0%	7.3%
200–499			9.2%	12.9%
500–999	6.9%	9.0%	8.6%	11.5%
1000 or more	74.4%	63.8%	72.0%	60.8%
Total	100%	100%	100%	100%

[1]1980: Up to 39 hours a week, 1990: up to 35 hours a week (usual working time)

Sources: Statistisches Bundesamt, Fachserie 4, Reihe 4.3.1., 4.3.2, 4.3.3; Fachserie 1, Reihe 4.1.1. Bundesanstalt für Arbeit, *Sozialversicherungspflichtig Beschäftigte nach Wirtschaftsklassen.*

of employees. The agreement comprises 13 pay groups (E1–E13). These are differentiated according to each company's job requirements; they are based on a broad job evaluation and are explained by examples. Since there is no agreed procedure for evaluating jobs, each firm has its own job evaluation system. Another agreement covers university-trained staff. It has been signed by a group of employee representatives, including the Deutsche Angestellten Gewerkschaft (DAG) the industry's scientific staff union and the IG Chemie, Papier, Keramik.

When the national pay agreement, instituting a uniform pay system, was introduced in 1987 it was hailed as an historic step forward, since it was the first agreement to abolish the distinction between workers and salaried employees and to classify both groups according to a single grading system. As will be seen, however, this integration is only a formal one, as firms still differentiate between manual and non-manual workers in their personnel policy and their statistics.

Implementation of the national pay agreement differs from company to company. Most large companies use their own system of job grading and job evaluation for their own needs. It is employed regularly on the basis of agreements signed by management and the works councils.

Compared with other women in industry, women in the chemical industry are very well paid: the monthly gross earnings of full-time women manual and non-manual workers are the second highest of all manufacturing industries. Tables A.1 and A.2 (see Appendix) provide an overview. The overall sectoral wage dispersion of women in the chemical industry is positive, although the gender-specific wage differentiation has decreased only marginally since the beginning of the 1980s. As can be seen when analysing the case of the S Company below, high wages and a uniform classification system do not prevent occupational segregation and its effect on wage differentials.

4.2. THE S COMPANY

4.2.1 Employment structure[1]

Compared with other German chemical companies, the S Company is medium sized, employing 24 400 people worldwide, 12 000 of whom were in Germany in 1991. It has several plants in Germany and its headquarters are in Berlin. Employment in its German plants from 1982 to 1991 grew by 24.7 per cent. Growth was highest among AT employees (mainly research and development scientists; 56 per cent), average among salaried employees (+28 per cent) and very low among manual workers (+9 per cent) (see Table 4.2). Some important restructuring, however, had taken place, including the sale of certain lines of business. In 1992 these sales affected 2800 employees, who were offered new contracts by the new owners. In this case study we shall deal only with the situation in 1991, that is before restructuring.

Of the total number of staff employed in the German plants in 1991, 39 per cent were women. Women were heavily concentrated among the salaried employees: 70 per cent of all women were salaried employees, accounting for 52.6 per cent of all salaried employees. The proportion of women among AT employees was 13.3 per cent and among manual workers 21.3 per cent (see Table 4.2). In relation to the overall gender-specific composition of the chemical industry workforce, the S Company employs an average percentage of female workers, a high percentage of female salaried employees and a slightly higher percentage of women in AT positions.[2]

Table 4.2. Employment structure in the S Company[1]

	1982[2]		1991[2]		Distribution of all women employees (%)
	Total (1 000)	Women (%)	Total (1 000)	Women (%)	1991
Total employment	9631		12 009	38.8	4063 = 100%
Manual workers	3934		4313	21.3	22.6
Salaried employees	4219		5393	52.6	69.9
AT employees[3]	1478		2303	13.3	7.5
Apprentices	496	31.4	627	33.5	5.2
Temporary employees			457	—	
Part-time employees			906 (1990)	90.0	19.9

[1]Plants located in Germany. [2]End of year. [3]Includes university-trained employees covered by a special agreement.

The 1991 employment figure included 627 apprentices. The S Company offers apprenticeships in manual occupations, with two years' training for semi-skilled workers and three years' training for skilled workers, as well as apprentice in non-manual occupations. By the end of the 1980s the number of applicants for these had declined, but in 1990 and 1991 the number of candidates increased in Berlin as a result of unification. For occupations such as industrial clerk the S Company hires only young people with the highest school leaving certificate *(Abitur)* as apprentices. Women account for 33.5 per cent of all apprentices (a proportion which has not varied since the early 1980s) and are heavily concentrated in the non-manual occupations.

Approximately four per cent of the workforce have short-term temporary contracts, and 7.6 per cent work part-time. The latter percentage is slightly higher than the average for the chemical industry as a whole (6.3 per cent in 1990). Twenty per cent of the company's female employees work part-time, a higher figure than in the rest of the chemical industry. This is not surprising, however, since the company employs a higher proportion of women than the chemical industry average.

Shift work is common on the plants' production lines and the night shift was legally restricted to male workers. Female manual workers were prohibited from night work under the Hours of Employment Order of 1938. This regulation was abolished with the new Working-time Act in July 1994.

The labour turnover rate is about five per cent (excluding apprentices), that is about 600 employees a year. The sickness quota (time off due to sickness, excluding maternity leave) is quite high: in 1991 it was 10 per cent for manual workers and 4.5 per cent for non-manual workers, and had been increasing steadily since the early 1980s.

4.2.2 Characteristics of the internal labour market

The internal labour market in the S company comprises a number of clearly defined segments: the production department, the laboratories, the administrative units, the sales units and the research and development units are quite separate in terms not only of occupations but also of administration. The personnel management unit, for example, has separate sub-units responsible for the various parts of the labour force.

Like the other chemical companies, the S Company implements the national pay agreement in its own way, since it has its own job descriptions and employment ladders. It has not diversified the agreement by creating more pay groups as other chemical companies seem to have done.

The general distribution of employees in the S Company according to wage groups, which is shown in Table 4.3, is slightly different from that in

Table 4.3. Employees' distribution over pay groups, 1991[1]

Pay group	Chemical industry, West Germany		S Company	
	All employees (%)	Women (%)	All employees (%)	Women (%)
E1	4	11	1.3	(a) 4.2[2] (b) n.a.
E2	9	14	5.4	13.1
E3	8	7	3.1	3.4
E4	11	8	13.6	5.9
E5	6	4	4.1	2.3
E6	16	8	11.8	6.9
E7	9	6	5.6	2.5
E8	7	5	8.0	1.9
E9	7	11	11.9	20.8
E10	7	9	9.0	14.9
E11	7	8	10.8	13.1
E12	5	4	8.0	7.0
E13	4	2	7.4	4.0
Total	100	100	100	100

[1]Manual and non-manual employees. [2]Data refer to the Berlin plant only.
(a) 1988; (b) not available

the chemical industry as a whole: there is a lower percentage in pay groups E1 to E3, a higher percentage in E4, a lower percentage in E5 to E7, and a higher percentage in E8 to E13. Our interviews with company officials indicate that this fact can be explained by the different production lines in the company, which specializes mainly in pharmaceutical production and research and therefore has only a small pure chemical production. The fact that skilled chemical production workers are located in E6 and E7 may explain the higher share of those groups in other chemical companies. E4 is the largest group among the production workers in the S Company, and comprises workers involved in the production of ointment and pills. The higher proportion of employees in E8 and above is mainly due to the same reasons: a greater number of laboratory and sales staff and research assistants than in other chemical companies because of the different products manufactured. Table 4.3 shows the overall and the gender-specific distribution of employees in the S Company and the chemical industry as a whole. It will be noted that the company employs a larger proportion of women in the higher pay groups (E9 and above) than does the rest of the industry. This fact reflects not only the different production lines, but also the greater number of research-related positions and (since the data on women show the distribution in the Berlin plant only) the greater number of administrative units in Berlin.

Table 4.4 shows the distribution of manual and non-manual employees in the Berlin plant, and the proportion of men and women in the different pay groups. Each group will be discussed separately.

Table 4.4. Manual and non-manual employees over pay groups[1]

Pay group	Manual	Women (%)	Non-manual	Women (%)
E1	111	96.4	6	50
E2	402	83.8	—	—
E3	112	77.7	—	—
E4	535	22.8	41	75.6
E5	103	38.8	22	95.4
E6	351	8.0	186	81.2
E7	84	1.1	103	61.2
E8	270	—	85	57.6
E9			774	69.8
E10			543	71.1
E11			617	54.8
E12			407	44.5
E13			389	26.5
Total	1 968	36.7	3 173	58.8

[1]Data refer to the Berlin plant only, 1988.

4.2.2.1 Manual work

The national pay agreement for the chemical industry places manual workers in groups E1 to E8. E1 to E3 are for unskilled and semi-skilled workers; E4 and E5 require completion of a two-year apprenticeship; and E6 is the skilled workers' entry group, requiring completion of a three-year apprenticeship in the occupational field. The highest possible group for a skilled worker is E8; only a highly qualified worker can reach a higher group (up to E12). The wage groups are differentiated by job requirements, criteria being generally defined by the knowledge required, the diversity or complexity of the tasks and the degree of instruction given by the superior. There is no automatic promotion for manual workers to higher groups.

In the S Company mostly female workers are in E1 to E3 (85 per cent in 1988),[3] while E4 to E8 are male domains (85 per cent male). Seventy-four per cent of all female manual workers are graded E1 to E3; 92 per cent of all male manual workers are graded E4 to E8. Female workers in E1 to E3 do jobs described as 'requiring brief on-the-job training that can be done by other employees at any time' (E1), 'requiring a longer period – three months – of on-the-job training' (E2) and 'requiring some additional knowledge' (E3). These unskilled jobs are done by women who work in ointment and pill production, decanting, bottling and packing products, often on assembly lines. A remarkable number of these women are in fact skilled, having completed vocational training as a medical or dental assistant. The few men in these groups do supply, dispatch or transport work.

E4 seems to be the entry level for production-related (largely) male occupations. It requires 'knowledge and skills, which can be acquired through two years' formal occupational training in a recognized or equivalent training programme' and employees must be able 'to carry out assignments after detailed instruction'. The low proportion of females in this group stems from the fact that the S Company offers apprenticeships as chemical assistant and electrical systems installer only to males and mostly recruits its own apprentices. E5 is the highest group for semi-skilled workers; foremen are often in this group, and promotion to it is frequently related to length of experience in E4. Women in E5 are often forewomen in charge of women working on the assembly lines.

E6 to E8 are the wage groups for skilled manual workers (that is with three years' training), including foremen and highly qualified workers. The largest number of male skilled workers is in E6. Since most apprentices doing the vocational training course are – not surprisingly – male, only a very few women are to be found in these wage groups. In 1988 there were 29 women compared with 676 men (see Table 4.4).

Manual workers in the S Company do work which is highly segregated on the basis of gender. This is true as regards not only hierarchy but also tasks actually performed, for men and women work in different areas of production. Entry into the core skilled workers' group is not possible unless a person has appropriate vocational training in the chemical industry or holds the position of foreman or forewoman. The company prefers to hire as medical assistants women who have served an apprenticeship, because they have certain useful basic skills: they are accustomed to working with chemical material and antiseptic material, and to working with care; moreover, they understand the importance of pharmaceutical products and so forth. A medical assistant employed as an unskilled worker in groups E1 to E3 earns more in the S Company than in a private doctor's practice.

4.2.2.2 Non-manual work

The national pay agreement allocates non-manual work to all 13 wage groups and gives examples of the tasks involved. For example, E1 includes simple clerical work such as distribution of mail, E4 semi-skilled clerical work such as taking shorthand dictation and typing simple texts or operating telephone switchboards, and E9 skilled clerical work such as shorthand dictation and typing difficult texts or independently conducting routine correspondence. The S Company gives effect to these rather broad descriptions through a firm-specific agreement, signed by the works council, in which the wage groups for certain occupations are fixed. The agreement includes most non-manual occupations and defines the range in which employees carrying out specific tasks are grouped. Each group is explained separately.

A. Laboratory work for salaried employees in laboratories the S Company has the most detailed firm-specific agreement (with the works council) on job requirements and internal job ladders. It is considered to be necessary for implementing the national agreement at the firm level. As the job descriptions within the general pay agreement are not specific enough, the S Company developed its own scheme for laboratory employees, so as to have a more transparent system of job grading.

Under the national pay agreement, simple laboratory tasks may be classified in E1, E2 or E3, but the S Company places all its laboratory workers in E4 or above. The internal regulations differentiate between two groups:

- employees without specific vocational training. This group works in chemical/technical laboratories and medical/biological laboratories, and women's share in it is more than 50 per cent;
- employees with vocational training. This group works in research and development or in production-related development, and women's share in it is lower than in the first group.

The entry level for the first group of employees is E4, and the highest possible level is E7. The internal regulations provide detailed descriptions of the jobs associated with the different pay groups. By defining specific requirements they open the way to upward mobility even for employees who do not fulfil the general requirement for entry into E6, that is those who have not completed a period of vocational training in a specific occupation. The regulations state that to move up to the next group, a person must not only perform the tasks required but also have been employed in the group below for at least two years. There is no automatic promotion on the basis of seniority or merit, but a minimum period of employment is required in each group.

The situation is different for the second group. The entry level is E7, which generally requires employees to have completed three years' vocational training (requiring a higher level of abstract thinking than manual training) in the field of chemical laboratory work. After a year in E7 promotion to E8 is automatic; promotion to E9 is also automatic after a year in E8. The groups above may be reached only if job requirements justify higher remuneration. There is a detailed description of job requirements for those groups. Promotion depends on the extent to which an employee works independently, responsibility for apprentices, management of a laboratory, difficulty of the tasks performed and length of employment in a lower wage group. Skill requirements are increasing: some positions call for certificates of further training, for example as a chemical technician or engineer.

B. Clerical and administrative work the grading of clerical and administrative jobs is generally agreed between the management and the works council, but is not as detailed as for laboratory employees.

The S Company groups clerical and administrative employees in E4 to E13, although under the national pay agreement they could be in E1, E2 or E3. Employees performing simple clerical tasks which require two years' vocational training, are in E4 and E5. Secretarial work is graded from E6 to E13 (the company president's executive secretary has an AT position and is thus paid more than the highest collectively agreed wage). Most secretaries have completed three years' vocational training as a clerical employee, industrial clerk or data processing clerk.

Women are concentrated among those performing simple clerical tasks and among clerical employees, while a smaller proportion work as industrial clerks or data processing clerks. The personnel department is currently developing a scheme for secretarial work similar to the one for laboratory work. It will include detailed job descriptions, career ladders, minimum employment periods in certain groups, and so forth. Secretaries up to E9 have so far been grouped according to job requirements, with those above E9 dependent on the hierarchical status of their superior. A number of employees regard this as unfair, while others, especially the male superiors, reject the idea of pay groups dependent solely on job requirements.

Employees such as purchasing agents are grouped from E4 to E13, depending on their skills, years of experience and responsibility, and so forth. Data processing clerks and technical draughtspersons are graded from E7 to E13 and field staff (sales) in E12 and E13.

It could be said in general that the differentiation of occupations is quite broad, whereas the job descriptions (except for laboratory employees) are rather imprecise. When jobs are graded and allocated to a particular group, reference is made to the group's hierarchical structure but no comparisons are made between groups. This means that apart from the fact that a skilled clerical employee needs appropriate vocational training, the relative position of secretarial work is defined within the relevant groups, and there is no explicit reference to (or comparison with) purchasing agents, book-keeping assistants or other administrative or clerical occupations.

A study conducted by the women's officer, who is responsible for the implementation of affirmative action within the company, showed that equally trained clerical employees have different career paths. Whereas most of the female industrial clerks obtained positions as secretaries and moved up only very slowly, most of the male industrial clerks obtained positions in the sales area and moved up the career ladder quite quickly, especially when they accepted jobs in the company's foreign plants. Mobility plays an important, though not regulated, role in internal advancement.

In view of different promotion and career paths in the various occupations, it is clear that salaried women employees are more likely to be grouped in E6 to E10 (64 per cent of all women, compared with

30 per cent of their male counterparts). In E4 to E10 women's share is 70 per cent, and in E10 to E13 it is 44 per cent (see Table 4.4).

4.2.2.3 Grading and job evaluation for employees covered by the national pay agreement

Jobs are graded according to the national pay agreement. For manual workers there is a clear distinction between three groups (unskilled, semi-skilled and skilled), each with a narrow range of wage groups (only two or three different ones). The possibilities for upgrading jobs appear to be quite limited.

Examples of occupations/job titles:

Unskilled manual work
Non-manual work (including laboratories)
Semi-skilled work (2 years' vocational training)
- (a) manual
- (b) clerical
- (c) laboratories

Skilled work (3 years' vocational training)
- (a) manual
- (b) clerical (including secretaries)
- (c) laboratories

Highly qualified workers
Data processing
Purchasing agents
Sales field staff

With the exception of skilled laboratory employees, who (as already noted) are promoted automatically on the basis of seniority, the upward mobility of all employees depends on job description: only if a job, for example, requires specific knowledge and includes certain tasks is a better grading possible. Job evaluation is done by superiors and is not regulated; that is, there is no general rule regarding how and how often a superior has to evaluate jobs. Since the whole system is based on summary evaluation without clear definitions or distinctions, there is scope for superiors to make discretionary decisions. Indeed, within the given definition of the required skills, the allocation to a specific pay group involves a certain degree of discretionary power. As the personnel department has to take the final decision, the group to which a particular person is to be allocated is sometimes part of a bargaining process between a superior and the personnel department.

To summarize our findings, it appears that the formally integrated job grading for manual and non-manual workers has not abolished the differences between these two groups: the national pay agreement does not permit more upward grading for manual jobs, and the S Company does not make use of the (theoretical) possibility of downgrading clerical jobs. Differentiation within occupational positions is the norm. In manual work a completed apprenticeship in a recognized occupation or profession marks the main gender-specific segregation line; in non-manual work it is the entry position (after completion of a apprenticeship) in a specific occupational field that maintains gender-specific segregation.

4.2.2.4 University-trained employees

The salary agreement for university-trained employees covers only technical, medical and other science-related occupations. Since 1993 there have been two categories of such employees: PhD and non-PhD. In each one there is a seniority-based pay increase in the first five years of employment. Administrative or research employees with a university degree in business administration, management or the social sciences are treated in the same way, although there is no agreement covering them.

All university graduates are treated like AT employees with regard to their careers and salaries; that is, after the first five years of employment their pay is based solely on performance-related criteria. The superior assesses performance annually, and an individual's aspirations, progress and development are discussed with him or her. The result of this is an agreed plan for individual development. A total of 19.5 per cent of all university-trained employees are called AT employees, 447 (19 per cent) of whom are initially not covered by the salary agreement. Thirteen per cent of university-trained employees are female, but the corresponding figure for 'real' AT employees is only 4.7 per cent.

4.3. PAYMENT SYSTEM

Remuneration is negotiated at the regional level. For all pay grades E6 is the benchmark. In West Berlin E1 is approximately 85 per cent of E6, and E13 approximately 190 per cent. Starting at E5, there are automatic pay increases after a certain period of employment: after two, three, four or six years. E9 to E13 have three different subdivisions: technical employees, clerical employees and highly qualified workers. The wage rates for technical employees are higher than for clerical employees, and those for the third subdivision are between the two others. In the S Company women's

Table 4.5. Pay levels in the chemical industry, West Berlin (in DM)

Pay groups (E)	8/1988	9/1992		
E1. Over 18 years of age	2249	2740		
E2. Over 18 years of age	2364	2880		
E5.	2525	3076		
Pay guarantee 3 years*	—	77		
Pay guarantee 5 years	—	154		
E8	2751	3351		
Pay guarantee 2 years	—	201		
Pay guarantee 4 years		436		
Pay guarantee 6 years		670		
E9. Entry stage	2603	3215		
> 2 years	2850	3519		
> 4 years	3131	3867		
> 6 years (end stage)	3518	4345		
E13	4793	5898		
	E9 (%)	E10 (%)	E11 (%)	E12 (%)
Starting level	74	76	78	78
After 2 years' service	81	83	85	85
After 4 years' service	89	91	91	92
Final level	100	100	100	100

*Monthly regular supplement after 3 years' employment.

Sources: *Entgelttarifvertrag Berlin zum 1.8.1988* gem. Section 7, Bundesentgelttarifvertrag. IG Chemie, Papier, Keramik, 1987. Section 8. © F. Maier and S. Quack 1993.

share among clerical employees is 78 per cent, among technical employees 47 per cent and among highly qualified workers 15 per cent. Table 4.5 summarizes the different groups and their pay.

4.4. PERFORMANCE PAYMENTS AND WAGE SUPPLEMENTS

Piecework and wage premiums in production have been abolished, and all manual and non-manual employees are paid time wages at monthly rates. Wage supplements for overtime (+25 per cent per hour), regular night-shift work (+20 per cent), irregular night-shift work (+15 per cent), working on Sundays and public holidays (+60 per cent) and full continuous shift work (+10 per cent) are fixed in the national pay agreement. As we do not have any information about the number of people in the

S Company doing this kind of work and the relevant company regulations, we cannot assess the importance of these supplements for the employees.

Shift workers who have reached the age of 55 can take early retirement after 15 years on full continuous shift work or 20 years on partial continuous shift work. The firm adds a certain amount to the unemployment benefits (people who take early retirement being officially classified as unemployed), so that former employees receive 90 per cent (in the first year), 80 per cent (in the second year) and 70 per cent (in the third year) of their former net income. From the age of 58 they will receive full unemployment benefits until they reach the legal retirement age, which is 60 for unemployed people.

All employees receive a year-end bonus and additional holiday pay (a fixed sum of DM33 per day of holiday, the length of holiday being 30 working days).

Each year the S Company pays a discretionary bonus. In 1990 it was one per cent of the total wages bill and in 1991 it was 0.9 per cent (DM87.7 million). Each unit's superior receives a proportionate amount and distributes it among the employees. A percentage is earmarked for supplements paid according to age and length of service, and the remainder (about 42 per cent) is distributed according to the decision of the superior. Neither part may exceed a certain fixed sum for each employee, which is lower in the lower pay groups and higher in the higher ones. This bonus is not performance-related in the strict sense of that term. Truly performance-related payments are common only among AT employees and are based on management appraisal. Within that group the firm tries to encourage the use of management techniques such as management by objectives.

4.5. REGULATION OF PART-TIME WORKING

There is a uniform agreement in the chemical industry on the regulation of part-time working, which guarantees part-time workers the same hourly wages as their full-time counterparts. As long as they do more than marginal part-time work (marginal part-time workers work less than 15 hours a week, earn less than DM520 a month and are not subject to social security regulations), they receive pro-rata wages and wage supplements. The agreement states that part-timers have priority when a company is recruiting for full-time positions, and requires the employer to inform marginal part-time workers that they are not covered by social security regulations, including the fact that they have no access to the firm's health insurance scheme.

4.6. OTHER SOCIAL POLICY

The S Company has its own health insurance scheme, the advantage being that the contributions are lower than those of the public scheme but the entitlements are the same. In 1991 a total of 14 220 employees in German plants were members of the company scheme, plus 10 000 family members.

The company has its own kindergarten, with 175 places for children aged between three months and six years. In addition, the company offers shares to its employees at a better price than on the stock market, provides loans for house buying or building and has a well-developed social welfare department dealing with individual problems, including alcohol and drugs.

4.7. INTERNAL FURTHER TRAINING

Further training activities (not on-the-job training) in the S Company are quite extensive, and 5365 employees (44 per cent) participated in them in 1991. Most further training is closely related to firm-specific or job-specific needs and does not lead to a nationally recognized certificate. There are, for example, seminars on 'ecological thinking in laboratories', information technology, biochemical issues, working conditions, occupational health and safety, language training and management training, as well as 'train-the-trainers' seminars. Manual workers are more explicitly catered for with introductory seminars on data processing and chemical processes, and skilled manual workers who have completed vocational training and have at least five years' occupational experience can take part in seminars leading to the certificate for highly qualified workers.

Participation in training is voluntary, although certain jobs require training as a prerequisite. The overall level offered to employees is decided by the personnel department, as are the number of hours and the budget. In general, employees are entitled to participate in the training offered to their group. The actual decision (who takes part, for how long, and in what kind of seminar) is a joint decision of the superior and the personnel department.

In some of the S Company's plants the management has initiated 'quality circles' as a management tool. Group-based decision-making and problem-solving are seen as a means of improving the quality of work.

4.8. AFFIRMATIVE ACTION FOR WOMEN

As noted earlier, the S Company has a women's officer (appointed in 1990) responsible for implementing affirmative action at plant level. Such positions are common nowadays in large chemical firms. They are difficult, however, for the women are not elected by the employees, nor do they have a set of defined instruments or the right of intervention unlike the works councils. Since these women are located within the managerial hierarchy, both employees and management have difficulty in finding the 'right' relationship with them.

The S Company appointed a woman from inside and within a short time she developed a series of activities which led the personnel department to start developing guidelines for secretarial positions. The officer initiated seminars on vocational and individual life planning for secretaries, manual workers, forewomen, highly qualified female workers and clerical workers, and started working groups on secretarial work, women in management and women on parental leave.

4.9. SUMMARY AND CONCLUSIONS

For the purpose of implementing the national pay agreement at company level, the S Company developed its own grading system, but only for laboratory employees. This system is based on detailed job descriptions and includes seniority-based promotion. This is because of the need to agree on more precise job descriptions than are provided in the national pay agreements. However, the personnel department and the works council agreed on a ranking and grading system for all the different non-manual occupations. Interestingly, no comparisons are made between the different occupations, although they are integrated into the same grading system. The main issue for manual workers is vocational training in an essential vocation; skills acquired in a non-essential vocation such as that of medical assistant do not count in terms of grading. For non-manual workers the main issue seems to be the pay group they find themselves in immediately after vocational training. For example, along the secretarial path promotion follows the internal logic of a secretarial position's requirements, whereas the sales path follows a different logic. A uniform grading system does not prevent occupational and gender-specific segregation.

Notes

1. The following information is based on the company's internal and published reports and statistics, and on interviews with members of the personnel department conducted by F. Maier, A. Carl and A. Krehnke. We thank them for their cooperation.
2. As we do not have data relating to the different regional plants, we are not able to say whether there are regional differences resulting from the

different functions of the plants (the plants in western Germany are more production-related; the Berlin plant is the headquarters, does more research and development and has only some lines of production) and from different labour market conditions (Berlin is a metropolitan labour market with a higher share of female employment than in those areas of western Germany where the other plants are located).

3. These data refer to 1988 and only to the Berlin plant; it was not possible to obtain more recent data.

Part 2

Equal Pay in Italy

5 Introduction

Francesca Bettio and Paola Villa

The official figure in Italy for the economy wide gender gap was 27.5 per cent in 1991, a relatively low figure in Europe and the industrialized world as a whole. Yet the gap had been increasing during the 1980s, albeit slightly, rising from 21.6 per cent in 1983 (see Table 5.1). A number of factors account for this, some of which are still at work: the elimination of the flat wage indexation allowance, a renewed emphasis on performance-related pay and the increase in local-level bargaining, all tending to favour a greater dispersion of earnings.

The Italian case studies presented in this book highlight the important differences concealed in the aggregate figures, explaining the factors involved at the micro-level and revealing various combinations of levels and

Table 5.1. Ratio of female to male actual earnings (employees only) by category of employment (%)

	1983	1991	1983–91
Manual	79.28	70.76	–8.52
Clerical	75.69	73.09	–2.60
Senior clerical	68.93	73.39	+4.46
Managers	55.36	63.81	+8.44
University teachers	71.13	70.58	–0.55
Secondary school teachers	96.63	93.29	–3.34
Primary school teachers	85.29	81.57	–3.72
Regular soldiers	82.38	77.95	–4.43
Senior officers	58.48	56.87	–1.61
Regular officers	68.39	57.49	–10.90
Magistrates	68.00	55.91	–12.09
Members of Parliament	73.86	54.62	-19.24
Priests	n.a.	121.75	n.a.
Unspecified	77.41	69.90	–7.51
Total	78.39	72.53	–5.86

n.a. = not applicable.

Source: Ministero delle Finanze, *Dichiarazione dei redditi delle persone fisiche.*

trends in the gender pay gap. They cover three sectors – health services, telecommunications and banking.

The first study is of a public hospital in Rome, Hospital A, a small- to medium-size hospital (721 employees) sufficiently diversified in terms of the services it offers. A public hospital rather than a private one was chosen because the public health service has so far been largely dominant within the health sector in Italy.

The second case study is of the national telephone company, the Società Italiana per l'Esercizio delle Telecomunicazioni (better known as SIP), which operates the domestic telephone system under monopoly licensing. To cover the production side of the industry, the case study also deals – briefly – with ITALTEL, one of the largest Italian companies manufacturing telecommunications equipment, and one of SIP's main suppliers.

The final case study, which deals with the banking sector, is of a large savings bank and a medium-size cooperative bank (referred to throughout as BP Bank and CR Bank respectively).

The public hospital and the national telephone company are at one extreme, with an overall differential in annual earnings of less than 10 per cent, too low to have registered any significant increase of late. At the other extreme is banking, with a differential ranging from 35 to 20 per cent. It has, however, shown improvement over the last decade, and a further reduction will probably occur as women progressively gain seniority in this industry, where they are relatively new entrants. Finally, at ITALTEL, which is somewhat representative of large manufacturing firms, the differential has increased substantially since 1980 (from 7 to 18 per cent) but is still five points below the economy wide figure of some 23 per cent.

Thus, at the fine level of aggregation of the case studies, the gender pay gap may be higher but also significantly lower than the overall figure. This is because occupational segregation protects as well as hinders women's relative pay; for example, because women are underrepresented among non-manual workers, or because they are in the middle section of the grading scale in more than one industry. In other words, it is segregation between firms and between industries more than occupational segregation that seems to have a definite negative effect on women's relative earnings in the Italian context. With this in mind it may be easier to relate aggregate trends to the details of the case studies.

6 Health Services

Francesca Bettio[1]

6.1. THE INDUSTRY

6.1.1 Employment

The public health service (PHS) had a total of 836 500 permanent and temporary employees in 1990, 20 per cent of whom were in the private sector (see appendix Table A.3). Both public and private employment rose steadily between 1980 and 1990, by 11.8 and 26.3 per cent respectively. Women's share of employment also rose, or so we infer from partial data on public employment, which reveal an increase from 47.5 per cent in 1985 to 52.1 per cent in 1990.[2]

6.1.2 Collective bargaining and unionization

The recent move towards privatization of all previous public employment contracts[3] involves, of course, the whole of the PHS. What exactly the new legislation will imply is still very unclear: some experts believe that the changes are little more than cosmetic, while others stress that major innovations will result from the new rules.

On a formal level one of the main features that still distinguishes public employment contracts is the validity *erga omnes* of collective agreements signed with the most representative unions, since agreements must be translated into government action. In practice, this is not a very important feature since all collective agreements are valid *erga omnes* in Italy. It was of importance, however, in one respect, namely the nature of industrial relations in the public sector. Formerly, consent had to be sought from 'representative' unions on practically every significant aspect of the organization of work. However, strict criteria were used to characterize unions as 'sufficiently representative'. In practice, new, fringe or (usually) militant public sector unions could not take part directly in formal negotiations. Under the new, private contract all this will change and may cause greater dispersion in earnings by allowing more room for a larger number of unions and, in particular, their radical fringe.

Moreover, management used to have almost no discretion in the organization of work, since each significant decision had to meet with the unions' approval. The removal of this 'constraint', implied by the transition to the new contractual status, may lead to major innovations in, say, the organization of working time, thus threatening to erode one of the advantages that public employment still has for women.

The old contractual status continued to apply until the beginning of 1994, when the agreement in force since the end of 1990 expired. Around the latter period the level of unionization was fairly high in the PHS: 54 per cent of non-medical personnel and 77 per cent of doctors were represented by unions.[4]

Some of the changes implied by the transition to 'private law' labour contracts were anticipated for all public employment in 1983 (by the framework law on public employment). In the PHS in particular, local units were given additional discretion in some matters – specifically: overtime, training and retraining, turnover, group incentives, and work loads or grading under emergency conditions (for example during a strike). The move was clearly towards forms of local level bargaining, and the main result is that incentive pay is now a small (about five per cent) but not insignificant component of gross earnings in the industry, see Appendix Table A.4.

6.1.3 Grading and pay structure

The PHS is covered by a single collective agreement for all employees, including physicians. Employees are assigned to one of the following four occupational groups, each of which broadly defines a separate career path:

1) medical personnel, including physicians, biologists, pharmacists, health technicians (e.g. analysts in testing laboratories), nurses, health auxiliaries;
2) professionals: lawyers, architects, accountants, statisticians, etc.;
3) manual workers: porters, drivers, electricians, cooks, etc.;
4) administrative personnel: clerks and administration management.

The four groups have the same scale of 11 grades, but a specific group does not necessarily extend over the whole range. For example, professionals, who are usually graduates, are placed in the top three grades (9–11), as are physicians, pharmacists, biologists and any other graduates. Nurses, on the other hand, are in grades 4–8, while manual workers usually reach as far as grade 6.

Entry to any position is by public competition, but seniority may confer the right to automatic promotion up to a threshold that varies with each group. Furthermore, internal training may be compulsory for reaching higher grades or moving from one group to another; for example, in the case study hospital, unskilled workers recruited into the bottom grades of group 3 (manual workers) were required to have 400 hours of internal training in order to be promoted to grade 4 of group 1 (medical personnel). In general, internal training is provided for nurses and related occupations.

As in the rest of the public sector, the actual earnings of health employees have risen considerably in relative terms since the early 1980s and were higher in 1990 than in the economy as a whole (see Appendix Table A.4). If we set the average level of per capita gross annual earnings in the economy at 100, public employees' earnings stood at 114 in 1980 and 125 in 1990. Earnings in the PHS, on the other hand, reached 116 in 1980 and 135 in 1990. No doubt because of the share of physicians in total employment, average earnings in the PHS are thus consistently at the top of the public sector pay pyramid, as well as being considerably higher than average earnings in the economy as a whole (see Osservatorio del Pubblico Impiego, *Relazione 1992,* p. viii).

The composition of PHS pay is similar to that of public employees, in general. Both differ in a number of fundamental respects from the composition of private sector pay, although the current trend is towards convergence. In particular, basic components such as contractual minima and cost-of-living allowance traditionally had greater importance in public employees' pay, and so did seniority. By contrast, occupation-specific allowances, which represented the public sector equivalent of firm-specific allowances in the private sector, still count for much less.

The additional degree of freedom in the setting of pay granted to local units in the PHS since 1983 and the transition to a 'private law' contract for all employees will no doubt erode differences, but they are still relatively pronounced, as can be seen when the composition of pay in selected 'public branches' is compared with that in selected 'private branches' (Table 6.1). Contractual minima, cost-of-living allowance and seniority pay accounted for 41, 40 and 12 per cent respectively of average annual gross pay in public education (excluding universities), while the corresponding figures in the engineering industry were 26, 43 and 7 per cent. Firm-specific premiums, on the other hand, totalled 21 per cent in that industry, whereas they did not (yet) exist in public education.

One difference specific to the PHS industry in this respect is the importance of shift-work premiums in the pay of various occupations, nursing in particular. These premiums were increased considerably by the latest

Table 6.1. Structure of gross annual earnings, December 1990 (%)

	Contractual minimum pay	Cost-of-living allowance	Seniority allowance	Other benefits	Total central bargaining	Firm-specific allowance	Overtime, shifts etc.	Total
Banking	36	35	12	6	87	9	4	100
Education	41	40	12	7	100	0	0	100
Central government	39	42	10	2	92	0	8	100
Commerce	29	52	9	1	91	4	5	100
Cleaning services	30	56	5	0	91	3	7	100
Textile and clothing	28	53	4	0	85	12	3	100
Engineering	26	43	7	0	76	21	3	100

Source: Based on CNEL, *Retribuzione, costo del lavoro, livelli della contrattazione,* relazioni *sindicali* e politiche bei *redditi*, Roma 1991, Vol. 2, Table 4.14, p. 303.

agreement, ostensibly to ease the shortage of nurses affecting the north of the country during the 1980s. There exist, however, no data enabling a direct comparison to be made between the pay structure in the PHS and that in other industries. Consequently, we shall reconsider this matter separately.

Neither the dominant position of the PHS in the pay pyramid nor the bias in favour of the basic components of pay is gender neutral. The bias tends to reduce the gender pay gap within the PHS, while the dominant position tends to reduce the gap in the economy as a whole, given the importance of the PHS for female employment. More controversial is the net effect of shift-work premiums and overtime, which are so important in the health industry. As we shall argue below, and notwithstanding the feminization of nurses, they probably have a net adverse influence on women's relative earnings even within the health industry.

6.2. The case study hospital

6.2.1 Employment

Hospital A is a medium-size hospital created in 1970 out of an old people's home and is located in the historic centre of Rome. Like all other public hospitals in Italy, it is administered by the local health service unit – the Unità Sanitaria Locale RM1. The latter administers all hospitals, laboratories and surgeries in the same area. At the beginning of 1993 the hospital had 721 employees, including part-time and full-time physicians. Out of that total, 342 were women; there were no foreign or temporary workers.

6.2.2 Occupational breakdown

The hospital's staff numbers are more than its capacity for in-patients warrants: 160 beds, some 20 wards and auxiliary units, as well as support services and administration (Table 6.2). This is partly the result of a policy of featherbedding actively pursued during the 1970s throughout the PHS. In the early 1980s Parliament tried to introduce some order into hospital recruitment (Law No. 833/1978) by tying employment in each major occupational group (doctors, nurses, and so on) to the existing capacity (that is, number of beds). Such rules, however, can always be circumvented by creating small wards (fewer than 30 beds). In view of the need to ensure a minimum team per shift, mini-wards (as they are called) tend to absorb proportionately more personnel.

Preliminary to the examination of the wage structure and wage differentials in the hospital is the question of how representative its occupational

Table 6.2. Employment at Hospital A, by ward and service unit, 1992

	Employment		
	Total	% women	% highly skilled and physicians[1]
Management and support services	19	6.32	36.8
Wards and auxiliary units			
Anaesthesia and reanimation ward	42	57.1	47.6
Cardiology ward	11	63.6	54.5
Children's day hospital	12	100.0	25.0
Day hospital	4	75.0	0.0
Dental clinic	15	26.7	60.0
Delivery room and neonatal	27	96.3	3.7
Dermatology service	4	25.0	0.75
Ear, nose and throat ward	25	56.0	36.0
Emergency ward	30	10.0	26.7
Gastroenterology ward	34	52.9	32.4
Geriatric service	2	50.0	100.0
Gynaecological ward	45	68.9	42.2
Incubator room	27	74.0	3.7
Immunology and blood transfusions	14	64.3	50.0
Observation ward	17	52.9	5.9
Operating theatre	28	35.7	3.6
Out-patients' clinic	15	80.0	7.0
Orthopaedic ward	5	40.0	40.0
Paediatric ward	32	65.6	62.5
Rehabilitation service	1	100.0	100.0
Surgery ward	37	45.9	35.0
Urology ward	33	39.4	36.4
Ambulances	18	5.6	5.6
Blood and other tests	26	46.0	38.5
Electroencephalogram	2	50.0	0.0
Endoscopy	14	71.4	35.7
Lactarium	4	25.0	0.0
Pharmacy	11	36.4	45.5
Replacements	1	0.0	0.0
Statistical epidemiology	5	20.0	0.20
Training unit	6	83.3	16.7
X-rays	36	27.8	27.8
General services and administration			
Admission	4	50.0	0.0
Archives	2	0.0	0.0
Accounting and purchases	6	66.7	16.7
Cash book and daily turnover monitoring	9	88.8	0.0
Legal office	6	50.0	50.0
Kitchens	10	30.0	0.0
Maintenance	24	0.0	8.3

Table 6.2. (continued)

	Employment		
	Total	% women	% highly skilled and physicians[1]
Mortuary	2	0.0	0.0
Oxygen ramp	5	0.0	0.0
Parking	12	0.0	0.0
Porters	9	0.0	0.0
Storehouses and tools	5	0.0	0.0
Switchboard	6	0.0	0.0
Waste disposal and general services	4	0.0	0.0
Wardrobe and linen	5	40.0	0.0
Miscellaneous	10	50.0	20.0
Total	721	47.4	26.9

[1]Grades 7–11.

Source: Unità Sanitaria Locale RM1.

structure and pay structure are for a gender-specific analysis. Tables 6.3–5 are relevant in this respect.

Table 6.3 breaks down male and female employment by occupational group and, within each group, by skill grade. The same breakdown is available for the national PHS and the case study hospital, albeit in two different years – 1990 and 1992 respectively.

Obvious discrepancies must be discounted. Since the PHS occupational structure in establishments other than hospitals is necessarily different, some entries in the tables are necessarily empty. Veterinarians are perhaps the most obvious example of this fact. Since, moreover, the occupational breakdown is rather fine, some entries for the case study hospital often show fewer than three or four employees. With such small numbers, an index such as the percentage of women may be very misleading.

We calculated a coefficient of correlation as an index of the degree to which the hospital may be considered representative of the national PHS for our purposes.[5] The correlation is between the share of women in each occupation and grade within the national PHS and that in the case study hospital, as set out in Table 6.3. The value of the coefficient is 74.2, which inspires confidence in the representativeness of the study, but suggests caution as well.

One further question is why ‘non-standard’ employment (part-time workers, foreign workers and temporary employees in particular) is so underrepresented at the hospital.

Table 6.3. National public health sector and case-study hospital: Structure of employment by occupational group, grade and sex

Occupational group by grade	National public health sector (1990)			Hospital A (1992)		
	Male	Female	% Female	Male	Female	% Female
Doctors (full-time)						
Grade 11	8 548	464	5.15	9	1	10.00
Grade 10	23 784	4 567	16.11	45	23	33.82
Grade 9	24 018	10 399	30.21	37	20	35.09
Total	56 350	15 430	21.50	91	44	32.59
Doctors (part-time)						
Grade 11	1 507	31	2.02			
Grade 10	4 082	373	8.37	4	0	0.00
Grade 9	3 915	1 093	21.83	0	2	100.00
Total	9 504	1 497	13.61	4	2	33.33
Veterinarians						
Grade 11	652	2	0.31	–	–	–
Grade 10	1 375	45	3.17	–	–	–
Grade 9	3 141	285	8.32	–	–	–
Total	5 168	332	6.04	–	–	–
Pharmacists						
Grade 11	315	132	29.53	1	0	0.00
Grade 10	178	185	50.96	1	0	0.00
Grade 9	413	801	65.98	0	1	100.00
Total	906	1 118	55.24	2	1	33.33
Chemists						
Grade 11	329	115	25.90	–	–	–
Grade 10	1 442	1 127	43.87	–	–	–
Grade 9	2 620	4 428	62.83	1	5	83.33
Total	4 391	5 670	56.36	1	5	83.33
Trainers and coordinators						
Grade 8	553	1 266	69.60	1	1	50.00
Total	553	1 266	69.60	1	1	50.00
Inspectors						
Grade 7	1 335	118	8.12	–	–	–
Grade 6	4 937	1 171	19.17	–	–	–
Total	6 272	1 289	17.05	–	–	–

Table 6.3. (continued)

Occupational group by grade	National public health sector (1990)			Hospital A (1992)		
	Male	Female	% Female	Male	Female	% Female
Nurses						
Grade 7	3 802	18 258	82.77	2	26	92.86
Grade 6	49 297	111 552	69.35	59	111	65.29
Grade 5	–	–	–	25	47	65.28
Grade 4	23 323	32 556	58.26	–	–	–
Total	76 422	162 366	68.00	86	184	68.15
Health technician						
Grade 7	2 039	1 081	34.65	2	2	50.00
Grade 6	14 723	11 600	44.07	28	17	37.78
Total	16 762	12 681	43.07	30	19	38.78
Rehabilitation						
Grade 7	1 372	3 808	73.51	0	2	100.00
Grade 6	2 194	6 451	74.62	–	–	–
Grade 4	296	270	47.70	–	–	–
Total	3 862	10 529	73.16	0	2	100.00
Lawyers, etc.						
Grade 11	162	2	1.22	–	–	–
Grade 10	6	0	0.00	0	1	100.00
Grade 9	671	23	3.31	2	0	0.00
Grade 8	–	–	–	–	–	–
Grade 7	554	0	0.00	–	–	–
Total	1 393	25	1.76	2	1	33.33
Blue collar and technical						
Grade 11	33	2	5.71	–	–	–
Grade 10	74	35	32.11	–	–	–
Grade 9	340	204	37.50	–	–	–
Grade 8	0	4	100.00	–	–	–
Grade 7	179	898	83.38	–	–	–
Grade 6	3 884	4 944	56.00	3	1	25.00
Grade 5	4 324	380	8.08	27	0	0.00
Grade 4	42 705	16 439	27.79	29	6	17.14
Grade 3	22 069	36 803	62.51	84	62	42.47
Grade 2	18 320	23 437	56.13	–	–	–
Grade 1	186	158	45.93	–	–	–
Total	92 114	83 304	47.49	143	69	32.55

Table 6.3. (continued)

Occupational group by grade	National public health sector (1990)			Hospital A (1992)		
	Male	Female	% Female	Male	Female	% Female
Administration						
Grade 11	1 756	97	5.23	–	–	–
Grade 10	1 932	264	12.02	–	–	–
Grade 9	1 240	376	23.27	–	–	–
Grade 8	1 318	557	29.71	–	–	–
Grade 7	4 437	2 770	38.43	5	0	0.00
Grade 6	10 578	14 346	57.56	10	7	41.18
Grade 5	6	0	0.00	–	–	–
Grade 4	7 148	18 052	71.63	4	7	63.64
Grade 3	653	204	23.80	–	–	–
Grade 2	2 986	758	20.25	–	–	–
Grade 1	2	0	0.00	–	–	–
Total	32 056	37 424	53.86	19	14	42.42
Overall total	305 753	332 931	52.13	379.00	342.00	47.43

Source: Osservatorio del Pubblico Impiego, *Relazione 1990.*

6.2.3 Part-time workers

Only six employees, all physicians, worked part-time at Hospital A (Table 6.3). This is because in the public health sector part-time employment is an option practically only for physicians and was introduced mainly to legalize the widespread practice of working in a public hospital and, at the same time, for a private clinic. Part-time workers in this industry, therefore, are more often men: 14 per cent of all physicians employed in the PHS worked part-time in 1990, while the figure was only 8.8 per cent for women. The corresponding figures for Hospital A in 1992 were 4.2 per cent for male doctors and 4.3 per cent for female doctors.

6.2.4 Foreign workers

As already noted, there are no foreign workers at Hospital A, despite the fact that hiring foreign nationals (particularly nurses) is a feasible option. Our interviewees perceived a lower standard of foreign nurses, including their awkwardness with the Italian language. While this may well be the case, fear that employing foreigners will eventually lead to lower pay should not be ruled out, although this was never explicitly mentioned. Admittedly, the issue is less contentious now than it was a few years ago,

Table 6.4. National public health sector and case-study hospital: structure of employment by grade and sex only

Skill levels	National public health sector (1990)			Case-study hospital (1992)		
	Male	Female	% female	Male	Female	% female
11	13 302	845	5.97	10	1	9.09
10	32 873	6 596	16.71	50	24	32.43
9	36 358	17 609	32.63	40	28	41.18
8	1 871	1 827	49.41	1	1	50.00
7	13 718	26 933	66.25	9	30	76.92
6	85 613	150 064	63.67	100	136	57.63
5	4 330	380	8.07	54	47	46.53
4	73 472	67 317	47.81	31	13	29.55
3	22 722	37 007	61.96	84	62	42.47
2	21 306	24 195	53.17	0	0	0.00
1	188	158	45.66	0	0	0.00
Total	305 753	332 931	52.13	379	342	47.43

Sources: Osservatorio del Pubblico Impiego, *Relazione 1990*; Unità Sanitario Locale RM1.

when foreign workers were given access to employment in the PHS following widespread complaints about the scarcity of national applicants. The generous increases in shift-work premiums, mentioned earlier, may have already started to ease the shortage, and the more austere hiring policy of the 1980s and 1990s means that the question of recruiting foreign workers is less of an issue.

6.2.5 *Temporary employees*

No temporary employees worked at the hospital in 1992. This is hardly surprising since in 1990 they accounted for a mere 4.5 per cent of total employment and 3.5 per cent of female employment in the PHS at national level. This category has been omitted from our analysis for the following reasons: no occupational or skill breakdown is available for temporary employees; their incidence is low, especially among women; and no further information about them could be gathered from our case study. The figures given in all the tables thus refer to permanent employees, unless otherwise specified.

6.2.6 *Seniority*

We were unable to obtain seniority data for all the hospital's personnel, only for a random 15 per cent sample of employees in 1990 that excludes physicians. Seniority in this sample was marginally higher for women (14.9 years against 14.5 for men). This is consistent with the answers given by our interviewees when they were asked about relative female seniority. As emphasized earlier, seniority is not an issue for the gender pay gap in Italy in the private or the public sector, particularly not for the latter sector, given that its employment conditions are sufficiently advantageous to discourage staff from leaving.

6.2.7 *Pay and differentials*

On the whole, differences in employment between the case study and the PHS are not so dramatic, but before reaching any definite conclusion on this point we must investigate their repercussions for the grading and pay scales.

Let us first compare the pay structure in the PHS and the hospital, keeping in mind that the figures for the former refer to 1990 and those for the latter to 1992, and that the collective agreement was renewed in the meantime.[6] In the PHS the scale was 100 to 25.32, proceeding from the top grade 11 down to grade 1 (Table 6.5). In the hospital the scale was 100 in grade 11 down to 31.16 in grade 3, no employee being classified in the

Table 6.5. National public health sector and case-study hospital: structure of gross annual pay by grade

Skill levels	Gross annual pay: Full-time equivalent units (M + F)			
	National public health sector		Case-study hospital	
	000 lire	Index	000 lire	Index
11	82 666	100.00	94 796	100.00
10	63 480	76.79	76 068	80.24
9	48 928	59.19	56 476	59.58
8	34 409	41.62	56 100	59.18
7	33 710	40.78	36 219	38.21
6	30 179	36.51	37 082	39.12
5	25 050	30.30	38 077	40.17
4	24 316	29.41	34 839	36.75
3	22 798	27.58	29 540	31.16
2	22 048	26.67	—	—
1	20 929	25.32	—	—
Total	32 155	38.90	42 274	44.60

Sources: Osservatorio del Pubblico Impiego, *Relazione 1990*; Unità Sanitaria Locale RM1.

two bottom grades (Table 6.5). Even if, for the sake of comparison, we consider grades 11-3 only in the PHS, the range there remains marginally wider than in the hospital: 100 to 27.58.

In other words, the case study hospital has a definitely flatter pay scale. Contributory factors are to be found both in the existing differences in employment and in the changes introduced by the latest agreement. The first significant difference is the contracting out of some occupations graded at the bottom of the scale; other differences probably have a lower incidence in hospitals. Cleaners and messengers are an example. The current agreement classifies them in the two bottom grades (group 3); in the case study hospital, cleaning was contracted out, and no messenger worked there (or no one was classified as such). Returning to our earlier analysis of differences in employment, we can see that the fact of having zero entries in the hospital for several occupations has affected the wage structure; flattening it out.

Furthermore, the latest agreement appears to have favoured a general sliding up of employees along the grading structure, thus progressively emptying bottom grades: for example, nurses classified in the lowest grade for this occupation (grade 4) and with just one year's seniority were allocated to the next grade up.

The last source of difference is the gender-related distribution of employment in the grading structure, which may be taken as a substitute for a different pattern of segregation in the hospital in relation to the PHS. Having estimated average pay by grade at the hospital on the assumption that the share of women in each grade is the same as in the PHS, estimated values differ very slightly from actual values (Table 6.6), thus suggesting that the specificities of the hospital's pay structure do not conceal marked differences in the pattern of segregation. This result further confirms an earlier correlation exercise with employment data.

To summarize, relying on the case study hospital means analysing women's relative pay in a context of fairly 'compressed' skill and occupational pay differentials, with the inevitable implication of underestimating the industry-wide gender pay differentials. A 'flatter' pay scale has traditionally characterized the public sector in relation to the rest of the economy, but this phenomenon is more pronounced in the case study.

With this qualification in mind, turn to the analysis of pay differentials in the hospital (Tables 6.6–10). In important respects, the results are 'eccentric' compared with the standard findings on women's relative pay. In 1992 the overall gender pay gap at Hospital A was a mere 9.1 per cent. This figure is definitely low, since (a) comparisons are between earnings, not hourly wages, and (b) a large number of highly paid professionals are included, mainly physicians.

Table 6.6. Case-study hospital: gross annual pay by grade, all employees

Skill grades	Gross annual pay, all full-timers (male and female)			
	Actual Values		Simulated values share of women = national PHS	
	000 lire	Index	000 lire	Index
11	94 796	100.00	94 910.19	100.00
10	76 068	80.24	74 940.41	78.96
9	56 476	59.58	56 498.49	59.53
8	56 100	59.18	56 056.35	59.06
7	36 219	38.21	36 096.25	38.03
6	37 082	39.12	37 054.56	39.04
5	38 077	40.17	39 159.13	41.26
4	34 839	36.75	34 519.69	36.37
3	29 540	31.16	28 983.71	30.54
2	—	—	—	—
1	—	—	—	—
Total	42 274	44.60	42 166.16	44.43

Source: Unità Sanitaria Locale RM1.

Sensitivity analysis of the data in Table 6.7 reveals how far the overall gap is dependent on differences in the distribution of male and female employees across the grading scale, hence their respective occupational structure. First, if women were distributed as men are in the grading structure, while retaining their own grade-specific pay values, the overall gender gap would decrease to 0.6 per cent; that is, it would practically disappear. The reason for this is clarified by the next figure, namely the actual value of the gap that is obtained after doctors, pharmacists, various professionals and management have been excluded; by considering employees graded 1 to 8 only. The value in this case is 2.04 per cent, close to zero once more. Since physicians constitute the vast majority of those excluded, we may therefore conclude that among non-physician women have almost reached parity with men in the hospital.

And not only that. If we examine the gender pay gap in each grade and occupation (Table 6.8), we find a negative value (that is in favour of women) or one close to zero in half of the instances (eight out of 16 values) and, in particular, in two out of the top three grades. In other words, women who reach middle to high positions within each occupation not infrequently earn more than men, except that there are fewer of them in the highest-paid occupations. Once more we find that the problem is

Table 6.7. Case-study hospital: gross yearly pay by grade, 1992[1]

Grade	Men (No.)	Average pay (000 lire)	Women (No.)	Average pay (000 lire)	Women's relative pay (Men = 100)
11	10	95 130	1	91 450	96.13
10	50	73 742	24	80 913	109.73
9	40	56 583	28	56 324	99.54
8	1	52 473	1	59 726	113 .82
7	9	35 333	30	36 485	103.26
6	100	37 343	136	36 890	98.79
5	54	39 386	47	36 574	92.86
4	31	35 355	13	33 608	95.06
3	84	30 752	62	27 898	90.72
Total	379	44 360	342	39 963	90.09

[1]Full-time equivalent units.

Source: Unità Sanitaria Locale RM1.

Overall differential at Hospital A according to different hypotheses	
Actual gap, all employees	9.01
Actual gap, employees graded 1–8	0.06
Estimated gap (women's grading structure equal to men's)	2.04

[1]Male minus female pay in percentage of male pay; weighted average.

Source: Table 6, 7 for the data.

not the pay gap at every step of the ladder, but the uneven distribution of the sexes at the very top of the scale.

In order to gain further insight into these results, we have identified the most important pay components and calculated the gender gap for each of them (male component = 100). The components are:

1) basic pay, comprising contractual minimum, cost-of-living allowances and seniority pay
2) occupation-specific allowances, equivalent in public employment to firm-specific wage premiums in the private sector
3) premiums for overtime, shift work (nurses) or being on call (doctors)
4) group incentives, usually tied to some index of 'attendance'[7]

Table 6.8. Case-study hospital: gross yearly pay by occupation 1992 (full-time equivalent units: 000 lire)

Occupational group/grade	Males		Females		Relative female pay (Males = 100)
	Total	Yearly gross pay (1992)	Total	Yearly pay (1992)	
Doctors (full-time)					
Grade 11	9	95 917	1	91 450	95.34
Grade 10	49	73 899	23	81 756	110.63
Grade 9	37	57 334	22	58 206	101.52
Pharmacists					
Grade 11	1	88 054	0	–	n.a.
Grade 10	1	66 030	0	–	n.a.
Grade 9	0	–	1	57 626	n.a.
Chemists, etc.					
Grade 9	1	49 200	5	47 289	96.12
Trainers, coordinators					
Grade 8	1	52 437	1	59 726	113.90
Nurses					
Grade 7	2	34 181	26	37 712	110.33
Grade 6	59	38 999	111	37 977	97.38
Grade 5	25	41 438	47	36 574	88.26
Health technicians					
Grade 7	2	36 433	2	33 613	92.26
Grade 6	28	35 701	17	31 387	87.92

Table 6.8. (continued)

Occupational group/grade	Males		Females		Relative female pay (Males = 100)
	Total	Yearly gross pay (1992)	Total	Yearly pay (1992)	
Rehabilitation					
Grade 7	0	–	2	23 398	n.a.
Lawyers, etc.					
Grade 10	0	–	1	61 536	n.a.
Grade 9	2	46 389	0	–	n.a.
Manual workers and technicians					
Grade 6	3	31 258	1	32 598	104.29
Grade 5	29	37 617	0	–	n.a.
Grade 4	27	36 207	6	39 937	110.30
Grade 3	84	30 752	62	27 898	90.72
Administration					
Grade 7	5	35 353	0	–	n.a
Grade 6	10	33 991	7	33 639	98.96
Grade 4	4	29 604	7	28 184	95.20
Total	379	44 360	342	39 963	90.09

Source: Unità Sanitaria Locale RM1.

Table 6.9. Case-study hospital, 1992: women's gross annual pay by major component

Occupation/ Grade	Women (No.)	Gross annual pay				
		Basic wage	Occupation-specific allowance	Overtime and shifts premium	Group incentives	Total
Doctors						
Grade 11	1	96.10	0.66	0.33	2.92	100.00
Grade 10	23	90.93	0.45	2.66	5.96	100.00
Grade 9	22	90.73	0.72	2.89	5.66	100.00
Pharmacists						
Grade 11	0	–	–	–	–	n.a.
Grade 10	0	–	–	–	–	n.a.
Grade 9	1	82.71	0.00	2.17	5.12	100.00
Chemists, etc.						
Grade 9	5	94.63	0.00	0.00	5.37	100.00
Trainers, coordinators						
Grade 8	1	59.30	1.00	37.57	2.12	100.00
Nurses						
Grade 7	26	82.84	7.94	5.43	3.79	100.00
Grade 6	111	68.73	6.43	16.16	8.68	100.00
Grade 5	47	74.13	1.37	15.44	9.06	100.00
Health technicians						
Grade 7	2	98.84	0.00	0.03	1.13	100.00
Grade 6	17	87.94	0.67	5.83	5.56	100.00
Rehabilitation						
Grade 7	2	100.00	0.00	0.00	0.00	100.00
Lawyers, etc.						
Grade 10	1	89.83	0.00	0.00	10.17	100.00
Grade 9						
Manual workers and technicians						
Grade 6	1	89.71	0.00	0.05	10.24	100.00
Grade 5	0	–	–	–	–	n.a.
Grade 4	6	67.52	0.00	32.33	0.15	100.00
Grade 3	62	85.27	0.00	14.56	0.17	100.00

Table 6.9. (continued)

Occupation/ Grade	Women (No.)	Gross annual pay				
		Basic wage	Occupation-specific allowance	Overtime and shifts premium	Group incentives	Total
Administration						
Grade 7	0	–	–	–	–	–
Grade 6	7	90.76	0.00	0.00	9.24	100.00
Grade 4	7	93.75	0.00	2.48	3.78	100.00
Average		79.30	2.99	11.81	5.90	100.00

Source: Unità Sanitaria Locale RM1.

Table 6.9 breaks down female employees' pay into these four components. Basic pay accounts for 79.3 per cent of the average pay of female employees. This is consistent with the traditional importance of basic pay components in the pay of all public employees (Table 6.3). Occupational allowances, on the other hand, are significant only for nurses, and are partly justified by the risks involved. Their share in the average pay for women is small (2.99 per cent), but the maximum for skilled nurses is 7.9 per cent.

Of the three non-basic pay components, overtime and shift-work premiums have on average the highest share: 11.8 per cent. However, the amount of these premiums varies a great deal across occupations. They are relatively unimportant in the case of physicians, for the latter are more often on call rather than working shifts. By contrast, they are important for 'generic' nurses (grades 5 and 6), since less skilled nurses tend to work heavier shifts. The main beneficiaries, however, are relatively unskilled workers in grade 4 (auxiliary workers), who increase their pay by one-third through overtime and shift-work premiums. Clearly, the latter are used to increase pay for the bottom layer of the hospital's labour force, without any direct comparisons that might lead to a ratchet effect.

The distribution of the final component, group incentives, follows a less clear-cut pattern, since its value is more uniform (in absolute terms) across occupational groups and grades, and only marginally higher for employees in grade 6. This suggests that within the public sector the introduction of 'merit pay' has been a cover-up for pay increases rather than an effective form of incentive.

Table 6.10. Case-study hospital, 1992: relative female pay by pay component (corresponding component of male pay = 100; gross yearly pay)

Occupation/ Grade	Women (No.)	Relative female pay				
		Basic wage	Occupation-specific allowance	Overtime and shifts premium	Group incentives	Total
Doctors						
Grade 11	1	99.17	385.71	15.07	51.83	95.34
Grade 10	23	116.33	249.73	40.98	107.51	110.63
Grade 9	22	108.32	227.98	32.90	100.48	101.52
Pharmacists						
Grade 11	0	–	–	–	–	n.a.
Grade 10	0	–	–	–	–	n.a.
Grade 9	1	–	–	–	–	n.a.
Chemists, etc.						
Grade 9	5	98.99	0.00	0.00	63.57	96.12
Trainers, coordinators						
Grade 8	1	96.84	0.00	154.71	90.82	113.82
Nurses						
Grade 7	26	101.29	99.77	0.00	424.91	110.33
Grade 6	111	100.69	104.27	86.20	91.16	97.38
Grade 5	47	100.14	103.44	57.69	80.99	88.26
Health technicians						
Grade 7	2	102.13	0.00	6.44	14.84	92.26
Grade 6	17	99.93	22.81	35.19	89.36	87.92
Rehabilitation						
Grade 7	2	100.00	0.00	0.00	0.00	100.00
Lawyers, etc.						
Grade 10	1	–	–	–	–	–
Grade 9	0	–	–	–	–	n.a.
Manual workers and technicians						
Grade 6	1	95.02	0.00	3.69	4 412.78	104.29
Grade 5	0	–	–	–	–	–
Grade 4	6	105.24	0.00	122.68	97.07	110.30
Grade 3	62	99.37	0.00	60.07	95.33	90.72

Table 6.10. (continued)

Occupation/ Grade	Women (No.)	Relative female pay				
		Basic wage	Occupation-specific allowance	Overtime and shifts premium	Group incentives	Total
Administration						
Grade 7	0	–	–	–	–	–
Grade 6	7	99.09	0.00	0.00	109.20	98.96
Grade 4	7	98.14	0.00	0.00	39.72	95.21

Source: Unità Sanitaria Locale RM1.

Definite indications emerge when the gender gap is calculated component by component rather than overall (Table 6.10). In the case of basic pay, the gender gap is nil or negative for the vast majority of occupations or grades. In other words, if there were only basic pay, women would earn more or at least as much as men in most occupations. Since at this fine level of aggregation, disparities in basic pay are due almost solely to seniority, we have found here indirect confirmation that seniority is often greater for women. Occupation-specific allowances also tend to favour women: marginally in the case of nurses, considerably in the case of physicians. However, as noted above, their overall impact is modest.

The real counterbalancing factors are all linked to attendance and work schedules. Gender pay gaps in overtime and shift-work premiums as well as in incentive pay tend to be positive. They appear in fact to follow a pattern, whereby men in the lower grades within each occupation tend to compensate by taking the heavier shifts, working more overtime or having a higher attendance than women.

6.3. CONCLUDING REMARKS

Discussion of the gender pay gap in the PHS may be concluded by assessing the way it is influenced by three groups of factors – institutional, occupational and time-related.

Institutional factors continue to work unambiguously in favour of women: directly through pay structure, indirectly through seniority. A relatively compressed scale for contractual minima, together with the high incidence of the cost-of-living allowance, compresses skill differentials and thus gender-related differentials. At the same time job security, generous pensions and other benefits of public employment increase, if anything, the tendency for women in Italy not to quit a job once they have started it, with favourable implications for seniority and the related pay component.

Occupational segregation works both ways, since women are underrepresented at the top and the bottom of the scale in the PHS. Underrepresentation at the top, however, is dominant and is therefore responsible for a significant share of the gender pay gap in the health industry. Put differently, the gap is roughly proportional to the incidence of women among top-ranking physicians. This finding emerges clearly from the case study material and may well apply to the PHS in general, although the share of the gap accounted for by underrepresentation among physicians would be lower at the national level (the proportion of women at the bottom of the grading scale, it will be remembered, is higher in the PHS than in the case study hospital).

Finally, working time tends adversely to affect women's relative pay in the health industry as elsewhere. This is seen more clearly if we separate physicians and related occupations at the top from the rest of the workforce. Among non-physicians, women at the case study hospital would earn at least as much as men if it were not for the fact that men compensate for women's higher skills in terms of working time – more overtime, heavier shifts and higher attendance in general.

Notes

1. Dipartimento di Economia Politica, Università degli Studi di Siena.
2. As has been noted elsewhere (Bettio and Villa 1992), employment data by sex and separate industrial and occupation groups are available for the public sector only, and have been available only since 1985; they are published by the Osservatorio del Pubblico Impiego.
3. See Bettio and Villa (1993, section 2.1).
4. Data collected by the Osservatorio del Pubblico Impiego, Relazione 1990, Roma.
5. In calculating the coefficient, entries with no employees either at the national level or in the hospital were dropped; and to avoid the problem of small numbers we have considered only occupational totals (neglecting the distribution by grade) for pharmacists and professionals.
6. The overall *de facto* average figure for gross annual pay in the PHS in 1990 was 32 155 million lire versus 42 274 million lire in the hospital in 1992. Since no earlier data for the hospital are available, we cannot determine how

much of the difference is attributable, respectively, to a dissimilar wage structure, wage drift and the contractual rise granted in the meantime. Thus, not only was there little to gain by considering actual wage levels rather than indexes, but also we believe that comparing the pay structure is sufficient for our purposes.

7. Except in the case of testing laboratories, where other indexes of 'productivity' are feasible.

7 Telecommunications

Francesca Bettio[1]

7.1. THE INDUSTRY

In the context of the progressive privatization of the publicly owned industries (that is where assets are shared between the public and the State), the ownership and market structure of telecommunication services are changing rapidly. At the time of the study three major companies belonging to IRI, the former public holding, operate in the telecommunications industry, each one still operating under monopoly licensing: SIP (Società Italiana per l'Esercizio delle Telecomunicazioni) is in charge of the installation and servicing of the domestic telephone system; ITALCABLE is responsible for international telecommunications; and TELESPAZIO is responsible for communications via satellite. This study looks at the SIP.

Industry-level comparisons can be made only for 'communications' as a whole, which include (private) postal and courier services, and where SIP employees alone account for more than one-quarter of the total. The inclusion of postal and courier services suggests that the 18 per cent growth in employment during the 1980s shown in Appendix Table A.3 (the overall average was 5.72 per cent) overestimates the trend with respect to telephone and satellite communications alone.

Average earnings in the telephone and satellite area, on the other hand, are underestimated by the figure referring to communications as a whole, as the comparison with our own data for SIP employees reveals (see Appendix Table A.4 and Table 7.11). It should be noted in this respect that although SIP retains its main monopoly licence, it has lost other licences in recent years, and may soon be forced to share the domestic telephone system with other companies. Up to the time of the study, however, its more than 80 000 employees have most probably shared in the company's monopoly revenue. For example, they are paid 14 months' salary per year, the norm in Italy being 13.

In fact, average annual earnings at SIP in 1991 totalled 36 650 000 lire (Table 7.11), not including individual bonuses for intermediate management or top management's earnings. This figure exceeded by 27 per cent average earnings in the economy as a whole in the same year and was marginally higher than earnings in the public sector as a whole.[2]

7.2. THE NATIONAL TELEPHONE COMPANY

Like the hospital examined in the first case study, the national telephone company therefore belongs to a relatively well-paid employment sector, one that expanded considerably during the 1980s. Another similarity with the hospital is the concentration of female employment around the middle of the grading and pay scale, likewise implying a very small gender pay gap. There are, however, considerable differences between the two cases in terms of skills and in the occupational and gender composition of employment.

Women are still a minority in SIP – 17.7 per cent in 1992 (Table 7.1). The relatively high share of manual workers (21.7 per cent), practically all men (there are 106 women out of 18 950 manual workers), is part of the explanation. The expected underrepresentation of women among foremen and top and intermediate management – who make up 8.5 per cent of the labour force – is a second contributory factor. A third factor is high segregation, a feature that school curricula and a traditionally male environment probably help to perpetuate, as argued below.

7.2.1 Part-time and full-time workers

SIP is a complex organization, consisting of divisions and subdivisions and spread over the national territory (see Chart 7.1). In 1992 it employed 87 474 full-time equivalent workers, 17.7 per cent of whom were women (Table 7.1).

Part-time employment is low but not uncommon in this company, amounting to 4.6 per cent of total employment in 1992 (Table 7.2).[3] SIP distinguishes between 'heavy' and 'light' part-timers, the former working 50 per cent of normal working time and the latter 75 per cent. The ratio between the two definitely favours 'heavy' part-timers: one to three approximately.

Another choice available to part-timers is between two schedules: working each working day, half or three-quarters of the time, or working half or three-quarters of the working days in a week on a normal daily schedule. The company sets a limit of 12 per cent part-timers in any establishment and does not offer the part-time option to managers, shift workers or team workers, with the significant exception of telephone operators.

Chart 7.1. Organization chart: SIP, 1993

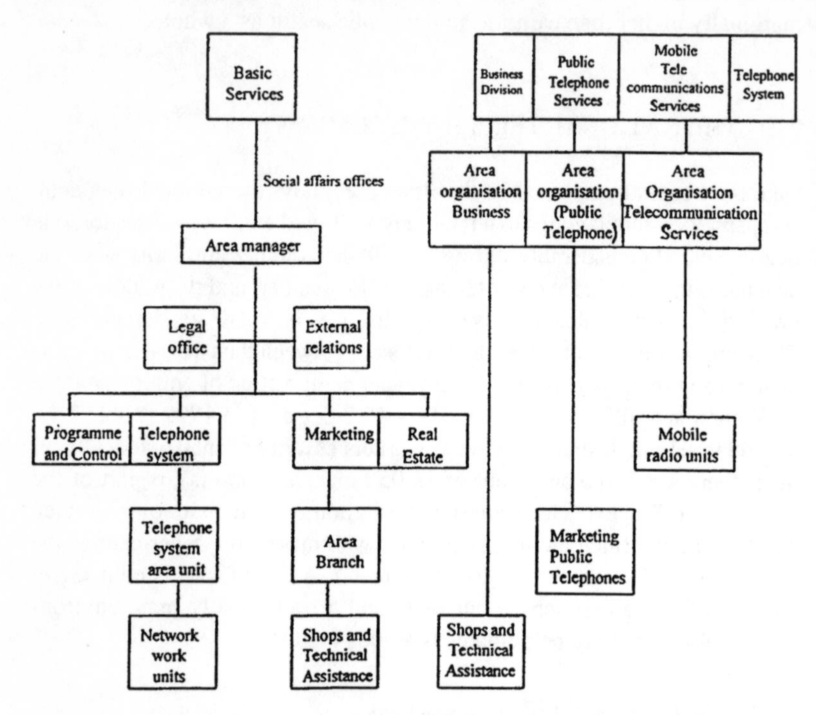

Wage and other conditions are generally not unfavourable to part-timers, thanks to recent legislation.[4] In particular, a strictly proportional criterion applies in relation to earnings. Thus, even if our data refer to full-time equivalents, we may assume that they do not give a particularly 'biased' picture.

Since part-time contracts are not particularly attractive for Italian firms, SIP, like most other firms in the country, 'grants' part-time status rather than demanding it. In addition, so we were informed, SIP has a definite preference for converting existing contracts from full- to part-time status rather than hiring on a part-time basis. Reportedly, the firm fears that employees may use part-time work as a form of easy access to permanent employment; that is, once hired as part-timers they may soon demand and obtain full-time status, with the help of unions and sympathetic legislation. Part-time work in this case is seen as adding rigidity to the labour contract rather than increasing its flexibility.

The company's fear may be a reaction to having pursued a policy of part-time hiring in the recent past. The gender composition of part-timers

Chart 7.1. (continued)

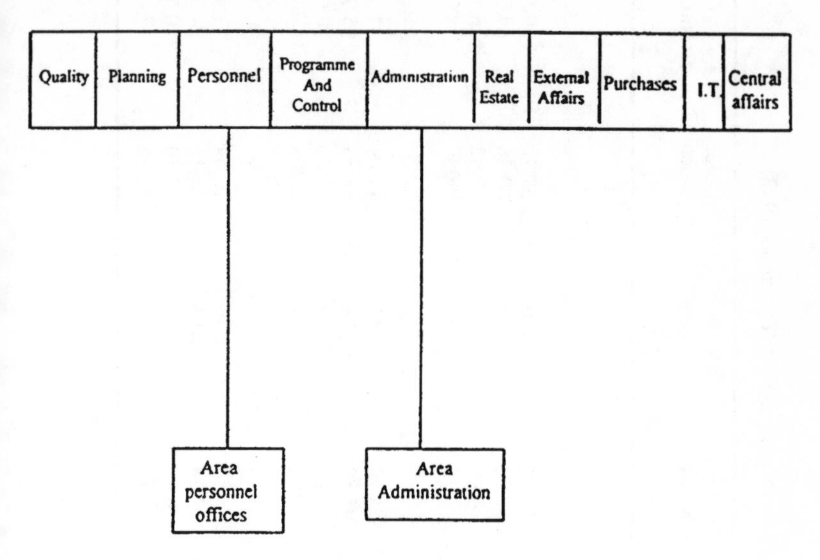

Source: adapted from information from case-study organization

and their distribution in the grading scale underscore this point. Women constitute by far the majority of all part-timers (77.49 per cent), but men's share is higher for 'heavy' part-timers (25 per cent) than for 'light' part-timers (13 per cent); the two typologies serve very different workers' strategies. 'Heavy' part-timers are concentrated in the bottom grades in clerical and technical occupations, that is among new, young entrants. The bulk of 'light' part-timers, by contrast, are women graded 6 or 7 – the majority of senior female personnel in the firm. In short, a not insignificant share of men are willing to enter as part-timers, but they differ from women in that they are less willing to stay on as part-timers.

7.2.2 Occupational segregation and the internal labour market

There are four major divisions in the company: basic (consumer) services; business; public telephones; and radio-mobile services. Each branches out at the regional level down to local sales, service and work stations. Nine additional units are responsible at the central level for overall planning, administration, personnel management and general services (Chart 7.1). In terms of employment (Table 7.1) the basic services division is by far the most important division (75 per cent), followed by the business

Table 7.1. SIP employees by major division, occupational category and sex, December 1992[1]

Divisions	Basic services	Business division	Public telephones	Mobile telecom services	Other divisions	All divisions
Occupational category						
Men (%)						
Managers and technicians	7.00	10.04	17.68	7.00	31.70	9.58
Clerks	59.59	89.95	82.32	93.00	60.36	64.26
Production Workers	33.41	0.01	0.00	0.00	7.92	26.16
All employees (no.)	54 962	9262	775	971	6059	72 029
Women (%)						
Managers and technicians	1.14	3.95	4.20	5.42	11.09	3.52
Clerks	97.98	96.05	95.80	94.58	88.55	95.79
Production workers	0.88	0.00	0.00	0.00	0.36	0.69
All employees (No.)	10 708	1214	191	74	3259	15 445
Share of Women (%)						
Managers and technicians	3.07	4.91	5.52	5.56	15.84	7.30
Clerks	24.26	12.28	22.24	7.17	44.11	24.22
Production workers	0.51	0.00	0.00	0.00	2.39	0.56
All employees (No.)	16.31	11.59	19.73	7.06	34.98	17.66

[1]Full-time equivalent units.

Source: SIP.

Table 7.2. SIP: part-timers by occupational group and grade, 1992

	Part-timers (50%)		Part-timers (75%)	
	Men	Women	Men	Women
Management				
Grade 1	0	0	0	0
Grade 2	0	0	0	2
Grade 3	0	0	0	0
Clerks and technicians				
Grade 4	2	2	3	4
Grade 5	12	8	17	28
Grade 6	23	166	37	294
Grade 7	52	423	53	495
Grade 8	79	235	13	70
Grade 9	622	1 468	5	19
Manual workers				
Grade 6	0	0	0	0
Grade 7	2	1	5	0
Grade 8	4	0	4	0
Grade 9	3	7	1	9
Grade 10	1	0	0	0
Total	800	2 310	138	919

Source: SIP.

division (12 per cent) and the central organization units ('other divisions' in Table 7.1; 10.6 per cent).

The distribution of female employees among divisions and units is far from uniform. Compared with men, they are better represented in the central units: clerical positions here are fairly mixed (44 per cent women) and women account for 16 per cent among intermediate and top management. In absolute terms, however, the vast majority of women (70 per cent) work in the first division (basic services) and almost exclusively in clerical positions. Mobile telecommunication services, which involve technical and other skills, are the least feminized division (seven per cent of women), followed by the business division.

A better idea of the existing occupational segregation is given by the distribution of male and female employees, respectively, along the grading scale and among narrowly defined occupations. Sixty-five per cent of women, as against 38 per cent of men, are to be found in clerical jobs graded 6 and 7 (Table 7.3). Moreover, 78 per cent of all women in the company are employed in the following five occupations:

administration clerk; commercial clerk, e.g. for drafting standard contracts with customers; telephone operator; recording and locating of faults reported by customers; 'technical auxiliary'.

The first three occupations are the main entry levels in the two typical career paths – as clerks or as telephone operators – for women at SIP. The

Table 7.3. SIP: distribution of employees by skill grade and occupational group, 1992[1]

Occupational category	Men		Women	
	Total	(%)	Total	(%)
Managers	802	1.11	21	0.14
Technicians and intermediate management	6 100	8.47	523	3.38
Clerks	446 282	64.26	14 796	95.79
Production workers	18 845	26.16	106	0.69
All employees	72 029	100.00	15 445	100.00
Skill grade				
Top management	802	1.11	21	0.14
Foremen and intermediate management				
Grade 1	1 335	1.85	71	0.46
Grade 2	1 579	2.19	180	1.16
Grade 3	3 186	4.42	272	1.76
Clerks and technicians				
Grade 4	2 492	3.46	383	2.48
Grade 5	8 854	12.29	900	5.83
Grade 6	13 298	18.46	4 641	30.05
Grade 7	13 939	19.35	5 435	35.19
Grade 8	6 903	9.58	2 187	14.16
Grade 9	797	1.11	1 250	8.09
Manual workers				
Grade 6	427	0.59	0	0.00
Grade 7	13 572	18.84	11	0.07
Grade 8	3 973	5.52	64	0.41
Grade 9	843	1.17	29	0.19
Grade 10	29	0.04	3	0.02
	72 029	100	15 445	100

[1]Full-timer equivalent units.

Source: SIP.

fourth occupation is a relatively new one for women and a slightly more technical version of the operator's job, offering slightly higher chances of promotion. Women gained access to it after periods of restructuring caused by the automation of various customer services previously attended to by operators. Those that were made redundant were given training and moved to the units in charge of programming, and repair and maintenance work, with the task of identifying, locating and recording the faults reported by customers.

For each of these occupations a career means promotion from entry grade 9 to grade 6. Seniority ensures automatic promotion to grade 7, the average length of service required being about five years. Higher seniority is necessary but not sufficient to reach grade 6; promotion is thus partly discretionary at this juncture and the chances vary from one occupation to another, with an upper ceiling which the firm imposes on the number of promotions. Thus, for example, promotion is generally easier for clerks than for telephone operators, and easier for operators in the repair and maintenance teams than for those involved in other customer services.

Grades 6 and 7 are in the middle-to-lower section of the grading scale at SIP. The company is a typical example of a well-structured internal labour market, defining career paths in terms of progression along a 10-grade scale, or sections thereof, for all employees except top managers.

Top management represent 1 per cent of all employees, include very few women (2.6 per cent) and are almost invariably recruited from within the firm, that is from intermediate management and foremen, graded 1 to 3. Top managers' salaries and conditions are separate from those of all other employees.

Intermediate management and foremen are usually recruited from among graduates, hired directly into grade 5 and moved up to grade 2 on the basis of seniority. A minority of intermediate management, roughly 10 per cent (we were told), come from a lower grade, and in particular from the position of assistant, that is a foreman in charge of a small local division or office. Assistants may be hired directly for this position and given grade 7 upon entry, eventually reaching grade 5 through seniority; or they may be promoted to the position from the lower ranks. Promotion from the bottom in this case involves a tiny minority of manual workers, telephone operators or clerks, who may be promoted to the position of assistant in order to progress further from grade 6.

In practice, grade 6 is the career ceiling for most manual workers and clerks, including telephone operators. In fact, manual workers reached the ceiling at grade 7 before the current agreement was signed; and they still enter one grade below everybody else in the company, at grade 10. Residual differences, however, will soon disappear, since the distinction between manual and non-manual workers itself is bound to be abolished at SIP, and all new entrants will soon be classified as non-manual.

So far, however, manual workers have been the bottom group. In terms of vertical segregation, therefore, women benefited from having left this group earlier. This happened when computerized technology was first introduced into the telephone operators' room. Previously, telephone operators had been regarded as manual workers operating on a particular type of assembly line. In fact, so we were told, the pace of work was as intense as on any typical assembly line and supervision was relentless. With the introduction of computerized technology, operators were promoted to non-manual status.

Another factor that continues to work in women's favour is seniority – of considerable importance for automatic promotion at SIP, with the exception of managerial positions at every level. As we have seen, discretion plays a part in promotion only at the last step in the ladder for most occupations. Because women's seniority is high in absolute terms at SIP (15.5 years), practically all of them will reach grade 7 and many of them eventually to progress to grade 6.

On closer inspection, however, we can see that differences in seniority do exist between men and women, despite the similarity in the overall averages (16 years for men, 15.5 for women: Table 7.4).

Women are much more 'junior' at higher grades than at intermediate grades (6 and 7 in particular), where the vast majority of them are to be found. In the bottom grades (8–10) the difference in women's favour is less marked, and in some cases men are more senior than women, for example among manual workers in grade 8, although, the number of women is too small to warrant any definite conclusion. Different factors are at work here. Higher seniority in the middle grades suggests that it is relatively more difficult for women to break through the ceiling represented by grade 6. By contrast, lower seniority for women at the top suggests that the company may have converted only recently to a policy of recruiting women for intermediate management positions.

In other words, lower seniority at the top may be a sign of impending vertical desegregation. On the other hand, we found that women are overqualified among intermediate management: their share of graduates is 60.4 per cent as against 33 per cent for men (Table 7.5). These two findings may not contradict one another. Typically, recruitment follows a wave-like pattern at SIP. Thus data referring to a single year may give distorted information if they conceal a recent number of hirings. In particular, the data in question showing a higher share of graduates among female intermediate management may conceal a combination of two recent developments:

Table 7.4. SIP: average years of seniority by skill grade, 1992

Skill Grade	Men	Women
Top management	21.09	15.11
Foremen and intermediate management		
Grade 1	21.03	16.04
Grade 2	21.06	11.09
Grade 3	22.11	14.00
Clerks and technicians		
Grade 4	18.08	16.03
Grade 5	19.11	23.03
Grade 6	15.05	22.08
Grade 7	13.04	17.09
Grade 8	2.11	3.02
Grade 9	1.07	1.11
Manual workers		
Grade 6	21.07	–
Grade 7	20.02	23.04
Grade 8	9.03	7.11
Grade 9	1.11	3.03
Grade 10	0.07	0.10
All employees	16	15.05

Source: SIP.

Table 7.5. SIP: foremen and intermediate management by level of education, 1992

Education	Women (%)	Men (%)
Graduates (17 years' schooling or more)	60	33
All non-graduate diploma holders (13 years' schooling)	33	61
Primary, lower secondary and other (less than 13 years' schooling)	7	6
Total	100	100

Source: SIP.

1) the company's shift to a policy of recruiting females as well as males for intermediate management positions
2) the consolidation of the tendency to recruit graduates only, men or women, for these positions.

Table 7.6. SIP: employees by level of education, 1992

Education	Men (%)	Women (%)
Graduates (17 years' schooling or more)	5	6
Non-graduate engineers (13 years' schooling)	39	4
Non-graduate accountants (13 years' schooling)	6	26
Other non-graduate diploma holders (13 years' schooling)	3	36
Primary, lower secondary and other (less than 13 years' schooling)	47	28
Total	100	100

Source: SIP.

This interpretation would tally with the previous findings of lower seniority for women at the top of the career ladder.

Education, however, does not consistently work in favour of desegregation. In terms of average number of years of schooling, women have a slight advantage over men: the incidence of graduates throughout the labour force is the same, however as most manual markers are men the incidence of the less educated (less than 13 years of schooling) is lower for women (Table 7.6). Women's disadvantage lies elsewhere, notably in their lack of 'technical' education. The core of the male labour force is currently recruited from among non-graduate engineers, very few of whom are women (Table 7.6). The net effect is fewer occupational prospects for women within the firm as well as fewer chances of proceeding beyond grade 6.

Internal training does not compensate for women's initial disadvantage in terms of formal 'technical' education. SIP organizes extensive training for its labour force, but men are the main beneficiaries. An example of this is what the firm calls 'basic training' (Table 7.7).

SIP organized 821 270 hours of basic training in 1992 for a total of 2088 trainees. However, women accounted for only 7.7 per cent of the trainees and had an even lower share of the total number of hours (6.4 per cent). Further evidence on this point concerns the share of women hired on youth training contracts (Table 7.8): almost half (46 per cent) of newly hired men enter as trainees, while the figure for women is 24 per cent.

However, the extent to which training and education involve segregation is questionable; they may instead mask less 'tangible' obstacles, gender hierarchy for example. The union official we interviewed told us of recent opposition by male workers at a local unit to the promotion of a

Table 7.7. SIP: basic internal training (annual hours and participants), 1992

Grade or occupational group	Participants			Per capita annual hours	
	Men	Women		Men	Women
	No.	No.	(%)	No.	No.
Manual workers	389	24	6.17	275.49	465.50
Clerks and technicians	755	17	2.25	354.75	343.53
Skilled clerks and technicians	788	108	13.71	503.38	301.76
All trainees	1932	149	7.71	399.41	332.90

Source: SIP.

woman to the position of foreman, despite her well-known skills and competence. The opposition was simply to the idea of having a woman in charge (men 'suffer', as the union official put it) and the company had to take a firm stand in order to confirm the promotion.

7.2.3 The gender pay gap

Whatever their true importance for segregation in the historical perspective and for women's future employment prospects, technical training and education do not appear to be disproportionately responsible for the gender pay gap at present. If they were, women ought to be heavily penalized in terms of grading, and hence of pay. This is not what our data suggest.

First of all, we shall summarize the grading situation. As noted earlier, the overwhelming majority of female employees are to be found in grades 6 and 7 (65.2 per cent). Compared with men, their distribution in the grading scale is 'heavier' at the bottom and much lighter at the top, especially if top management is included.

Differences at the bottom, however, are not dramatic. This is because of the disadvantage that still attaches to being a manual worker rather than a clerk, combined with the fact that female manual workers at SIP are so few. Differences at the top, on the other hand, are more pronounced, but the upper wage pyramid is still sufficiently flat at the top (Table 7.9) to effectively 'protect' women's relative pay.

To translate the above facts into numbers, we have simulated the gender pay gap according to different hypotheses and compared it with the actual

Table 7.8. SIP: turnover by major company division, 1992[1]

Divisions	Men			Women		
	New hirings and moves to permancy		Separations	New hirings and moves to permancy		Separations
	Total	(Including youth training contracts)	Total	Total	(Including youth training contracts)	Total
Basic services	444	161	725	158	15	303
Business	172	71	96	34	9	23
Public telephones	138	101	3	7	4	1
Radio-mobile services	12	5	14	3	1	7
Other	777	373	801	287	88	412
Company	1543	711	1639	489	117	746

[1]Full-time equivalent units.

Source: SIP.

Table 7.9. SIP: contractual minimum monthly pay by grade, 1991 and 1994

Skill grade	Contractual minimum pay			
	1992		1994	
	000 lire[1]	Index	000 lire[1]	Index
1	1 739.7	100.00	2 135.0	100.00
2	1 630.8	93.74	1 982.7	92.87
3	1 529.6	87.92	1 838.6	86.12
4	1 385.5	79.64	1 540.3	72.15
5	1 297.7	74.59	1 445.1	67.69
6	1 222.3	70.26	1 363.5	63.86
7	1 148.2	66.00	1 283.3	60.11
8	1 037.2	59.62	1 147.1	53.73
9	889.5	51.13	963.1	45.11
10	740.7	42.58	802.0	37.56

[1]Fourteen, not 12 months, are paid to each employee. The contractual minimum includes basic salary, a monthly allowance for managers (grades 1 to 3) and the yearly group incentive equivalent to that paid in July 1991

Source: Collective agreement.

gap. According to the figure for average *de facto* gross yearly earnings that we received from SIP, women's earnings are on average 5.3 per cent lower than those of men. This gap is lower still than the one we found in the hospital, despite the feminization of the main component skilled workers there (that is nurses).

The figure of 5.3 per cent is an underestimate for at least two reasons. First, top management is not considered; second, the figures for wages that we received from SIP, henceforth referred to as actual figures, exclude all discretionary 'premiums' paid to employees. SIP was clearly unwilling to disclose this kind of information.

Attempts to remedy these two drawbacks were made by estimating the true differentials on the basis of 'informed guesses' made by trade union officials. The results are set out in Table 7.10.

As these figures show, neither the inclusion of managers' pay nor that of premiums for intermediate management dramatically lowers women's relative pay. In the hypothesis most unfavourable to women, the pay gap would increase by two percentage points (from 5.3 to 7.8 per cent).

We must, however, set aside these estimates for a moment and refer to actual figures (that is figures that exclude managers' earnings and

Table 7.10. Women's relative pay at SIP, December 1991 (men's pay = 100)

Actual figure: no top manager, no discretionary premiums	94.67
Hypothetical figure, including discretionary premiums; no top management	94.16
Hypothetical figure, including discretionary premiums and top management	92.7–92.2

Source: Based on data in Table 7.11 and estimates by union officials.

premiums in order to proceed with the analysis). The actual gender pay gap is 5.3 per cent in this case, as noted, and it is interesting to compare it with the value we would get on the basis of the contractual pay scale. If women and men received earnings strictly proportional to the wage scale laid down by the collective agreement (Table 7.9), while retaining their respective distribution along the grading scale, women's relative earnings would be just 3.5 per cent lower than those of men. In other words, the grading structure *per se* penalizes women only to the extent of 3.5 per cent.

The other major determinant of the pay gap is differences in working time. To visualize this, we have broken down the actual pay gap into three components: actual basic pay (contractual pay plus seniority allowance); overtime and allowances for being on call; and non-discretionary, collective wage premiums. The first two components are fairly obvious. The third is a novelty in the pay of SIP employees; it depends partly on the employee's rate of 'attendance', and partly on the productivity of the unit in which he or she works.

Table 7.11 reports the actual gap as the sum of these three components. Basic pay contributes 2.1 percentage points to the differential. In theory, major differences in actual basic pay are due to grading or to seniority, or

Table 7.11. SIP: average annual pay and its components, December 1991 (000 lire)[1]

	Gross annual pay			
	Basic salary	Overtime and allowance for on-call	Group incentives	Total
Men	33 562	1380	1708	36 650
Women	32 794	402	1502	34 698
Women, men = 100	97.71	29.13	87.94	94.67
Components of differential[2]	2.10	2.67	0.56	5.33

[1]Full-time equivalent units. [2]Male component-female component/male total; per cent.

Source: SIP.

both. We know for certain that seniority ought not to make a vast difference, since the average figure is practically equivalent for women and men. Grading, on the other hand, should result in a gap higher than the actual two percentage points: our simulation suggests 3.5 per cent, as noted. As no further data are available, we cannot identify exactly what acts as a partial compensation for the gap that we would expect on the basis of grading alone. At any rate, this 'unaccounted for' compensation is sufficiently small not to warrant major speculation.

Overtime and work-schedule-related allowances, on the other hand, penalize women by adding 2.7 points to the differential, that is more than basic pay, while collective premiums have a marginal incremental impact (+0.5 points).

The overall picture is sufficiently clear, despite the inevitable lacunas in the analysis. As in the case of the hospital, the two major components of the gender pay gap are underrepresentation at the top more than overrepresentation at the bottom, and differences in the work schedules. If women had the same working schedule as men the overall pay gap at SIP would decrease to five per cent or less, even if we considered top management and took discretionary premiums into account. There are three key reasons for such a small gender pay gap:

1) the fact that women are located in the middle of the grading scale, because of the pattern of segregation that prevails below managerial ranks, including the underrepresentation of women among manual workers;
2) the importance of automatic promotion through seniority;
3) a pay scale which remains sufficiently flat despite the recent introduction of group merit pay and the payment of individual incentive bonuses to intermediate and top management.

To a degree, all three elements are common to the health sector, as we have previously noted. This comes as no surprise, since SIP has been close to the public employment sector in terms of industrial relations, on account of its mixed ownership status. In addition, its employees have certainly shared in some of the company's monopoly revenue, and on a fairly egalitarian basis.

7.3. ITALTEL, THE MANUFACTURING COUNTERPART OF SIP

Before concluding it may be worthwhile comparing the picture at SIP with that at one of its suppliers of electronic components, ITALTEL. This firm is one of a handful of firms that have complied with the legislation on affirmative action by providing data on female and male personnel. The comparison with SIP based on these data has the advantage of shifting the focus from the service to the industrial sector, and although the data are very scanty, they bring out some notable points.

With its 16 761 employees in 1989, 37.8 per cent of whom were female, ITALTEL is a very large firm in Italian manufacturing, despite the fact that approximately 44 per cent of jobs have been lost through restructuring since 1979 (Figures 7.1–7.3). Like SIP, ITALTEL operates under the umbrella of IRI, the former public holding now threatened with progressive dismantling.

As elsewhere in the medium-to-large segment of electronic engineering, restructuring at ITALTEL has involved job losses primarily for manual workers, so that the share of white-collar workers (including technicians) was nearly 50 per cent at the end of the 1980s. In fact, while manual workers continued to lose their jobs until 1988, the non-manual segment has been increasing since 1985. The shift in favour of non-manual work is not so much the result of more administration versus actual production, as of technological progress creating the need for technical jobs in support of actual production, for example research and development or quality development (Figure 7.5).

The reason may be different, but the outcome is the same as we observed in the case of SIP: manual workers are becoming a smaller contingent every year. Unlike at SIP, however, women are not benefiting either in terms of employment or pay. Their share of jobs at ITALTEL dropped from 42.2 per cent in 1982 to 37.8 per cent in 1989, solely on account of the non-manual segment, where they continued to lose ground throughout the 1980s. By contrast, female manual workers suffered relatively fewer losses, with a consequent increase in their share.

This was probably the single most powerful factor driving down women's relative pay throughout the 1980s. Average earnings for women peaked at 92 per cent in 1979, falling to 82 per cent in 1989 for two reasons: manual workers were and are graded lower on average, and the actual pay gap between manual and non-manual workers widened in the intervening period.[5]

As elsewhere, seniority does not explain lower pay for women. At ITALTEL in 1989 more than 90 per cent of female employees had worked in the firm for at least ten years, compared with 77 per cent of men (Figure 7.4). Naturally, a 'younger' male population is also the result of more recruitment of men over the past decade.

Figure 7.1. ITALTEL, total employment (no.)

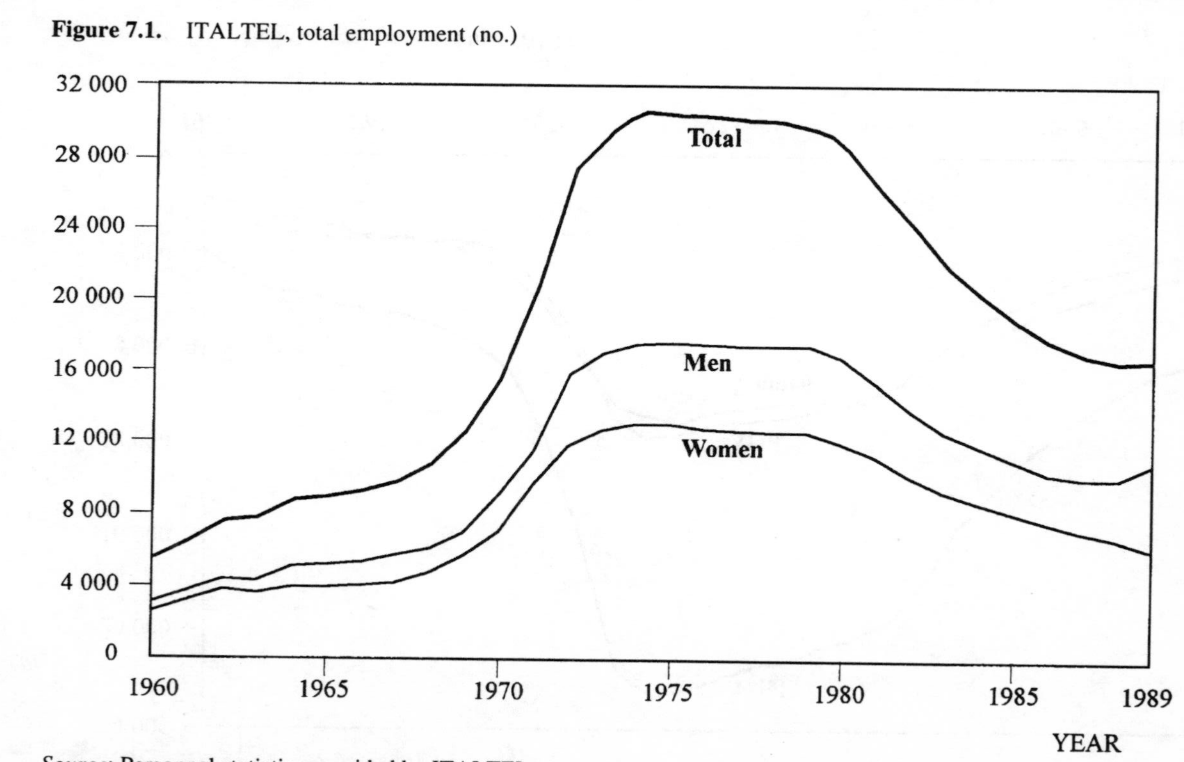

Source: Personnel statistics provided by ITALTEL

Figure 7.2. ITALTEL, manual workers (no.)

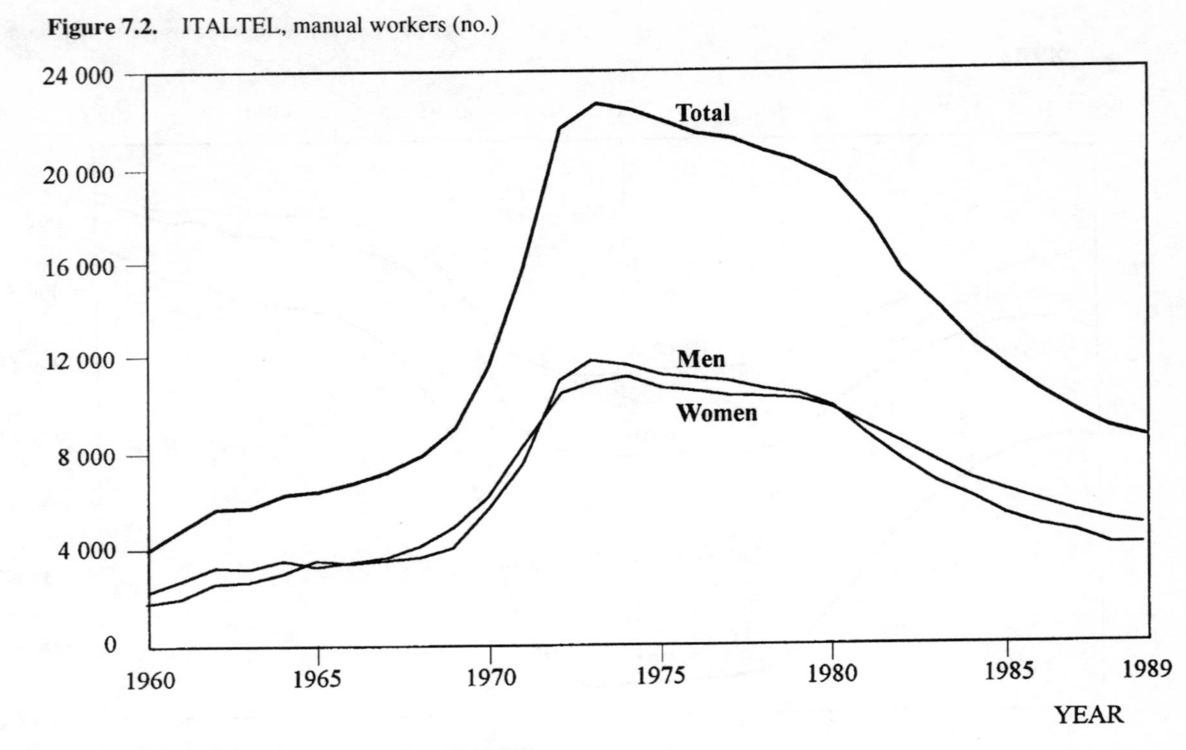

Source: Personnel statistics provided by ITALTEL

Figure 7.3. ITALTEL, non-manual workers (no.)

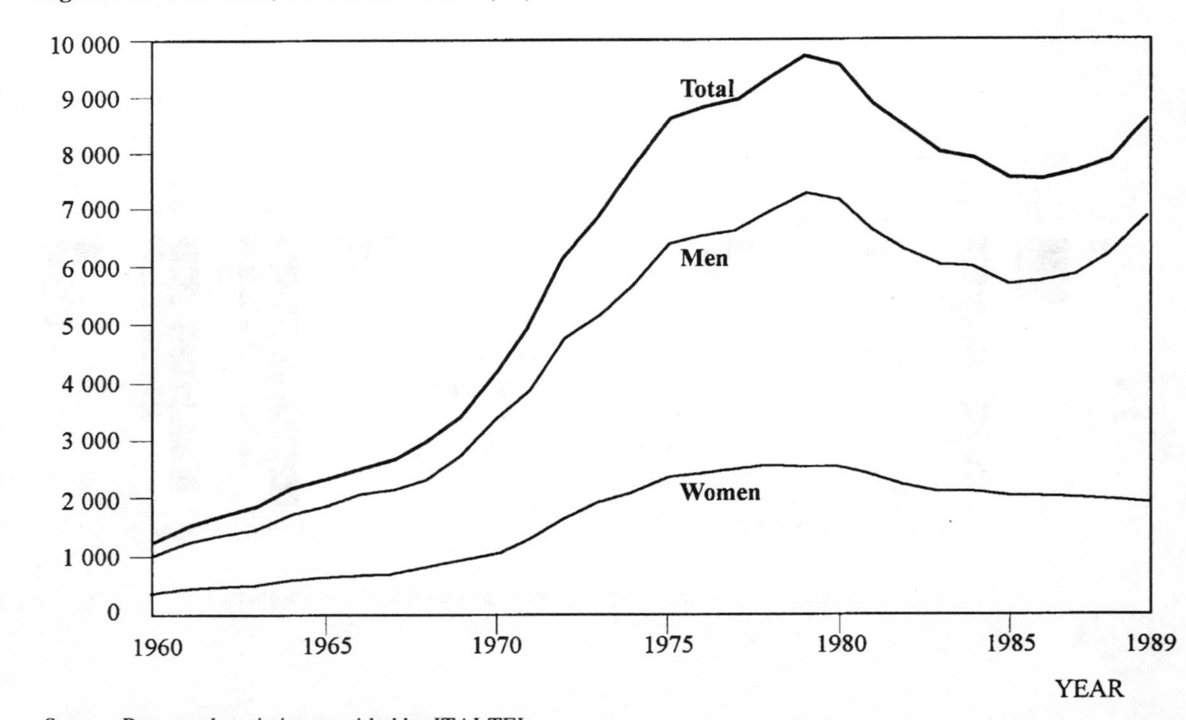

Source: Personnel statistics provided by ITALTEL

Figure 7.4. ITALTEL: distribution of employees by age and seniority, 1989

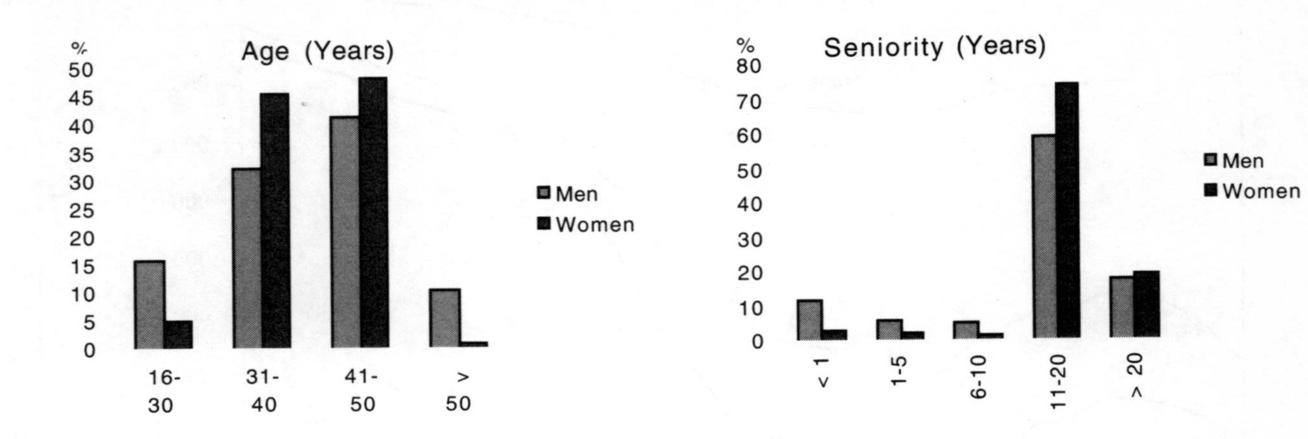

Source: Personnel statistics provided by ITALTEL

As elsewhere, technical education in particular partially explains lower upward mobility, hence lower pay for women. Forty per cent of men at ITALTEL have either a non-graduate diploma or a Bachelor of Arts degree, as against 10.6 per cent of women. Their respective distribution among the company's divisions suggests that engineering and related 'technical' subjects are dominant for men. For example, the research and development division alone employs over 1,500 men (Figure 7.5).

Thanks to the support of a female top manager (so much of an exception that she was often in the newspapers) a programme of affirmative action was drawn up in 1986 and may well have been inspired by the deterioration of women's relative employment and pay conditions. However, no measure was actually taken before 1988, and thus the data examined so far could not possibly be influenced by the implementation of the programme.

Two points of general interest may be drawn from this brief analysis of ITALTEL. First, the share of women in manufacturing as a whole follows opposite trends to those of ITALTEL: it is increasing among non-manual workers and decreasing among manual workers. This explains why the male-female gap in earnings increased at ITALTEL much more than in the industry and in the economy as a whole. If, then, ITALTEL is at the bottom end of the spectrum, in a few cases a deterioration in relative pay of over ten percentage points within manufacturing may be expected. By similar reasoning, it may be expected that the upper ceiling for the gender pay gap at the firm level will often not be in excess of the aggregate, national figure of 27.5 per cent.

Second, the case of ITALTEL illustrates how much the deterioration (or improvement) in women's relative earnings may come to depend on the pattern of segregation for manual versus non-manual workers. It also reinforces the suggestion arising out of our analysis of SIP that segregation of women in higher education is hindering both their employment and their career chances in manufacturing and in industry-related services. Both at SIP and ITALTEL most (male) new entrants, in fact, are hired as 'technicians' provided that they have received some kind of higher education in technical subjects.

Notes

1. Dipartimento di Economia Politica, Università degli Studi di Siena.
2. Note that the data in Appendix Table A.4 comparing earnings for the three industries chosen refer to 1990 for reasons of homogeneity, whereas the figures in the text refer to 1991 and are based on national accounts statistics

Figure 7.5. ITALTEL: employees by main occupational group, 1989

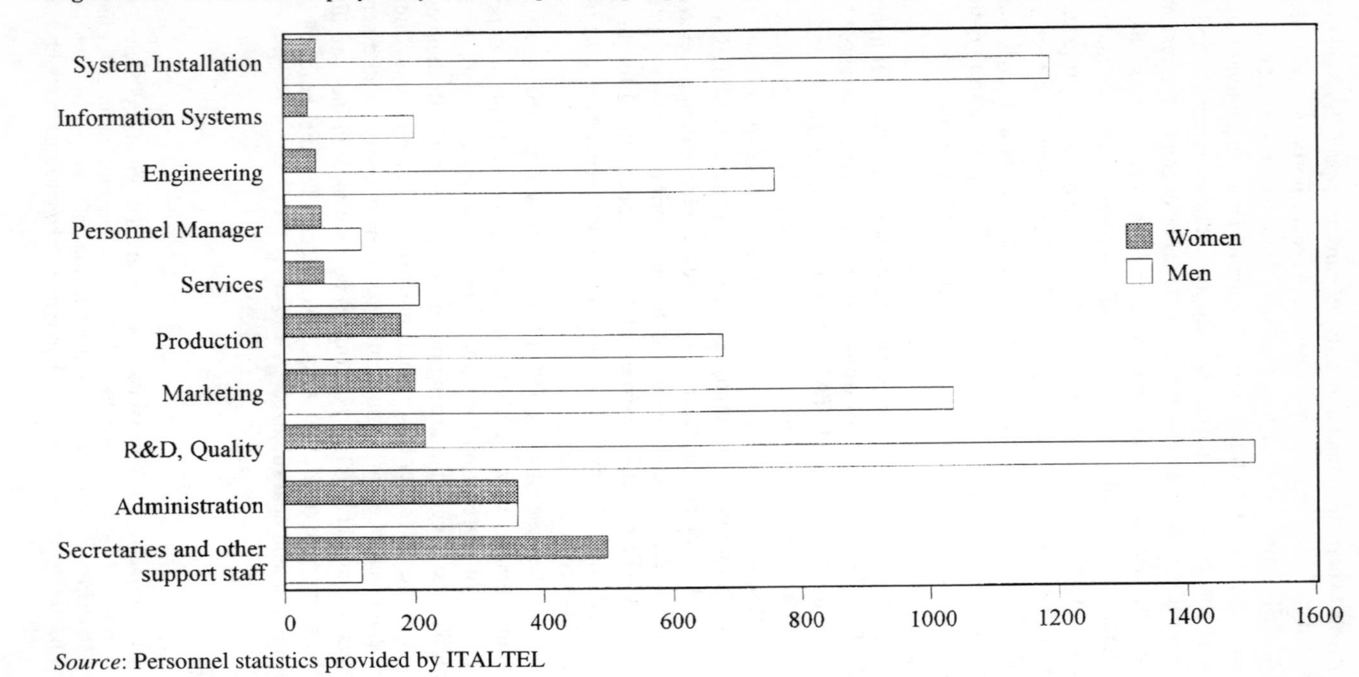

Source: Personnel statistics provided by ITALTEL

or on the figures given to us by SIP. Note, moreover, that the data in Table 7.11 refer to the communications industry, which includes private postal services as well as telecommunications, and thus underestimate earnings in the latter.

3. If we convert the figure for total employment in Table 7.1, measured in full-time units, into actual employees by using the data on the volume and time schedule of part-timers (Table 7.2), we arrive at a figure of 90,848. Part-timers in Table 7.2 total 4,167, i.e. 4.6 per cent of actual employees.
4. See the reports prepared for the European Commission on atypical employment in Italy (Villa 1988 and 1989).
5. See Bettio and Villa (1993, sections 1 and 2).

8 Banking

Paola Villa[1]

8.1. INTRODUCTION

Unlike for the two previous case studies, it was not possible to collect detailed data on earnings by gender in banking. We have therefore tried to compensate for this, at least partially, by analysing three sources of information.

The first source comprises aggregate data from a sample of 123 banks, provided by the banks under Law No. 125/1991 on equal opportunity and affirmative action.[2] The quality of these data is good with regard to employment information (employment structure by occupational category, recruitment, departures, training, upward mobility); however, the quality of data on earnings and employment structure by skill grade is extremely poor. This source, even though unsatisfactory in many respects, is very important since it allows for the first time an analysis of banking disaggregated by gender.

Collective agreements constitute the second source. In particular, detailed information on the rules governing the determination of earnings was extracted from an analysis of (i) the national collective agreement for savings banks and (ii) the latest enterprise agreement for a large savings bank. Both agreements are still in force.

The third source comprises qualitative information and some detailed data on the structure of the internal labour market for two banking institutions: a medium-size cooperative bank referred to throughout as BP Bank, and a large savings bank, referred to as CR Bank. Unfortunately, it was not possible to obtain individual data on earnings for the following reasons:

- Individual data are not easily made available in banking. The secrecy of information on earnings has to be explained by the fact that a large part of them are individually determined through a complex system of bonuses related to annual evaluation of individual job performance.
- Average aggregate data, by skill grade and gender, are not normally produced by the personnel department; in fact, this was the reason

most frequently adduced by banks for not completing some sections of the questionnaire provided for by Law No. 125/1991.

To facilitate the exposition, the main conclusions on banking are briefly summarized here. In this industry, average earnings continue to be high, although the differential with other sectors has decreased considerably over time. The entry of women into this industry, from which they were previously almost excluded, can be seen as an important improvement in their position in the labour market. However, despite this progress in terms of the overall share of employment, the earnings gap by gender is relatively wide in banking, certainly wider than in other industries. Earnings differentials are to be explained partly by the average lower seniority of women, since they have entered the industry in large numbers only recently, and partly by the greater difficulties they experience in career advancement. In short, the fact that women have now entered banking in large numbers does not imply a process of career advancement similar to that of their male colleagues. Data available both at the aggregate level and at the enterprise level clearly show the existence of vertical segregation. This implies that it is more difficult for women to be promoted to the high-pay positions, and almost impossible for them to fill the very top ones.

8.2. THE INDUSTRY

8.2.1 Employment in the industry

The banking sector employs over 32 000 people (1992 data), equal to 2.5 per cent of total employment in services. As is widely acknowledged, the Italian banking system is relatively underdeveloped, compared with that of other European countries (Villa 1990). This explains the significant expansion of credit institutions over the last 15 years (see Table 8.1), which has involved the introduction of new technologies, the reorganization of banking services, radical changes in the division of labour, an increase in employment and changes in employment policies.

Until very recently, employment in banking was traditionally regarded as an archetypal 'good male occupation'. Earnings were high, always occupying the very top positions in the ranking of industries by pay level. Employment was stable and offered good prospects for career advancement for employees willing to stay with the same employer. Entry was always at the bottom of the career ladder, and advancement was internal to

Table 8.1. Employees by economic activity: banks, service and all activities, 1975–91 in 000s

	Banks[1]	Services[2]			All activities[2]		
	T	F	T	%F/T	F	T	%F/T
1975	216.3	2827	8 738	32.3	5612	19 635	28.6
1985	306.2	4318	11 550	37.5	6756	20 742	32.6
1991	326.1	5175	12 853	40.3	7490	21 592	34.7
Total increase 1975–91	+109.7	+2348	+4 115		+1878	+1 957	
Percentage increase 1975–91	+50.7	+83.1	+47.1	+8.0	+33.5	+10.0	+6.1

Note: (F) Female and (T) total employment
Sources: [1]Banca d'Italia, *Relazione Annuale, Appendi* (various years) (data taken from the balance sheets of banks. [2]ISTAT, *Rilevazione campionaria delle forze di lavoro.*

the bank, with seniority playing a crucial role in upgrading. As a result, banking represented a typical internal market, which women were unable to enter.

In the last two decades, in a situation of rapid expansion of employment in the banking sector, Italy has experienced for the first time a significant increase in female employment, in both absolute and relative terms. The share of women employed in banking was about 10 per cent in the early 1970s, whereas at present it is between 20 and 30 per cent in most banks (see Table 8.2).

As pointed out elsewhere (Bettio and Villa 1992), at the national level banking employment data are not disaggregated by sex. The best approximation available is the aggregate 'credit, insurance and services to firms', which shows a large increase both in the number of people employed and in the rate of feminization over the period. Data available for samples of banks (see Tables 8.2 and 8.3) confirm this: the overall expansion of employment in this sector has been considerable; women have taken advantage of this expansion in greater numbers; and therefore the share of women employed in banking has increased substantially. Even though the rate of feminization in banking remains low, compared with the rate recorded for non-manual jobs in services,[3] the expansion of female employment in this high-pay sector is remarkable.

Table 8.2. Trends in the share of women employed in banking in a sample of banks, selected years

Bank	Year	Total employment (T)	Share of women (F/T%)
Banca Popolare di Milano[1]	1975	n.a.	10.70
	1982	4 274	20.19
	1984	4 291	22.28
	1987	4 368	25.43
	1990	5 476	28.25
	1991	5 551	29.04
Banca Popolare di Abbiategrasso[1]	1981	398	6.43
	1986	491	10.79
	1991	580	15.69
Cariplo[1]	1969	5 558	4.14
	1980	9 167	22.46
	1986	9 866	27.99
	1991	14 933	33.23
Credito Italiano[1,4]	1982	14 977	24.78
	1985	14 447	24.97
	1989	13 868	26.32
	1991	(12 303)*	29.90
Banca Nazionale del Lavoro[2,4]	1981	21 834	15.55
	1986	23 448	17.72
	1991	(15 517)*	25.22
Comit[2,4]	1986	16 111	19.70
	1991	(13 381)*	24.82
Banco di Roma[2]	1985	n.a.	20.30
	1991	9 857	28.59
Cooperative bank in North Italy[3]	1983	2 511	21.71
	1986	2 614	27.38
Savings bank in North Italy[3]	1980	1 055	30.60
	1987	1 269	35.40

Notes: n.a. = not available. *Total employment does not include all employees; figures are therefore not homogeneous with figures for previous years

Sources: [1]Data provided to us by the trade unions (FIBA-CISL). [2]Frey *et al.* (1988). [3]Ambrosini, *et al.* (1989). [4]Data for 1991 provided by OML, Regione Lombardia, on the basis of the questionnaires completed in accordance with Law No. 125/1991.

Table 8.3. The share of women employed in a sample of banks by legal category, 1976, 1984 and 1991 (%)

	Cooperative banks	Foreign banks	Savings banks	Private banks	Public banks	Financial societies
1976[1]	20	16	25	16	22	n.a.
1984[1]	34	19	29	18	25	n.a.
1991[2]	22.08	n.a.	37.56	24.33	25.05	40.44

Notes: n.a. = not available.

Sources: [1]Sample of 76 banks: Turati (1986), data reproduced in Chiesi *et al.* (1989, p. 127). [2]Sample of 123 banks: author's estimates based on data provided by OML, Regione Lombardia.

8.2.2 Earnings in banking

Earnings are high in banking compared not only with other industries in Italy, but also with earnings in other countries. If annual labour costs per head are taken as a substitute for earnings per employee, then the evidence indicates that average pay is much higher in Italy than in Germany and the UK (Table 8.4). For 1990, put the average labour cost per employee (per year) equal to 100 for Italy, the figure is 75 for Germany and 62 for the UK.

The data set out in Table 8.4 do not allow inferences about trends in relative earnings over the long run. However, on the basis of other information available, it seems plausible to hypothesize that the earnings gap between Italy and other European countries was even wider in the 1970s. Presumably some compression took place over time.

At the very beginning of the 1970s, gross earnings in banking were extremely high in Italy, roughly three times the average pay in the private sector (see Table 8.5). Over the last 20 years, however, the wage differential has narrowed dramatically: in 1990, gross earnings in banking were less than twice those in the private sector. This narrowing took place mainly from the beginning of the 1970s up to the early 1980s. The wage indexation system, on the one hand, and increasing competition within the banking industry, on the other, were among the major factors responsible for it. Further compression can be expected over time, in view of the increasing competition from abroad.

Despite the steady reduction in relative terms, banking remains a high pay industry compared with other industries in the country, and compared with banking in other European countries. In fact, according to INPS data,

Table 8.4. Annual labour cost per employee in banking: Italy, Germany and the UK, 1983–90

	1983	1987	1988	1989	1990
(a) Millions of lire, current prices					
Italy					
Large banks	45.75	64.77	69.64	71.54	77.24
Savings banks	52.46	72.78	72.38	71.48	80.69
Total banks	44.36	63.80	68.64	69.49	77.18
Germany					
Large banks	34.64	48.46	52.26	54.19	57.97
Savings banks	25.51	35.69	37.42	37.05	39.56
Total banks	32.09	48.23	52.83	53.99	58.33
UK					
Total banks	34.28	38.61	44.85	47.57	48.12
(b) Index numbers for total banks					
Italy	100	100	100	100	100
Germany	72	75	76	77	75
UK	77	60	65	68	62

Source: Prosperetti and Durante (1993) p. 33.

non-manual workers in banking in Italy have the second highest average annual earnings (see Bettio and Villa 1993, table 3).

Along with the decline in relative earnings, there has been (as already mentioned) a significant expansion in the share of women in banking (Bettio and Villa 1992); it now stands at about 26 per cent. It remains to determine whether these two trends are related, and if so, in what way.

First consider the reasons why women entered banking. According to an 'optimistic' interpretation, they started entering because of a change in management's attitude. More precisely, Italian banks were becoming increasingly interested in the image they presented to their customers, and concerned about sex segregation. Consequently, they started to favour the entry of women into banking.

This does not sound like a plausible explanation. In fact, the rate of feminization is relatively high in banks where recruitment is through open competition (such as the two banks considered here), compared with the low rates recorded in banks where recruitment is based on discretionary screening (Bettio and Villa, 1992). A more 'pessimistic' interpretation seems therefore to be more plausible. This would consider the entry of

Table 8.5. Gross earnings per unit of employment, selected industries, 1970–90 (index numbers)

	Goods, services for sale	Credit and insurance	Communications	Textile industries	Hotels, catering etc.	Public administration
Old series						
1970	100	283.9	165.5	72.8	57.5	151.4
1973	100	262.8	155.5	78.1	64.4	138.6
1976	100	227.9	119.4	81.1	68.7	112.8
1979	100	197.0	127.0	85.4	71.3	112.1
1980	100	195.9	132.2	83.9	68.3	116.9
New series						
1980	100	191.2	131.1	77.4	61.6	110.7
1981	100	183.2	122.5	78.1	60.5	116.7
1982	100	174.8	122.2	78.8	64.1	116.7
1983	100	188.7	118.6	80.1	61.5	113.8
1984	100	181.6	118.0	81.5	65.3	112.5
1985	100	184.5	112.4	80.6	62.0	110.4
1986	100	188.3	105.5	79.8	62.6	110.1
1987	100	188.5	101.5	78.3	61.4	111.4
1988	100	188.3	102.3	77.1	60.2	114.6
1989	100	181.8	105.9	73.8	58.4	113.0
1990	100	187.6	112.0	74.6	59.9	121.6

Note: Employees only; the data refer to the so-called regular unit of employment.
Sources: For the old series: Faustini (1988, p. 134); for the new series: ISTAT (1989, pp. 140–8); ISTAT (1991, pp. 182–92).

women into banking as the indirect outcome of a relative deterioration in employment conditions in this industry. The changes in the nature of 'banking jobs', in relative earnings and in the status attached to employment in banking have reduced over time the industry's capacity to attract 'primary' workers, that is highly qualified male resources. Banks therefore have increasingly to fill their vacancies by recruiting from the 'secondary' segment of the labour market, which comprises an increasing number of highly qualified women.

8.3. THE INSTITUTIONAL FRAMEWORK FOR WAGE DETERMINATION

In banking, collective bargaining takes place at two levels. At the national level, general collective agreements lay down the basic conditions for employment in the sector. At the plant level, decentralized agreements can be negotiated for (i) the implementation of what is laid down at the national level, and (ii) the improvement of the conditions (including pay rates) defined in the national agreement. For the bank considered here (CR Bank), a plant agreement was signed which significantly improved pay and conditions in relation to the national agreements. Throughout the banking sector two separate national collective agreements are negotiated: one for managerial staff and one for clerical workers and auxiliary staff.

8.3.1 Grading structure

Banking has a complex hierarchical structure, which is divided into categories of employment, grades and classes. The national collective agreements specify six categories of employment: managers, assistant managers (*funzionari*), senior clerical workers (*quadri*), clerical workers, subordinate staff (*subalterni*) and auxiliary workers. The general characteristics of the tasks to be performed in each category are also defined. Categories are subdivided into grades and classes at the plant level (usually through collective bargaining) and the allocation of workers to grades is determined at that level.

Both BP Bank and CR Bank operate a typically hierarchical structure. Table 8.6 shows the latter's hierarchical structure. BP Bank has a similar structure, but with a larger number of grades for senior clerical workers.

Table 8.6. Categories and grades in CR Bank

Category of employment	Number of grades per category
Managers	4
Director General	
Central Director	
Subsidiary Director	
Subsidiary Vice-Director	
Assistant managers	4
Authorized Agent 1a	
Authorized Agent 2a	
Authorized Agent 3a	
Authorized Agent 4a	
Senior clerical workers	1
Clerical staff	
Head clerk (Grade 1)	4
Head clerk (Grade 2)	
Clerk (Grade 3)	
Clerk (Grade 4)	
Subordinate staff	6
(delivery persons, messengers, safe staff, drivers)	
Auxiliary staff	7
(guards, manual workers, cleaners)	
Total	26

Source: CR Bank, Contratto integrativo aziendale, 1988.

8.3.2 Entry

Both banks operate a typical internal labour market with entry at the lowest grades, and career progression depending on promotion from within through the grading structure.

If subordinate and auxiliary staff are excluded from the analysis, it could be argued that in banking there is only one large internal labour market: to become a top manager one has to start working in banking as a clerical worker when relatively young, and remain with the same bank throughout, moving up through the hierarchical structure step by step. This can be easily understood if we consider the procedures used for filling vacancies. At CR Bank, there are four such procedures:

1) open competition (advertising the vacancy outside the bank);
2) internal competition (advertising the vacancy only inside the bank);
3) internal discretionary choice (the next line manager will decide which employee will be appointed for the vacancy);
4) hiring on the market (screening discretionally).

The last procedure is rarely used, and only when the other three procedures are not relevant. This can be the case when a highly qualified person is needed, and there is nobody in the bank who might possess the required skills. Both the national and the plant agreement make this point very clearly. For example, in the CR Bank agreement, it is stated that 'up to grade 3 managers, the Administration can hire people external to the bank only when internal deficiencies occur'. It follows therefore that the standard procedures for filling clerical positions and managerial positions are internal competition (based on qualifications and/or written examinations) and internal discretionary choice. As a result, entry in most cases is through open competition for the bottom-grade clerical positions, with screening based on both educational level and written examinations.

8.3.3 Appraisal system

As in banking in other countries, an appraisal system is used to evaluate the performance of all employees. The results of the annual appraisal are crucial since they are used, together with seniority, for automatic upgrading, upgrading by internal upward mobility, and determination of the annual bonus and other wage supplements. The national collective agreement states that at the end of each year the bank must prepare the annual appraisal and communicate its results. The overall evaluation has to be expressed as follows:

(a) outstanding; (b) very good; (c) good; (d) satisfactory; (e) mediocre; (f) unsatisfactory. Each employee is informed solely of the overall evaluation, not of the reasons justifying it. Only in the case of an unsatisfactory appraisal is an employee entitled to receive a summary of the reasons, and possibly to appeal.

8.3.4 Pay structure

As already mentioned, the national agreements set out the earnings structure (defining its minimum components) and minimum pay conditions by category of employment. Through plant bargaining it is possible both to improve what is set at the national level and to integrate it, for example by introducing new pay components. In the case of CR Bank, the outcome is a very complex pay structure resulting from:

1) a further subdivision, within each category, of each grade into classes of pay (for example, both managers and assistant managers are placed in four grades, each with ten classes of salary);
2) a long list of pay components, each determined differently;
3) the combination, for the determination of many different pay components, of seniority and annual appraisals.

In particular, the main components for the determination of earnings are the following:

1) basic pay (monthly pay as defined in collective agreements), which differs in terms of category, grade and class;
2) wage indexation allowance up to 1992 (in July of that year the collective agreement on the indexation system was abolished; this implies that the wage indexation allowance has not changed since then and will soon be incorporated into the basic pay);
3) seniority bonus for employees in medium- to high-level clerical positions, from which it is possible to move upwards only through promotion; this bonus can be interpreted as a way of compensating senior clerical workers with few prospects of advancement (see below for more details);
4) seniority allowances, which are intended to increase monthly earnings through seniority. These are determined differently by category, but they apply similarly to all employees, that is, if a person stays with the same bank, he or she will receive a pay increase once every two years, up to a maximum of 12 increases. Since seniority allowances are cumulative, earnings tend to increase significantly with seniority;
5) responsibility allowances, which are paid monthly to all managers and clerical workers in specific positions involving responsibility either for a team or a special service;
6) bonus for graduates: all graduate employees' monthly earnings are increased by a lump sum, which differs by category (ranging from a minimum of 100000 lire per month for clerical workers to over 500000 lire per month for managers). This means that if two people are employed for the same job, but one is a graduate and the other is not, the first will receive a higher salary (independently of everything else);

Table 8.7. CR Bank: merit bonus scheme

Merit bonus for employees with less than 10 years' seniority	
Managers and assistant managers	190% of monthly earnings (December)
All other employees	235% of monthly earnings (December)
Additional merit bonus for all employees with over 10 years' seniority	
10–15 years' seniority	+ 10%
15–20 years' seniority	+ 20%
20–25 years' seniority	+ 30%
Over 25 years' seniority	+ 40%

Source: CR Bank, Contratto integrativo aziendale, 1988.

7) merit bonus: a merit bonus scheme has been introduced for all employees. It is paid at the end of the year to all those employees who have been appraised as 'very good' in the annual appraisal. This bonus, which is calculated as a percentage of total earnings in January, is differentiated by category of employment and by seniority, as summarized in Table 8.7.

8.3.5 Automatic processes: internal career and pay increases

Three automatic processes are outlined in the collective agreements: automatic upgrading; automatic pay increases (seniority bonus); and seniority wage increases (seniority allowances). The latter apply to all employees and are determined exclusively in terms of years of seniority within the bank. Traditionally, they are granted every two years; and this seems to be a general rule in Italian collective agreements. But there are wide differences within Italy with respect to the potential weight of seniority allowances in total earnings. In fact, the difference among industries can be substantial in terms of the total number of these increases (ranging from between two and five to between 10 and 12). The role which they play in banking has always been considerable: the national collective agreement sets out 12 two-yearly seniority wage increases.

Whereas seniority allowances apply to all employees and depend only on the number of years a person has been employed in the bank, automatic upgrading and automatic pay increases do not apply to managers, assistant managers or senior workers, but depend on a combination of skill grade, seniority and appraisal. For the sake of simplicity, we shall confine our analysis to clerical staff. If one analyses the complex system of rules and conditions, one could argue that these two automatic processes are designed to guarantee all clerks some sort of upward mobility. In particular: (a) an employee hired as a clerk enters at skill grade 4; (b) after a specified period (which varies according to the results of annual appraisals) he or she will be promoted to grade 3; and (c) after a specified period (which varies according to the results of annual appraisals) he or she will be promoted to grade 2.

Since it is not possible to progress further on the basis of 'automatic' rules, and since a bank's general strategy is to have a stable and loyal labour force, a scheme for automatic pay increases has been introduced for clerical workers graded in skill grades 2 and 1. As usual, the scheme is based on a combination of skill grade seniority, bank seniority and appraisal, as summarized in Table 8.8.

8.3.6 Promotion

Like the setting of wage rates and wage rises, the process of upgrading – from one grade to another as well as from one category to another – is defined by a set of rules laid down in the collective agreement. These are based on two fundamental principles: seniority and merit evaluations. Up to the position of deputy head clerk some upward mobility is guaranteed through collective bargaining by linking upgrading to seniority; the relevant rules (based always on a combination of years of seniority and the results of the annual appraisals) are set out in collective agreements. This implies that the process of upgrading as far as the position of deputy head clerk is certain, even though the time required can vary, depending on annual appraisals. For further advancement, there is no automatic rule; nevertheless, both seniority and merit evaluation continue to play an important role.

8.3.7 Non-pay conditions

Paid holiday entitlement varies according not to the category of employment but to seniority: for up to five years' seniority the entitlement is 20 working days; for six to 10 years it is 22 working days; and for over 10 years' it is 25 working days.

The standard working week is 37 hours and 30 minutes over five days. Daily starting and finishing times are set through national agreements (starting times can vary between 08.15–8.30 and finishing times between 16.45–17.00).

Table 8.8. CR Bank: seniority bonus

Category of employment	Conditions	Monthly wage increase
Clerk (skill grade 2)	Seniority in skill grade 2: 3 years; annual appraisal: "outstanding" (for all three years)	6.5% of basic pay
Clerk (skill grade 1)	Seniority in skill grade 1: 5 years; annual appraisal: "outstanding" (for all five years)	6.5% of basic pay
	Depending on bank seniority, the seniority bonus (paid monthly) is further increased as follows:	
	Bank seniority of 26 years	+ 50,000 lire
	Bank seniority of 28 years	+ 25,000 lire
	Bank seniority of 30 years	+ 25,000 lire

Source. CR Bank, Contratto integrativo aziendale, 1988.

8.4. THE GENDER WAGE GAP

Unfortunately, as mentioned at the beginning of this case study, data on earnings by gender are not available for the banking industry. Furthermore, statistical information on pay structure is not available. This is because all banks have categorically refused to provide detailed data on earnings (by gender and by skill grade), contrary to Law No. 125/1991. In the Lombardy region in particular, to which 123 questionnaires were dispatched, no bank provided data on earnings by skill grade; 18 refused to give any statistical information on pay; and the other 105 indicated some sort of gross average annual earnings for men and women without specifying the categories of employment considered. The data, as summarized in Table 8.9, are quite approximate and tend very likely to overestimate women's average pay.

According to these data, the 'average' earnings ratio between women and men is equal to 70.37 per cent for the whole sample, ranging from an average minimum of 65.51 per cent in the case of financial societies up to an average maximum of 74.25 per cent in the case of cooperative banks. The wage gap by bank fluctuates between 60 and 80 per cent, with most banks recording a ratio of approximately 65 or 70 per cent. To evaluate these results, it is useful to consider the case of CR Bank, which employs a high proportion of women and is quite perceptive about their position within the organization. One would expect in this case a better earnings ratio than that recorded for the whole sample. However, data for CR Bank give a ratio equal to 65.71 per cent. Having checked the figures for CR Bank, we believe that the data from the sample set tend to underestimate the true magnitude of the wage gap. The fact that savings banks in general, and CR Bank in particular, show relatively high figures for women among senior clerical workers supports this argument.

Three main factors could explain this wage gap in banking: a lower average seniority of women due to the fact that they have entered banking only recently; a significantly different attitude towards the internal labour market; and problems of vertical segregation, preventing access to the top positions.

As will be argued in the following sections, the second factor has to be rejected. In general, women have adapted fully to the prevailing pattern: they are employed full time (part-time work is almost non-existent); they enter the bank just after finishing their studies; and they show attachment both to their job and to the bank. In fact, the turnover rate for women is extremely low.

The lower seniority of women, on the other hand, might explain part of the earnings gap. This is certainly the case at CR Bank, where women

Table 8.9. Annual average earnings in a sample of Italian banks by gender and category of bank, 1990–91 (annual earnings in lire)

Category of bank	Male (M)	Female (F)	F as % of M	Number of banks in sample	Total employment[1]	
					M	F
All banks in sample	59 191 311	41 653 270	70.37	105	129 367	55 924
Cooperative banks	52 147 956	38 722 423	74.25	15	13 697	4 042
Small banks	54 703 100	38 265 253	69.95	7	935	434
Savings banks	65 461 106	44 701 847	68.29	6	13 698	8 780
Public banks	62 063 093	43 533 913	70.14	8	63 263	26 619
Private banks	54 847 837	38 113 150	69.49	38	34 873	13 673
Financial societies	53 875 263	35 295 354	65.51	31	2 901	2 376

[1]Total employment does not include managers

Source: OML, Regione Lombardia (Law No. 125/1991 data).

have been recruited in large numbers (see Figure 8.1) and therefore have on average a lower seniority than men (Table 8.10). Since earnings in banking are linked to seniority to a large extent, one would expect – for the same job positions – higher earnings for more senior workers. Of course, the higher the rate of recruitment of women, the greater the role one would expect seniority to play. Unfortunately, the available data do not allow this to be verified. While seniority may correctly be assumed to account for part of the pay gap, it cannot explain all of it. Other indicators suggest that some vertical segregation exists; and women's low relative pay is therefore due to the greater difficulties they have in career advancement.

As shown in Contini and Revelli (1992, pp. 220–8), where data (referring to annual earnings in 1985) for a sample of large banks were analysed, the distribution of earnings in banking suggests the existence of a long hierarchical structure. However, the process of upgrading is quite diversified by gender (see Bettio and Villa 1993, figure 4): men are distributed along all grades of earnings up to the very top, while women are concentrated in the medium to low grades. Thus the distribution of banking employees by class of earnings and gender is very asymmetrical, with men having a sort of monopoly position for the best-paid grades.

We shall now investigate the distribution of employees along the hierarchical structure, our assumption being that to some extent women have no access to the best paid positions.

Table 8.10. Average seniority by skill grade and gender, CR Bank, October 1989 (number of years)

Category and skill grade	Female	Male
Assistant managers		
Authorized Agent 1a	–	28.4
Authorized Agent 2a	–	27.9
Authorized Agent 3a	22.3	25.3
Authorized Agent 4a	19.0	22.7
Senior clerical workers	17.0	20.6
Clerical staff		
Clerks 1a	14.5	18.6
Clerks 2a	9.4	12.0
Clerks 3a	1.4	3.3
Clerks 4a	2.6	6.4
Total employment	8.6	16.2

Source: CR Bank.

Figure 8.1. Employment by gender in CR Bank

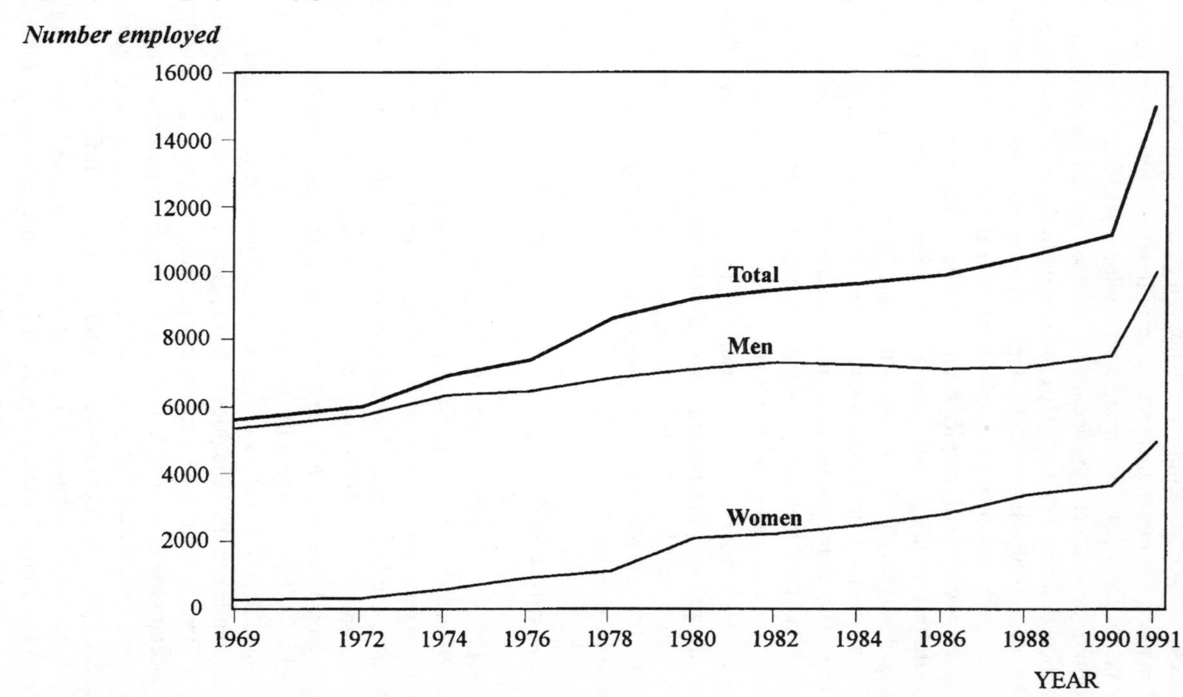

Note: In 1991 there was an acquisition of another small bank
Source: Case-study bank

8.5. THE INTERNAL LABOUR MARKET

The labour market prevailing in banking can be described as a typical internal market: the hierarchical structure is long and diversified; recruitment, except for a few very specific professional positions, is only from the bottom; and career advancement processes are all internal, up the hierarchical structure (step by step) and related to the employee's seniority. The relationships between the bank and its employees are structured so as to ensure stability of employment. On the one hand, the bank guarantees security of employment; on the other hand, employees appreciate this security, show strong motivation for internal career advancement and stay with the bank for a long time. As a result, both the regulation of salary progression and career advancement are linked to seniority. The entry of women into banking has not modified this picture. Like men, they are recruited at the bottom of the hierarchical structure; they are employed full time, usually working in the front office; and they receive intensive training. They seem to have adjusted fully to the pre-existing pattern: they display strong motivation for an internal career, and have a very low exit rate. Nevertheless, there is a remarkable difference between the positions occupied by men and those occupied by women.

8.5.1 The career ladder

Table 8.11 shows for the sample of 123 banks considered the share of women by category of employment (managers, senior clerical workers, clerical workers, manual workers). Overall, women are highly concentrated among clerical workers, accounting for 32.7 per cent of the total; the figure falls to 13.5 per cent for senior clerical workers, and to 4.7 per cent for managers. These data indicate a more favourable picture in the case of savings banks, and a more unfavourable one in the case of cooperative banks: some degree of access to senior clerical positions is evident in the first case, while certain difficulties seem to persist in the second case. Data from CR Bank and BP Bank support this picture, as shown in Table 8.12. The concentration of women in certain jobs can be better demonstrated if we consider the distribution of employment by skill grade and gender. Tables 8.13 and 8.14, containing data for CR Bank and BP Bank, show how in both cases the large majority of women are concentrated in the middle to low ranks for clerical jobs. This distribution is not justified by differences in education. In fact, like men, women tend to be highly qualified.

Table 8.11. Employment structure by gender in a sample of Italian banks, 1991

	Sample size	Managers			Senior clerical workers			Clerical workers			Manual workers			Total employment		
		F	T	F/T %	F	T	F/T %	F	T	F/T %	F	T	F/T %	F	T	F/T %
Cooperative banks	18	131	4 011	3.27	184	2 297	8.01	5 798	21 197	27.35	33	326	10.12	6 146	27 831	22.08
Small banks (rural banks)	7	10	194	5.15	16	114	14.04	402	1 212	33.17	16	43	37.21	444	1 563	28.41
Savings banks	7	156	3 561	4.38	443	2 036	21.76	8 205	16 415	49.98	44	1 543	2.85	8 848	23 555	37.56
Public banks	9	948	20 117	4.71	953	7 886	12.08	26 387	84 987	31.05	489	1 884	25.96	28 777	114 874	25.05
Private and foreign banks	46	487	10 801	4.51	748	5 710	13.10	14 458	47 522	30.42	19	553	3.44	15 712	64 586	24.33
Financial societies	36	143	1 225	11.67	166	556	29.86	2 562	5 299	48.35	1	22	4.55	2 872	7 102	40.44
All banks in sample	123	1 875	39 909	4.70	2 510	18 599	13.50	57 812	176 632	32.73	602	4 371	13.77	62 799	239 511	26.22

Note: F = female; T = total employees
Source: OML, Regione Lombardia (Law No. 125/1991 data).

Table 8.12. The structure of employment by gender in CR Bank and BP Bank, 1991

	M (no.)	F (no.)	MF (no.)	F/MF (%)	% distribution F	% distribution M
Managers						
CR Bank	2 464	102	2 566	3.98	2.06	24.71
BP Bank	887	44	931	4.73	2.74	22.71
Senior clerical workers						
CR Bank	902	218	1 120	19.46	4.39	9.05
BP Bank	516	64	580	11.03	3.99	13.21
Clerical workers						
CR Bank	5 322	4 602	9 924	46.37	92.74	53.37
BP Bank	2 434	1 498	3 932	38.10	93.28	62.33
Manual workers						
CR Bank	1 283	40	1 323	3.02	0.81	12.87
BP Bank	68	0	68	0.00	0.00	1.74
Total employment						
CR Bank	9 971	4 962	14 933	33.23	100.00	100.00
BP Bank	3 905	1 606	5 511	29.14	100.00	100.00

Note: M = male employees; F = female employees; MF = total employees
Source: OML, Regione Lombardia (Law No. 125/1991 data).

Table 8.13. Employment structure by category of employment, rank and skill grade, BP Bank, 1984 and 1991 (%)

	1984		1991	
	Male	Female	Male	Female
Managers	0.8	–	1.0	–
Director of branch	0.9	–	1.0	–
Deputy director of branch	1.1	–	1.2	–
Assistant managers				
Authorized Agent 1a	2.2	–	1.9	0.1
Authorized Agent 2a	3.1	0.1	3.2	0.4
Authorized Agent 3a	4.6	0.6	4.9	0.7
Authorized Agent 4a	6.4	3.0	9.7	1.6
Average rank III	18.3	3.7	21.9	2.8
Senior clerical workers 1	–	–	13.3	4.0
Head clerk	8.5	5.3	6.7	4.8
Average rank II	8.5	5.3	20.0	8.8
Deputy head clerk	24.2	17.1	26.2	27.1
Head of division	23.0	33.6	12.9	25.0
Clerk (Class 1)	15.0	34.1	11.7	31.4
Average rank I	62.2	84.8	50.8	83.5
Clerk (Class 2)	3.3	2.8	1.9	1.9
Ushers	4.1	3.1	2.6	3.0
Auxiliary staff	2.8	0.3	1.8	–
Total	100	100	100	100
(Number)	(3 335)	(956)	(3 898)	(1 606)

Note: Some qualification grades have not been translated because they are specific to the Itailian banking tradition. As the hierarchical system has developed, new terms (such as *procuratore* have been introduced.)
Source: BP Bank.

Data available for BP Bank reveal not only that a high percentage of women have a Bachelor of Arts degree, but also that their average educational level is higher than that of their male colleagues (see Table 8.15).

8.5.2 Entry

The progressive feminization of the banking sector does not seem to be due to new labour management strategies pursued by banks. In fact,

Table 8.14. Employment structure by category of employment and skill grade, CR Bank, December 1991

	M	F	MF
Managers	1.31	–	0.88
Assistant managers	23.40	2.06	16.31
Senior clerical workers	9.05	4.39	7.50
Clerical staff			
Clerk 1a	15.11	16.00	15.41
Clerk 2a	22.10	50.02	31.38
Clerk 3a	14.37	26.60	18.44
Clerk 4a	1.79	0.12	1.23
Subordinate and auxiliary staff			
Technicians	0.53	–	0.35
Subordinate staff[1]	10.43	0.68	7.19
Manual workers	0.51	0.12	0.38
Guards	1.16	–	0.78
Cleaners, etc.	0.23	–	0.15
Total	100	100	100
(Number)	(9 971)	(4 962)	(14 933)

[1]Delivery persons, messengers, drivers, safe staff
Note: M = male; F = female; MF = total
Source: CR Bank.

Table 8.15. Employment in BP Bank by education level, 1983 and 1991

	1983			1991		
	M	F	MF	M	F	MF
University	6.8	3.5	6.1	11.8	12.0	11.9
Secondary school	63.0	67.5	63.9	65.7	69.9	66.9
Compulsory education	30.2	29.0	30.0	22.5	18.1	21.2
Total	100	100	100	100	100	100
(Number)	(3 385)	(880)	(4 265)	(3 898)	(1 606)	(5 504)

Note: M = male; F = female; MF = total.
Source: BP Bank.

women have entered this sector, where it is compulsory to hire by open competition (see Bettio and Villa 1992), more rapidly than other sectors. Data on employment in banking by legal category (Table 8.3) show that the proportion of women employed by public and savings banks is high in relation to that recorded for foreign and private banks. This is confirmed by data drawn from our sample (see Table 8.16).

The case of CR Bank well illustrates this point. The percentage of women entering on open competition has been increasing over time, and now accounts for between 60 and 70 per cent of the total.

Given their high educational level (compared with that of men) and the fact that they often achieve better results in the written and oral examinations, the final ranking shows a majority of women at the top of the recruiting list. As a result, more women than men are hired (see Table 8.17).

8.5.3 Exit

As mentioned before, the labour force in banking tends to be very stable. In general, the turnover rate is notably low, and hence seniority is very considerable. The same pattern seems to apply to women (see Table 8.16): once they have entered a bank, they tend to stay.

8.5.4 Training

Training is very intense in banking, involving both new entrants and employees in top positions. Data in Table 8.18 show that on average 88 per cent of female employees and 106 per cent of male employees are involved in some training activity.

Differences among banks in training activities depend, of course, on the services provided and specific training requirements, the bank's personnel policy, its rate of expansion, and hence the total number of staff recruited. Of course, the higher the entry rate, the greater the amount of training is likely to be.

If an equal proportion of men and women were participating in training activities, one would expect higher figures for women, given their higher entry rate in the period considered. Thus, it is quite surprising to see that they are relatively less trained, and this is the case for all groups of banks except savings banks (see Table 8.18). It may be concluded from these data, although they are very aggregate and approximate, that men are necessarily involved at a higher rate in advanced training courses. This, of

Table 8.16. Total employment, entries and leavers in a sample of Italian banks, 1991

	Sample size	Total employment				Entries						Leavers					
		M	F	MF	F/MF (%)	Em	Ef	Emf	Ef/Emf (%)	Ef/F (%)	Em/M (%)	Xm	Xf	Xmf	Xf/Xmf (%)	Xf/F	Xm/M (%)
All banks in sample	123	176 712	62 799	239 511	26.22	16 179	10 866	27 045	40.18	17.30	9.16	9 082	2 629	11 711	22.45	4.19	5.14
Cooperative banks	18	21 685	6 146	27 831	22.08	2 684	1 049	3 733	28.10	17.07	12.38	1 141	245	1 386	17.68	3.99	5.26
Small banks (rural banks)	7	1 119	444	1 563	28.41	290	93	383	24.28	20.95	25.92	38	7	45	15.56	1.58	3.40
Saving banks	7	14 707	8 848	23 555	37.56	1 917	1 873	3 790	49.42	21.17	13.03	1 001	370	1 371	26.99	4.18	6.81
Public banks	9	86 097	28 777	114 874	25.05	4 687	3 539	8 226	43.02	12.30	5.44	4 172	1 044	5 216	20.02	3.63	4.85
Private and foreign banks	46	48 874	15 712	64 586	24.33	5 030	3 308	8 338	39.67	21.05	10.29	2 389	703	3 092	22.74	4.47	4.89
Financial societies	36	4 230	2 872	7 102	40.44	1 571	1 004	2 575	38.99	34.96	37.14	341	260	601	43.26	9.05	8.06

Note: Male = male employees; F = female employees; MF = total employees; Em = male entries; Ef = female entries; Emf = total entries; Xm = male leavers; Xf = female levers; Xmf = total leavers

Source: OML, Regione Lombardia (Law No. 125/1991 data).

Table 8.17. Hirings by gender in BP Bank and CR Bank

	Hirings			Employees
	F	MF	F (%)	F (%)
BP Bank				
1983	23	66	34.9	20.8
1990	215	358	60.1	28.2
1991	141	265	53.2	29.2
CR Bank				
1990	425	826	51.0	n.a.
1991	536	937	57.2	33.23

Note: F = female; MF = total
Sources: BP Bank and CR Bank

Table 8.18. Formal training in a sample of Italian banks, 1991 (no. of employees in training per year)

	Sample size	Training					
		Tm	Tf	Tmf	Tf/Tmf (%)	Tf/F (%)	Tm/M (%)
All banks in sample	123	187 793	55 271	243 064	22.74	88.01	106.27
Cooperative banks	18	40 083	8 169	48 252	16.93	132.92	184.84
Small banks (rural banks)	7	916	395	1 311	30.13	88.96	81.86
Savings banks	7	17 037	11 256	28 293	39.78	127.22	115.84
Public banks	9	53 598	14 684	68 282	21.50	51.03	62.25
Private and foreign banks	46	72 405	18 695	91 100	20.52	118.99	148.15
Financial societies	36	3 754	2 072	5 826	35.56	72.14	88.75

Notes: Tm = trained male employees; Tf = trained female employees; Tmf = trained employees (total); M = male employees; F = female employees.
Source: OML, Regione Lombardia (Law No. 125/1991 data).

course, can be expected to have a negative impact on women's career advancement.

8.5.5 Career advancement

As already mentioned, women enter the bank roughly with the same level of education and the same motivations as men. They display attachment to their jobs and concern about career advancement. However, all the available data indicate that vertical segregation is still noticeable. Data on employment structure by skill grade and gender (see Tables 8.13 and 8.14) show a concentration of women in the lower clerical grades.

Until 10 years ago, the concentration of women in the lower grades was the result of a rigid division of labour, with women allocated to jobs that offered few prospects of advancement. However, as the result of technological changes in the last decade women are now initially allocated to the same jobs as men: when they join a bank, they start working at the counter. Thus there are no differences.

Moreover, promotion is automatic, as provided in the collective agreements, up to a certain grade (deputy head clerk). This explains why a large number of women reach this position. To progress further, however, one needs to be promoted on the basis of an evaluation by the head clerk. The same holds good for all remaining steps in the hierarchical structure. Discretionary power here is obviously great, and usually (despite similar training, capabilities, seniority, and so on) men tend to be preferred to women. Consequently, women need much longer to reach the same grade.

The case of BP Bank illustrates this point well. Let us take, as an example, the position of procuratore di 3a, (assistant manager in grade 3 (see Table 8.19)). This position, which can be considered to be at the bottom of the high-qualification grades, is occupied by the largest number of women reaching a high position: 14 (compared with 305 men). The women in this grade are four years older than the men (51.7 and 47.1 respectively); they have a higher bank seniority (30.8 and 23.3); and they also have a higher grade seniority (4.7 and 3.7).

Data on upgrading, both at the aggregate level (Table 8.20) and at the micro level (Table 8.2), confirm this result: vertical mobility is more difficult for women than for men. The percentage of upgrading among women is systematically lower than among men, and this is mainly due to discretionary evaluations.

Since in the last 10 to 15 years highly qualified women have entered banking in large numbers and at the same time earnings in the industry have declined significantly in relative terms, the persistence of vertical

Table 8.19. Average age, average bank seniority and average grade seniority by sex, BP Bank, 1991

	Average age		Average bank seniority		Average grade seniority	
	M	F	M	F	M	F
Managers	53.0	–	26.7	–	2.9	–
Director of branch	53.0	–	29.1	–	2.7	–
Deputy director of branch	51.4	–	28.7	–	2.8	–
Authorized Agent 1a	50.5	36.8	27.7	1.2	2.9	1.2
Authorized Agent 2a	48.8	51.6	25.3	28.2	3.2	4.8
Authorized Agent 3a	47.1	51.7	23.3	30.8	3.7	4.7
Authorized Agent 4a	44.8	47.9	20.4	26.1	3.3	3.3
Average rank III	46.6	49.2	23.6	27.1	3.2	3.8
Senior clerical workers 1	41.7	–	0.9	–	0.9	–
Senior clerical workers 2	41.7	39.4	17.7	17.7	1.8	1.8
Head clerk	46.1	47.3	21.5	26.1	3.5	4.0
Average rank II	43.2	43.7	18.9	22.3	2.4	3.0
Deputy head clerk	42.0	37.1	16.8	14.8	4.1	3.4
Head of division	37.1	31.7	10.5	8.9	2.6	3.7
Clerk (Class I)	30.2	25.8	4.6	2.4	2.3	2.0
Average rank I	38.0	31.2	12.4	8.4	3.3	3.0
Clerk (Class I)	42.4	34.7	10.9	7.3		
Ushers/auxiliary staff	37.9	29.2	6.8	3.6		

Note: Some qualification grades have not been translated because they are specific to the Italian banking tradition. As the hierarchical system has developed, new terms (such as *procuratore* have been introduced.)
Source: BP Bank.

Table 8.20. Upgrading by gender in a sample of Italian banks, 1991 (no. of employees upgraded)

	Sample size	Upgrading					
		Um	Uf	Umf	Uf/Umf (%)	Uf/F (%)	Um/M (%)
All banks in sample	123	56 596	15 303	71 899	21.28	24.37	32.03
Cooperative banks	18	7 439	1 676	9 115	18.39	27.27	34.30
Small banks (rural banks)	7	393	136	529	25.71	30.63	35.12
Savings banks	7	5 010	2 317	7 327	31.62	26.19	34.07
Public banks	9	24 002	6 153	30 155	20.40	21.38	27.88
Private and foreign banks	46	18 459	4 353	22 812	19.08	27.70	37.77
Financial societies	36	1 293	668	1 961	34.06	23.26	30.57

Notes: Um = upgraded male employees; Uf = upgraded female employees; Umf = upgraded employees (total); M = male employees; F = female employees
Source: OML, Regione Lombardia (Law No. 125/1991 data)

segregation could be interpreted as the result of an attempt to 'protect' the best paid positions. As it is no longer possible – owing to increasing competition from abroad – to defend the relative position of the credit sector with respect to the rest of the economy, protection of the best paid jobs in banks has taken place, penalizing women.

Notes

1. Dipartimento di Economia, Università degli Studi di Trento.
2. This law deals with both direct and indirect discrimination. To improve knowledge about women's position in the labour market, it requires all firms with a staff of over 100 to compile every two years a detailed statistical report on male and female personnel, providing information on employment structure, earnings, employment contracts, recruitment, lay-offs, training, career advancement, and so on.
3. According to the labour force sample survey (ISTAT 1991), the share of women in non-manual jobs (employees only) is 45.3 per cent.

Table 8.21. Upgrading at BP Bank by gender, hierarchical layer and motivation for upgrading (%)

	Internal competition		Automatic upgrading (by seniority)		Promotion by internal evaluation		Discretionary upgrading		Other reasons	
	M	F	M	F	M	F	M	F	M	F
Rank III	34.3	35.5	—	—	29.4	—	100	—	21.1	7.0
Rank II	64.8	64.5	—	—	15.5	15.5	—	—	54.6	32.5
Rank I	—	—	100	100	48.3	75.2	—	—	23.3	60.5
Clerk (Class 2)	—	—	—	—	6.8	9.3	—	—	—	—
Auxiliary staff	0.9	—	—	—	—	—	—	—	—	—

Source: BP Bank.

9 Concluding Remarks

Francesca Bettio and Paola Villa

For heuristic purposes consideration may be given to a tripartite segmentation of the labour market in Italy against which to evaluate the results of the case study analysis. In terms of both pay and employment conditions the case study identifies a middle to upper segment, a lower segment and a marginal segment. Public employment, and employment in mixed private/public companies such as SIP or ITALTEL, in large firms or in profitable industries such as banking, which are sheltered from international competition, belong to the middle to upper segment. Manufacturing firms in industries highly exposed to international competition (textiles, for example), or small firms throughout the economy, would typically range from the middle to lower segment of our scale; very small manufacturing firms or private services, especially those resorting to the 'informal' (or black) labour market, would belong to the marginal segment.

The difficulty presented by the case studies is that we would place them all in the middle to upper segment. Hospital A, BP Bank, SIP and ITALTEL are medium- to large-size concerns in services or manufacturing. All of them, moreover, are highly structured internal labour markets in which employees share some of the company's revenue: because the concern is a monopoly (SIP) or an oligopoly (ITALTEL) operating under a mixed private/public regime; because it is part of the highly protected segment of public employment (the hospital); or because it is sheltered from international as well as internal competition (banking). Moreover, two of them – health services and the national telephone company – belong to industries with one of the lowest values for the earnings gap between men and women: public administration and the transport and communications industry.

On the other hand, trends in the gender pay gap impinge on factors that are common to all segments, for example the manual versus non-manual workers dichotomy. The cases thus offer indirect information about other segments, provided that these are covered by collective agreements. Coverage is ensured for most of the lower segment, but not the marginal segment, for which reliance is entirely on general data and information.

With these qualifications in mind we may now summarize our overall findings. From an international perspective, and within formal employment, the gender pay gap in Italy (27.5 per cent in 1991) is lower compared to other European countries, despite the post-1985 increase. Admittedly, it does not take into account 'unofficial' bonuses accruing to intermediate and top management, but we have ascertained in the case of SIP that these would add at the most one or two points to the 'official' gap. There is no good reason to suppose that SIP is unrepresentative in this particular respect.

A very slight difference in seniority (there are significant differences in banking but merely because women have entered the industry quite recently), combined with pay scales that remain relatively flat in most cases, has produced a modest pay gap. Fewer women work in Italy than in other industrialized countries, but those who do work display an uninterrupted pattern over the life cycle similar to that of men, and their earnings are much closer to those of men. When comparing Italy with other Western nations, one may wonder in fact whether the trade-off in that country is between fewer but better jobs for women or between better careers and fewer children, or both (Italy currently has the world's lowest fertility rate).

Segregation is probably the most important determinant of the pay gap. The second most important determinant is differences in what we have called called 'attendance', that is overtime, heavy shifts, on-call duties, and so forth. Merit pay is of some importance within the middle to upper segment, but things may be different in small firms of the lower segment on which we have no relevant information.

Nor can the relative contribution of each of these three components be quantified. Nevertheless, some guesses have been made by working backwards from the firm to the national aggregate. In the case-study hospital, for example, segregation *per se* has a very small impact: estimates are that it 'explains' 2.04 gap points out of a total of 9.01 (i.e. about 22 per cent). This means that the remaining seven points are accounted for by differences in attendance or in group incentives ('official' merit pay). The data for SIP, on the other hand, suggest that seven points for differences in attendance and incentive pay may be a high figure, since we have estimated an overall gap of 7.8 per cent, all inclusive, but the picture may be different in small firms. For the sake of argument, however, assumptions have been made that a figure of between 7 and 10 points is representative; that is, in each firm and industry women would earn 7 to 10 per cent less solely because of attendance and merit pay. Since in three out of four cases reviewed differences in seniority between men and women were either negligible or favoured women, and since in the fourth case (banking) differences favouring men are temporary, hardly any part of the gender gap may be thus accounted for. We may therefore conclude that between 63 and 75 per cent of the economy-wide gender gap in average earnings is attributable to segregation at all levels: occupational, inter-firm and inter-industry.

The above guess – for obvious reasons preference is given to calling it a guess rather than an estimate – may seem high in comparison with the modest importance that our evidence from 2 out of 3 case studies would attribute to occupational segregation alone. And this impression is probably correct, particularly since overrepresentation among non-manual workers is a feature of segregation that systematically acts in favour of women, as all our cases indicate. Nevertheless, it is well known that women are definitely overrepresented in small firms and in low-pay industries, and it is therefore reasonable to hypothesize that inter-firm and inter-industry segregation rather than occupational segregation may be largely responsible for the overall gender pay gap.

However small the role of occupational segregation, the disadvantage for women here comes from underrepresentation at the top of the occupational pyramid rather than from overrepresentation at the bottom. In other words, on balance, lack of upward mobility is the dominant feature, and is sustained by two intertwined factors: the intangible inertia of the social hierarchy and segregation in school curricula. Banking is probably the clearest example of how an organization which is very hierarchical at the top finds it particularly difficult to make room for women. But a similar difficulty is manifest at SIP, still a predominantly male organization: men 'suffer' – as the union official put it – if a woman is in charge. In this latter case, however, even before social hierarchy materializes as an obstacle, lack of formal and on-the-job technical education acts as an immediate barrier to upward mobility for women.

Finally, differences in 'attendance' – overtime, and so on – are not only an explicit component of the pay gap, but are also mentioned by unions and managers as a further, indirect obstacle to upward mobility. The reason is not always clearly identified, but appears as a mixture of signals and idiosyncratic acquisition of skills. That is, doing overtime or being available to work unsocial hours may signal greater dependability or give the worker extra knowledge and familiarity with the firm's procedures, mechanisms and needs, thus amounting to an idiosyncratic skill. When the overall gap is as small as in some large firms in Italy, this component may be relatively important but fairly difficult to remove.

Future trends in the gender pay gap are thus mainly tied to trends in segregation on the one hand and institutional changes affecting pay on the other. Current data indicate that desegregation of school curricula is under way. As a result, upward mobility for women should be enhanced. On the other hand, the expansion of low cost services may place more women at the bottom of the scale than at present and outweigh their entry into well-paid industries such as banking. In other words, while male manual workers are slowly disappearing both in manufacturing and in industry-related services and are being replaced by young male 'technicians', women may well be taking their place in low cost services. In view of these opposing trends, we should expect that future diversification among women will partly offset the tendency for the gender gap to reopen on account of increasing pay dispersion.

References

M. Ambrosini, M. Colasanto, and G. Gasparini (eds) *Tecnologia, organizzazione e lavoro: Uno studio di casi nel settore creditizio-assicurativo* (Milan: F. Angeli 1989).

F. Bettio, and P. Villa, *Occupational segregation: The case of Italy* (Brussels: European Commission Network on the Situation of Women in the Labour Market 1992) DG V/B/4.

—— *Wage determination and sex segregation in employment: The case of Italy* (Brussels: European Commission Network on the Situation of Women in the Labour Market 1993) DG V/B/4.

M. Chiesi, M. C. Federici, N. Lelli, R. Memoli, and P. Settimi (eds) *Diverse, non disuguali* (Rome: Edizioni Lavoro 1989).

B. Contini, R. Revelli, *Imprese, occupazione e retribuzioni al microscopio* (Bologna: Il Mulino 1992).

G. Faustini, 'Le graduatorie delle retribuzioni lorde settoriali', in *I salari in Italia negli anni ottanta: Rapporto della Commissione Carniti* (Venice: Marsilio 1988).

L. Frey, R. Lirraghi, T Treu 'Politiche del personale e valorizzazione femminile, in *Quaderni di Economia del Lavoro* (1988) No. 30.

ISTAT 'Conti Economici Nazionali; Occupazione e redditi da lavoro dipendente 1980–88', in *Collana d'informazione* (1989) No. 29.

—— 'Occupazione e redditi da lavoro dipendente, anni 1980–90', in *Collana d'informazione* (1991) No. 42.

L. Prosperetti, and G. Durante, *Retribuzioni e costo del lavoro nelle banche italiane ed europee* (Rome: ASSICREDITO 1993).

P. Villa, *Le donne nelle occupazioni atipiche* (first report) (Brussels: European Commission Network on the Situation of Women in the Labour Market 1988) DG V/B/4.

—— *Le donne nelle occupazioni atipiche* (second report) (Brussels: European Commission Network on the Situation of Women in the Labour Market 1989) DG V/B/4.

—— *La valutazione dell'impatto della realizzazione del mercato unico eureopeo sull'occupazione femminile nel settore del credito: Il caso dell'Italia* (Brussels: European Commission Network on the Situation of Women in the Labour Market 1990) DG V/B/4.

Part 3

Equal Pay in the United Kingdom

10 Payment Systems and Gender in the United Kingdom: Case Study of a Chemical Company

Colette Fagan[1]

This study presents the findings of a case study of a chemical company in the north-west of the United Kingdom, where a belt of chemical companies are located. The company studied introduced an integrated grading and payment structure in January 1993. This kind of overhaul of 'human resource management' has received a great deal of attention in British and American literature in connection with the search for flatter and more flexible organizations. The case study was carried out as part of a comparative analysis of payment and grading systems in Germany, Italy and the UK.

10.1. OVERVIEW OF EMPLOYMENT IN THE CASE STUDY AND THE UNITED KINGDOM CHEMICAL INDUSTRY

The chemical industry in the UK employs a total of 297 000 people, which accounts for 1.5 per cent of all employment (1.9 per cent of male employment and one per cent of female employment) (Table 10.1). The share of all employment concentrated in the chemical industry has remained broadly stable over the period since the mid-1980s. Men hold 68 per cent of the jobs in this industry, whereas the overall male share of employment in all manufacturing industries is 70 per cent. In contrast, women hold 48 per cent of all employment in the UK and 56 per cent of employment in the service sector.

The company studied manufactures photographic materials, chemicals and equipment.[2] It has shifted away from the production of colour film in order to develop a niche market, specializing in black and white and related products for professional photographic activities. The company is a subsidiary of one of the largest paper companies in the world.

Table 10.1. Comparison of the employment profile in the chemical industry and the case study

Employment profile	All UK	Chemical industry	Case study
Employment concentration			n.a.
% of all male employment in UK	100	1.9	
% of all female employment in UK	100	1.0	
% of all employment in UK	100	1.4	
Employment segregation			
% female share of workforce	52	32.0	35.0
% part-time employment rate	27	5.2	2.5–3.0
% Union density rate of employees*			
Workplace – less than 25 employees		11.0	n.a.
Workplace – 25 or more employees		38.0	86.0
All workplaces	37	34.0	n.a.
% of employees employed at workplace with > 25 employees[a]	47	88.0	n.a.
Total employment	20 839 500	297 200	1 208

n.a. = not applicable; * = 1991 data for chemical industry and UK; all other data for chemical industry and UK are for September 1992.

Sources: Rubery (1993), appendix (1991 Labour Force Survey); *Employment Gazette 1993: Labour Market Data* (Department of Employment Census of Employment), table 1.4, S12; personnel department, case study.

It is a research-oriented company with an explicit Total Quality Management philosophy and focuses on client-led development of products in order to sustain and develop the current niche market. At the time the case study was conducted the photographic market in the UK was depressed and hit by the recession. However, an internal financial brief for management notes that the company is maintaining its market share and concludes that this places it 'in a strong position to respond rapidly to eventual recovery in key business segments' (Managerial briefing document 1992, Appendix 1).

Just over 1200 people are employed at the workplace in five functional divisions: Finance, Human Resources, Research and Development, Production and Engineering, and Information Technology. The workforce covers a wide spectrum of skills and tasks, from the person who sorts the post, through laboratory technicians to scientists and world experts in narrow and specialized fields of chemistry. The sex composition, part-time rate and union density rate for the company studied are compared in Table 10.1 with those for the industry as a whole. On the first two comparisons the company is broadly similar to other companies in the industry, but a striking difference is its much higher level of unionization compared with the aggregate level for the industry as a whole.

Four unions are recognized at the case study workplace: the Amalgamated Electrical Engineering Union, the Association of Professional, Executive, Clerical and Computer Staff, General Municipal Boilemakers (GMB) and the Manufacturing, Science, Finance Union (MSF). Single table bargaining has replaced a two-tier system of bargaining, initially stimulated by the need for round table discussion in order to implement a redundancy programme set up by the company's head office in the United States. The personnel manager stated that the adoption of single table bargaining made it easier to develop and implement the integrated grading system.

10.2. GRADING AND PAYMENT SYSTEM

On 1 January 1993 a new, integrated grading and payment structure was introduced. This reform was instituted partly in response to significant job changes across the site in the previous 18 months, which had included a programme of redundancies. The new structure is a central component of a comprehensive programme of personnel policies adopted in 1992, summarized in Appendix 1.

The main impetus for the introduction of this new system was the desire to reorganize the way in which the workforce was managed and an explicit

Box 10.1: The flexibility clause

Flexibility and cooperation are essential parts of your employment contract. It is a condition of employment that the Company has the right to transfer an employee permanently or temporarily to a different job of a similar nature ... In order to maintain and improve operational efficiency, all employees must share skills and knowledge. When necessary, employees will be asked by management to perform basic maintenance, administrative and service tasks, provided you have the ability, are trained and it is safe to do so.

Source: Staff Handbook, p. 11.

concern to increase functional flexibility, particularly among manual (blue-collar) workers. Its introduction was described as the adoption of a Human Resource Management strategy which was congruent with the company's Total Quality Management philosophy – namely, minimizing hierarchies and empowering the workforce in order to sustain a competitive edge in quality product markets. To this end, a new flexibility clause was introduced as part of the integrated grading system (see Box 10.1). This overhaul of the grading of the workforce coincided with substantial capital investment and a reorganization of the production process.

Consultations and negotiations concerning the revision of the pay and grading structure lasted two years. The main issue was the size of the increase in the total wage bill in connection with integrated grading, greater functional flexibility and the reduction in job demarcation through the introduction of the flexibility clause. The unions wanted a larger increase in real wages to compensate for the loss of job demarcation.

10.2.1 The pre-1993 grading and payment system

Five separate grading structures were in place and these are listed below, together with a general indication of the job requirements according to the Standard Occupational Classification (OPCS, 1990).

- *Managerial and professional*

  Managerial jobs require a significant amount of knowledge and experience related training associated with the efficient functioning of organizations and business (many managers do not have a university degree, although graduates are becoming more common). Managerial staff include general managers as well as specialist managers (in such fields as marketing and sales, personnel, purchasing, computer systems, and production). Professional occupations require a degree or equivalent qualification, with some occupations requiring postgraduate qualifications and/or a formal period of experience-related training, for example accountants and engineers.

- *Clerical*

  Clerical and secretarial jobs require a good standard of general education. Some occupations require further vocational training to a well-defined standard (for example typing).

- *Laboratory technicians*

  This grading structure encompasses junior posts requiring a good standard of general education, and associated professional jobs requiring a high-level vocational qualification, both of which involve some task-related training.

- *Craft workers (blue-collar)*

  Craft jobs are differentiated from other manual jobs by a substantial period of formal work-based training, such as an apprenticeship (for example, electrical and electronic engineering trades).

- *Operatives and semi-skilled workers (blue-collar)*

  The requirements for these manual jobs are the knowledge and experience necessary to operate vehicles, industrial plant and equipment, to assemble products and to carry out routine tests. Some jobs involve simple and routine tasks, while others call for experience related or task related training.

All the craft workers were men and the managerial grades were also male dominated, particularly among the senior grades. Nearly 100 per cent of the clerical workers were women and 70 per cent of the operatives. Laboratory technicians constituted a more mixed grading structure, with women accounting for 45 per cent of this occupational workforce, although they were disproportionately concentrated in the lower grades. The concentration of women in a narrower range of jobs than men and the male dominance of higher-grade jobs reflect broader patterns of segregation found in the wider labour market (see, for example, Rubery *et al.*, 1992; Rubery and Fagan, 1993).

Each grading structure was associated with a separate salary structure, which was associated in turn with different systems of job evaluation and varying elements of performance-related pay. The unskilled and semi-skilled manual workers were graded using a factor-based job evaluation system. No job evaluation scheme operated for the craft grades where grading was based on formal qualifications gained through apprenticeships rather than on job content. The clerical and managerial grade systems were based on the Hay evaluation scheme. In these two white-collar areas a system of performance related pay was in operation, but not in a systematic way. In some parts of the company it functioned virtually as an automatic two per cent incremental change, regardless of individual performance. The laboratory technician grading was based on a combined system, with a task-oriented assessment rewarded by regrading rather than by a performance pay supplement.

Figure 10.1 shows the relative basic rates of pay in 1991; shift and overtime premiums are excluded. The junior monthly staff (JMS) grading range encompasses unskilled and semi-skilled operatives and clerical workers. The pay and grading for laboratory technicians (Lab), craft workers and apprentices (Craft and S/S) and managerial and professional staff (MSS) are shown separately. The managerial staff had two linked payment structures, one which covered grades 3 to 12 and a second-tier 'contract' pay range covering the higher grades.

While the relationship between the two payment structures covering monthly senior staff produced a smooth, upward-sloping curve, the pattern of overlap was much more ragged at the lower end of the payment distribution. All unskilled, semi-skilled and clerical workers earned between £8,397 in grade A and £11,997 in grade L. Grades H to L overlapped with the bottom of the higher level white-collar (managerial and professional) grades. Comparing these with the laboratory grades, we see that the junior laboratory grades overlapped with the salary range for grades B to H (LTA1 to LTA3), while the senior grades LT1 and LT2 were on a par with grade F and grade K. The starting salary for junior craft workers was slightly below that for senior laboratory technicians, while a qualified (time-served) craft worker ranked much higher and earned more than the bottom three managerial and professional grades (grades 3 to 5).

However, this figure does not show the effect of adding in additional payments such as working-time additions for shift working and overtime. Shift payments would have been concentrated among unskilled and semi-skilled workers and among production team leaders in the craft grades. Overtime payments were also concentrated in those grades.

Figure 10.1. Relative rates of pay, 1991 (basic 37.5 hours per week)

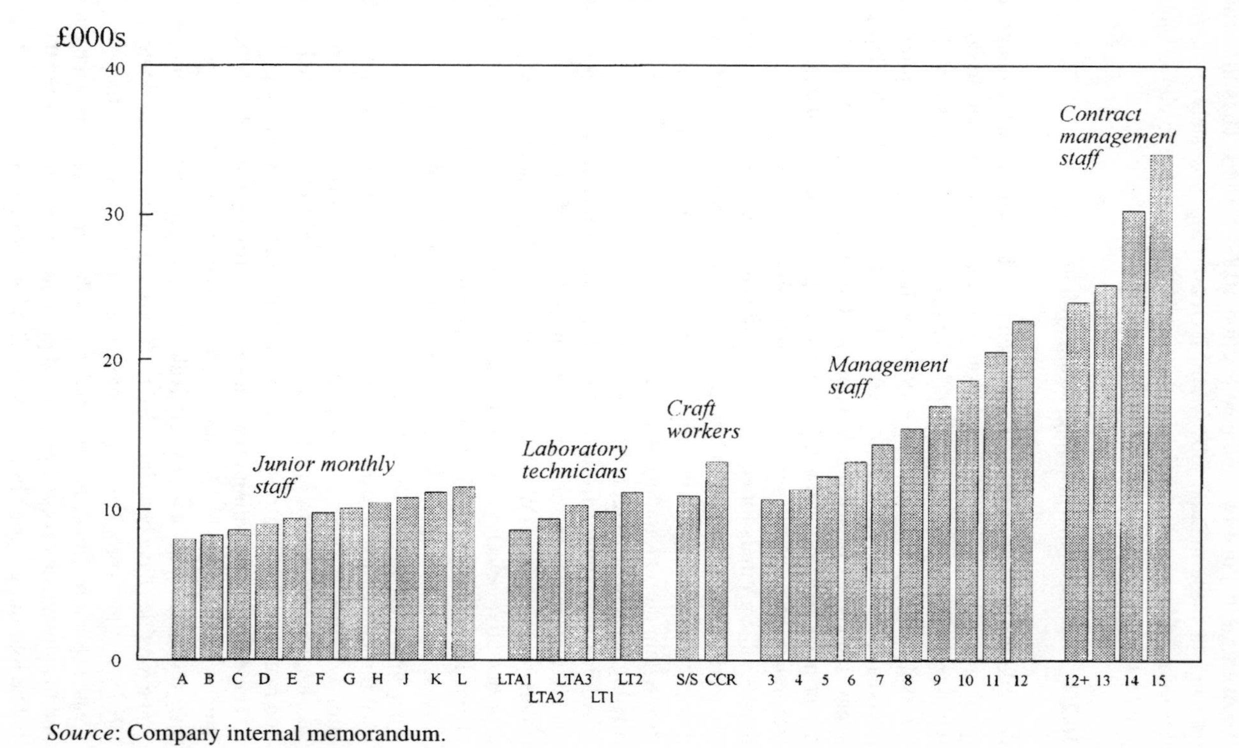

Source: Company internal memorandum.

Women account for more than half of the shift workers, while most of the overtime is done by men (see Section 10.2.4 below). Thus the actual earnings in these manual jobs would increase proportionately more than those for other jobs; in particular they would rise relative to clerical jobs, where working-time additions were rare.

10.2.2 The 1993 integrated grading system

A single job evaluation scheme was used in order to develop the integrated grading structure. The job evaluation procedure was designed to comply with the 'spirit as well as the letter' of equal pay on the basis that the old job evaluation systems made it very likely that an equal value claim would eventually be lodged (Managerial briefing document 1992, p. 6). The personnel manager stressed that flexibility rather than sex equality issues was the primary reason for the adoption of integrated grading. Indeed, while integration of employees into one grading structure addressed some of the more visible grounds for equal value claims, an overt and radical comparable worth exercise was not envisaged: 'A pecking order of jobs similar to that in each of the old structures is expected. That is to say present relativities within current grading structures should be maintained'. (Managerial briefing document 1992, p. 6)

Advice was sought from the Equal Opportunities Commission about which was the best scheme to adopt and an off-the-shelf evaluation scheme was adopted (Work Profiling System). The scheme chosen uses a representative selection of jobs for the evaluation. The job holder and his or her line manager work through a system to identify what the job involves. Once they agree on the job content a form is filled in and a computer analysis weights the final score. Effectively the same factors were used throughout the scheme. The union was not involved in the job evaluation exercise. A system for appeals against individual grading decisions was established, and in practice an appeal needed to be supported by the line manager if it was to succeed. A total of 22 appeals were lodged.

The generic streamlining produced a shift from some 100 job titles to between approximately 120 and 130. The result of the evaluation process is that job descriptions are now equivalent to a specification of competency. Some job titles have been included in the grading system which do not actually exist at the workplace, for example senior accountants. The purpose is to create explicit reference points which reveal the linkages between the grades and to cultivate an expectation of fluid promotion channels between them.

The jobs are grouped into a system of 11 grades covering manual, clerical, technical and all managerial jobs. No individual employee is paid above grade 11 and on an individual contract (but board members are on different contracts). There are some group staff on site who are not employed by the UK company and are therefore on different contracts; for example, the marketing manager for Africa is paid from the Brussels office. The resulting wide grades were designed to increase functional flexibility by reducing the demarcation associated with the previous narrowly defined jobs, to establish clear development ladders for all employees and to remove the anomalies which could result in promotions between the separate grading structures being associated with a reduction in wages (see Figure 10.1).

Table 10.2 examines how women and men are distributed across the new grading structure and the sex segregation of each grade.

Table 10.3 provides example job titles and entry requirements for each of the grades in the Research and Development division, plus grades 1 and 2.

Grades 1 and 2 are basic operative grades: everyone in grade 2 is a packing line operative, and together they account for just under four per cent of the workforce. Just over five per cent of the female workforce and three per cent of the male workforce are found in these two lowest grades. Women account for half of the workforce in both of them. This means that the sex share of this part of the job hierarchy is mixed, but that women are overrepresented in these grades relative to their 35 per cent share of the overall workforce.

Jobs evaluated as semi-skilled are found in grade 3, with a higher evaluation of the skill content for jobs put into grade 4. Nearly 60 per cent of female employees are employed in grades 3 and 4. Nearly a third of all men are also concentrated in these grades, but they are more dispersed across the higher grades. The majority of grade 3 workers are women and in grade 4 women are still overrepresented relative to their share of the workforce (43 per cent compared with 35 per cent). Most of the women in these grades are in junior clerical and laboratory technician jobs. Male-dominated production jobs in these grades include general operative jobs such as warehouse operators and fork-lift truck drivers; courier mail service operators and trained craft workers are in grade 4.

By grade 5 we see a further increase in the male share of the grade, although the female share is just over the women's share for the total workforce (38 per cent compared with 35 per cent). This grade accounts for 12 per cent of all men and 13 per cent of all women employed at the workplace. More senior clerical and laboratory workers are found in grade 5, along with some specialized posts such as systems analysts in marketing. This is the highest grade for semi-skilled (non-managerial) production

Table 10.2. Concentration and segregation in the integrated grading structure, 1993

Grade	% concentration of employment			% female share of grade	Total number of employees	Example job titles
	Men	Women	Total			
1	0.1	0	0.1	0	1	Operatives, mainly on packing line
2	2.8	5.4	3.8	51	45	
3	19.8	44.7	28.6	55	345	Clerical; laboratory technicians; warehouse operators; drivers
4	10.0	13.6	11.3	43	136	
5	11.7	13.4	12.4	38	149	Clerical; laboratory technicians; non-managerial production jobs such as night shift team leader in warehouse; systems analyst in marketing
6	14.9	7.8	12.3	22	150	Graduate scientists, including laboratory workers; craft and production supervisors/managers such as process control technician. (Graduate entry grade for professionals)

Table 10.2. (continued)

Grade	% concentration of employment			% female share of grade	Total number of employees	Example job titles
	Men	Women	Total			
7	8.7	6.4	7.9	28	95	Professional, e.g. accountants, information technology specialists, personnel; production supervisors/managers
8	8.3	4.2	6.9	22	83	Professional as for grade 7; shift managers
9	10.9	2.8	8.0	12	97	
10	6.9	0.7	4.7	5	57	Section and departmental managers
11	3.8	0	2.5	0	30	
not classified*	2.0	0.9	1.7	20	20	
Total = 100%	783	425	1 208	35	1 208	

* = not classified (includes individuals for whom a grading position has not yet been decided as well as company directors).
Source: Personnel records, case-study.

Table 10.3. Examples of job titles and entry requirements in the integrated grading structure

Grade	Example job titles	Entry requirements	Overtime bonus + merit payment	Fringe benefits
1	Site 'manager' (operative)	Literate	O/T paid	—
2	Packing operator	Good GCSE in English and Maths (min.)	O/T paid	—
3	Junior analytical technician	Four good GCSE grades	O/T paid	—
4	Senior research assistant	Four GCSE + ONC or "A" levels	O/T paid	—
5	Research technician	Four GCSE (incl. chemistry) + ONC/experience	O/T paid	—
6	Graduate scientist	Relevant degree	O/T paid	—
7	Research scientist I	Degree + experience or PhD	O/T paid	—
8	Research scientist II	PhD + experience	O/T paid	—
9	Research scientist III	As above	O/T paid	—
10	Section leader	As above but with management skills	No O/T paid	Car
11	Department manager	As above (experience obviously greater)	No O/T paid	Car

ONC = Ordinary National Certificate. Jobs in grades 3–11 are in Research and Development. All employees are eligible to join the company pension scheme. All employees are eligible for variable element of pay payments; the total cost to the company is approximately 2 per cent of the payroll.
Source: Personnel records, case-study.

workers, such as team leaders of the night shift in the warehouse. It is also the highest grade for clerical workers.

Women are underrepresented in grade 6 and above. Grade 6 is the lowest grade for graduates. This grade also includes senior laboratory workers, most of whom are men at this level, and craft workers, for example a process control technician in emulsions and a universal operator in the coating department. Grade 7 encompasses professional and some production supervisory/management jobs. From grade 8 upwards the male domination of the jobs increases sharply, associated with managerial and more senior professional posts.

10.2.3 The new payment structure

The new salary structure was designed to emphasize the link between pay and company performance rather than individual bonuses based on quantitative output: 'The company's aim is to pay salaries which are competitive, relate to the achievement of business objectives and encourage and reward individual performance'. (Staff Handbook, p. 4)

In the new structure each grade has three levels (see Box 10.2). Level 1 is the entry level, level 2 is the normal level or 'rate for the job' and level 3 is designed to be occupied by a small minority of employees who are either awaiting promotion or possess a special skill which is neither required at level 2 by the majority of staff nor relevant for promotion to a higher grade, for example a bilingual qualification.

Figure 10.2 maps the highest and lowest salary point for grades 1 to 9, which resulted from taking staff out of their separate grade and payment structures (shown in Figure 10.1) and slotting them into their new grade at their pre-existing salary level following the job evaluation exercise.[3] The variation in the width of the earnings dispersal for different grades is evident, indicating the previous undervaluation of some jobs relative to those in other payment and grading structures. The dispersal, and implicit discrepancy, is widest in grade 5, where the top and bottom salary points do not fit into the upward trend between grade and salary range shown in the figure. This is the highest level grade in which women are still overrepresented relative to their share of the total workforce.

Table 10.4 compares the estimated pre-existing salary range reproduced as Figure 10.3 with the new salary levels which were introduced in January 1993. The streamlining of the new payment system is evident, with the differential range within each grade having been compressed by replacing the pre-existing upper salary with a lower maximum salary (level 3) and raising the minimum salary in each grade from 3 upwards.

Box 10.2. The new grade levels

Level 1
This is the entry level. The time spent at this level will vary according to the job and the individual (from a few weeks to two years). Once the individual is able to fully perform the job as described in the job evaluation process to the appropriate standard he/she will proceed to level 2.

After one year in this level the individual may be eligible for lump sum performance payments.

Level 2
This is the level at which an individual is fully performing all the elements of the job to a consistently acceptable standard. This will be the level occupied by the majority of people.

'Continuous improvement' is a requirement of maintaining this level. The individual will receive training in new methods of work to improve both his/her working methods and flexibility (this may be considered the 'rate for the job').

Level 3
A small minority of employees will occupy this level. As a general guide, if more than 10 per cent of a job population is found in level 3 then a reassessment of the job's grade should be carried out.

Entry to level 3 is restricted to two types of job holder:

(a) the individual possesses all the necessary skills, knowledge etc. to move to a higher grade and is putting these to good use in the present post. Hence, the individual is ready for promotion but there is no appropriate vacancy;
(b) the individual has specialist skills above those required by all job holders but not relevant to a higher graded job. These skills are not required by all normal level 2 job holders and will not be required by them in the foreseeable future. These additional skills are of sufficient importance to set the individual apart from other holders of the same job.

Source: Extract from internal personnel document explaining the new grading and payment structure, January 1993.

The more regular pattern of smaller differentials for each grade under the new structure is illustrated in figure 10.3. The differentials between the grades produce a smoother line, although these vary. Thus the differential between the grades on the basis of the normal (level 2) rate for each grade and the entry rate (level 1) for the grade above is between 8 and 11 per cent for all grades except between grades 3 and 4 (0.4 per cent), 4 and 5 (2.6 per cent), and 7 and 8 (4 per cent).

What is the gender impact of the integrated grading and payment structure? Who benefited from the transition and who is likely to benefit in the

Figure 10.2. Current Salaries in New Grades

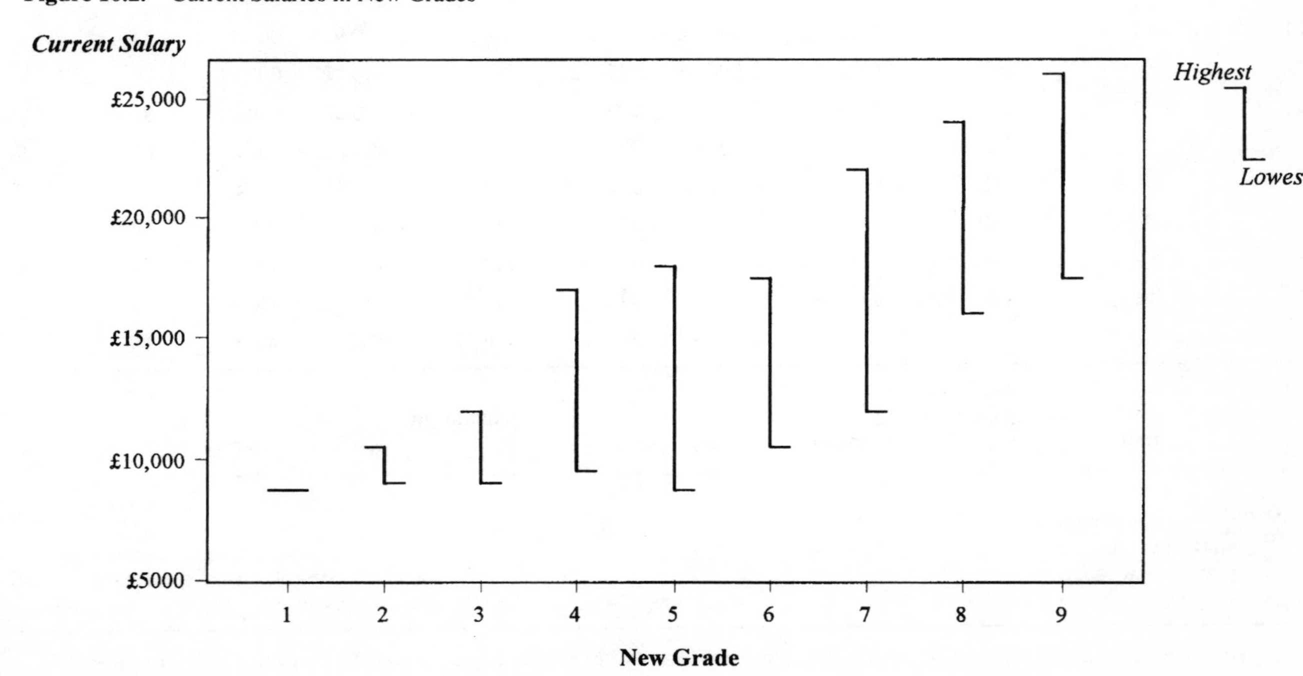

Source: See Table 10.4

Table 10.4. Pre-existing and revised salary ranges for the new grading system (in £ sterling), and distribution of 'losers'

Grade	% female share of grade	Pre-existing salary range (when posts regraded into new system*)			New salary levels				Distribution of 'losers'†† (those who received a zero pay rise in the transition)	
		Lowest	Highest	% differential	Level 1	Level 2	Level 3	% differential levels 1–3	% of grade	% distribution of 'losers'
1	0	8 700	8 700	n.a.	7 742.50	8 150.0	8 557.5	10.5	..	..
2	51	9 000	10 500	16	8 761.85	9 223.0	9 684.15	10.5	44	15
3	55	9 000	12 000	33	10 070.0	10 600.0	11 130.0	10.5	13	34
4	43	9 500	17 000	79	10 640.0	11 200.0	11 760.0	10.5	6	6
5	38	8 700	18 000	107	11 495.0	12 100.0	12 705.0	10.5	4	4
6	22	10 500	17 500	67	13 309.0	14 300.0	15 015.0	12.8	6	7
7	28	12 000	22 000	83	15 309.0	16 550.0	17 791.0	16.2	16	12
8	22	16 000	24 000	50	17 280.0	19 200.0	21 120.0	22.2	8	11
9	12	17 500	>26 000	>50	21 285.0	23 650.0	26 015.0	22.2	17	12

Table 10.4 (continued)

Grade	% female share of grade	Pre-existing salary range (when posts regraded into new system*)			New salary levels				Distribution of 'losers'[††] (those who received a zero pay rise in the transition)	
		Lowest	Highest	% differential	Level 1	Level 2	Level 3	% differential levels 1–3	% of grade	% distribution of 'losers'
10[†]	5	..	..	..	26 015.0	28 616.5	31 477.15	21.0	..	..
11[†]	0	..	..	..	31 477.15	34 642.87	38 107.16	21.6	..	..
								Total 'losers' grades 2–9	12	100

n.a. = not applicable. *These figures are estimates derived from a graphical presentation in a company document, reproduced as figure 3. [†]No data for grades 10 and 11 were provided in the company document, in part because the new salary levels had not been agreed at the time. In the second interview, the personnel manager provided the agreed salary levels for these grades: grade 10 equal to the top of grade 9, and a 10 per cent differential between each level in both grades 10 and 11. Estimated salary ranges were derived using this information and involved making the assumption that grade 11 starts roughly equal to the top of grade 10, following the practice adopted from grade 5 upwards in the structure. [††]No data were available for grades 1, 10 and 11, which account for over 10 per cent of the male workforce and less than one per cent of the female workforce.
Sources: Information leaflet for employees on the new pay and grading structure prior to its implementation in January 1993; memorandum to departmental managers; interview, personnel department.

Figure 10.3. Proposed 1993 Salary Levels

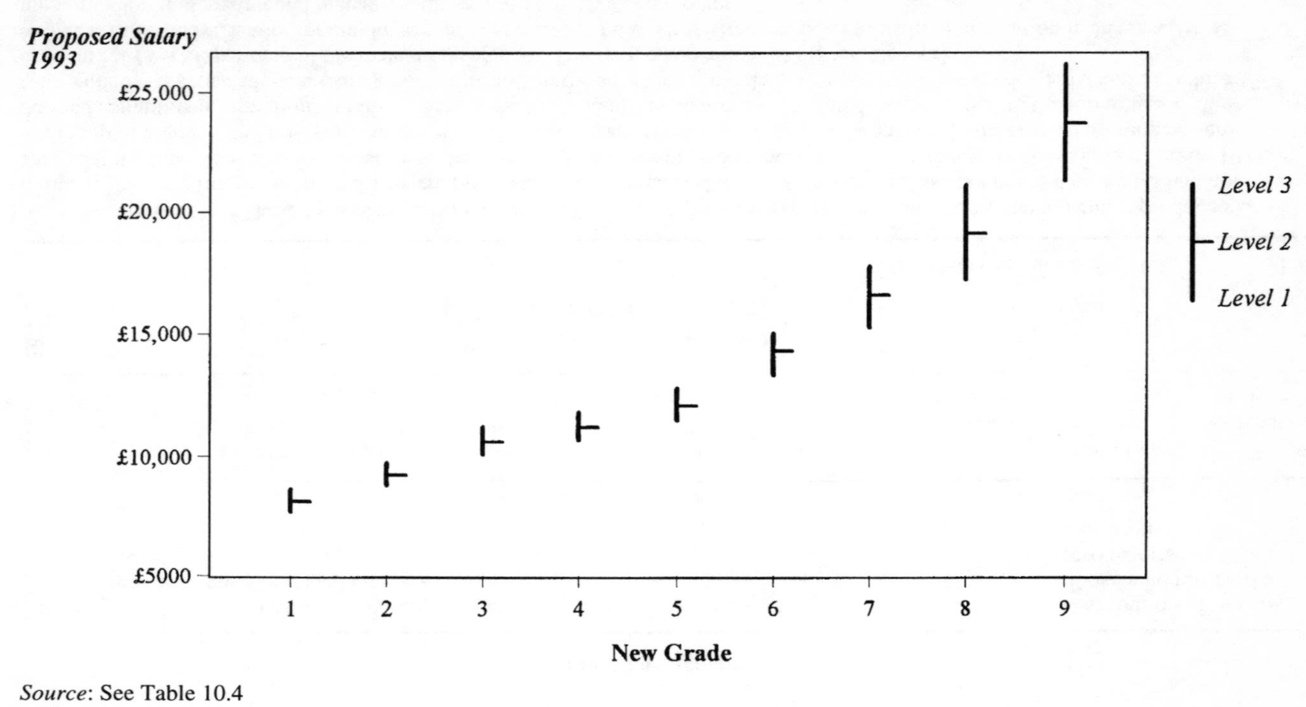

Source: See Table 10.4

future? The introduction of the new structure increased payroll costs by 4.4 per cent during 1993 (3.5 per cent over and above the 1992 pay costs across the site). Salaries were capped during the transition in order to keep the maximum individual rise at 10 per cent. A total of 203 employees were capped by this 10 per cent ceiling, 79 per cent (160) of whom were men. While men's salaries were disproportionately constrained relative to their share of the workforce, twice as many men as women received the maximum 10 per cent pay rise: 21 per cent of men compared with 10 per cent of women. Most of the men who were capped to a maximum 10 per cent rise were production managers/supervisors who had been re-graded from team leader positions because their jobs had expanded to include responsibility for expensive capital equipment.

While one occupational group of men was more likely than women to receive the maximum pay rise, another group of men was more likely to receive the minimum pay rise. The personnel manager stated that a higher percentage of men than women had their wages frozen. Unfortunately, a breakdown by sex of those who received a zero wage increase was not available, but it was possible to provide a breakdown by grade (see Table 10.4). Overall, about 12 per cent of the total workforce received no wage increase. The last column in Table 10.4 shows the incidence of 'losers' – employees who received no wage increase – within each grade and their distribution across the grades.

Employees in grade 2 (operatives) were much more likely to be 'losers' than those in any other grade; 44 per cent of these employees received no wage increase. Fifteen per cent of 'losers' were from this grade, although grade 2 accounted for only 4 per cent of all employees. 'Losers' were also disproportionately concentrated in grade 3, where there were 34 per cent of 'losers' compared with 29 per cent of all employees. Over 50 per cent of women employees compared with 22 per cent of male employees are found in these grades (see Table 10.2). Although women account for just over half the workforce in grades 2 and 3, most of the 'losers' and those receiving only a small wage rise in these grades were men, particularly operatives. This was a result of the job evaluation scheme which removed the previous evaluative emphasis on factors connected with moving heavy weights, associated with male-dominated jobs such as warehouse operatives. In contrast, most women in production jobs were packing films, which did not involve moving heavy weights. In addition, overtime premiums were reduced and this has fed through into lower total salaries, particularly for men in these grades. Slightly more male than female employees in these grades worked overtime (see Section 10.2.4 below) and much longer overtime hours were worked by men on average.

Further losses which remain to be resolved in the phasing-in period relate primarily to male-dominated jobs in these lower grades. While individual pay anomalies are scattered throughout the new hierarchy, the most significant one concerns about 50 operators in the warehouse, most of whom are men. For the pay of these operatives to match their grade they need to be held down until the grade levels have risen by three per cent. Since the personnel department expects to be negotiating pay settlements of 1 to 1.5 per cent over the next few years, this adjustment would take three years.[4]

However, it is not simply that the higher grades have been protected while the lower grades have lost out, for 'losers' are also overrepresented in some of the higher grades. The risk of being a 'loser' was higher in grades 9 and 7 than in grade 3, and 35 per cent of 'losers' were concentrated in grades 7 to 9, although these grades account for only 23 per cent of all employment. These are male-dominated professional and managerial grades, and again most 'losers' were male employees. At this level of the hierarchy the reason they lost was primarily to do with dismantling the complex and fragmented systems of performance-related pay.

Those employees who were placed in the middle grades 4 to 6 (and grade 8 to a lesser extent) seem to have benefited most from the integration of previously fragmented and segregated job hierarchies. The risk of being a 'loser' was much lower for employees in the middle grade, an incidence of between 4 and 6 per cent. These grades accounted for 36 per cent of all employees and only 17 per cent of all 'losers'. According to the personnel manager, there were proportionally more winners in grades 4 and 5 'where rates have been traditionally lower than their "value"'. More than half the employees in these grades are male, but the female share is higher than the overall female share of the workforce. Together, grades 4 and 5 account for 27 per cent of all female employees – primarily as laboratory technicians and clerical workers – and 22 per cent of all male employees.

From Figure 10.1 we can see that the previous salary range for laboratory technicians was from just over £8000 to just under £12 000, while the basic salary for trainee craft workers (S/S) was about £11 000 and just under £14 000 for craft workers. Table 10.4 shows that the new salary range for laboratory technicians starts at £10 070 (grade 3, level 1), which is the entry rate for the lowest-grade white-collar employees such as junior analytical technicians, the standard rate being £10 600 (grade 3, level 2). This is a significant increase in the starting salary. It is also a gain relative to trainee craft workers, for although they start one grade higher (grade 4) than laboratory technicians, the standard wage rate of £11 200 is similar to their basic wage under the old system. There was a smaller increase at the upper end of the salary range for laboratory technicians, with a salary of just over £12 000 in grade 5. Graduate laboratory workers, other graduate professional jobs and craft workers are located in grade 6 on a standard salary of £14 300. The wage increases for laboratory technicians mean that they are now well paid relative to equivalent posts in other companies where separate grading systems still operate. The regrading has also explicitly ranked the highest-level laboratory workers alongside other graduate professionals (grade 6) and reduced the wage differentials between laboratory work grades and the more male-dominated craft grades.

There were a larger number of grades for clerical jobs than for laboratory technicians, and the new system has compressed the range for clerical workers. The grading of secretaries has also been standardized across departments as a result of integration. The compression and new salary range have benefited those clerical workers who were in the lowest grades under the previous system; however, a few secretaries had been in senior grades before the integration and they lost out in the transition. By putting clerical workers in grades 3 to 5, the integration has explicitly ranked them alongside laboratory technicians and skilled production workers, but below the graduate and craft jobs in grade 6.

Some male-dominated production jobs have also benefited from re-evaluation and the integrated system. The rationalization of the grading of section leaders in production areas resulted in a higher grading and large pay increases for those team leaders who were found to have responsibility for managing expensive capital equipment, placing them in grades 6 and 7. This expansion of job content associated with changes in the production process may lead to further re-evaluation.

10.2.4 Performance bonuses and working-time premiums

Performance bonuses and working-time premiums are other important elements of the wage structure. The new wage structure has moved away from performance related pay, which was assessed by the personnel department as an ineffective incentive under the previous system. Promotion and training will form the primary reward for performance. Exceptional performance ('outstanding individual effort') is to be rewarded through a formalized system of specific, one-off cash payments at the end of the year. These payments will be made from a fixed budget set at a predetermined percentage of functional payroll costs linked to overall company performance. Such a payment is more likely to affect lower-grade staff, since it is a reward for performance in the current post and where the alternative rewards of training or promotion are not possible. Since women are currently overrepresented in the lower grades they stand to benefit most from these bonus payments, but the actual outcome depends on the implementation of the scheme. For example, options for training to enhance promotion prospects may not be seriously considered as an alternative recompense; or a disproportionate share of the payments may go to men in these grades.

Shift workers are found in grades 2, 3, 4 and 6, with shift managers in grade 9. Grades 2 to 4 are female-dominated and women account for 60 per cent of all shift workers. Shift workers are contracted to work 38.25 hours (compared with 37.5 hours for other employees) in order to allow a daily 15-minute hand-over period. The main shift pattern is the 5D2 rota (five days rotation: 0600–1400, 1400–2200), for which a premium of 16.5 per cent is payable on top of the basic salary. A new shift pattern has been introduced in order to permit specific machinery to be operated 12 days out of 14. Crews work in 12-hour blocks, including three weekends in eight, with weekly hours thus totalling 41 on average. A 28 per cent premium is paid for this working-time arrangement, and a similar premium is received by those working nights.

All employees except those in grades 10 and 11 are eligible for overtime payments. Authorized (ad hoc) overtime is compensated at the rate of time and a half (including a shift premium where appropriate), by time off in lieu, or by a combination of these agreed with the line manager. Sunday working is paid at a premium of double the basic rate including shift premiums where appropriate. Special premiums are paid for working on statutory holidays.

Sixty-eight per cent of employees who had worked at least one hour of overtime between April and November 1993 were men (Table 10.5). Grade 3 accounted for 41 per cent of all employees who had done overtime, a figure disproportionate to the 29 per cent share of employees who were concentrated in that grade. This pattern applied to both sexes. Apart from in grade 3, the distribution of overtime working by men broadly followed that for all male employees across the grades, whereas for women it was slightly higher in grade 4 and slightly lower in grades 5 and 6. Compared with the female share of each grade, a lower share of women worked overtime in every instance.

10.2.5 Summary of the gender impact of integration

The integration of separate and sex-segregated grading and payment structures into a uniform grading system where most employees in each grade

Table 10.5. Distribution of employees who worked at least one hour of overtime, April–November 1993

Grade	Distribution of employees working overtime by grade			Female share of employees working overtime
	Women	Men	All	
2	7	3	4	49
3	56	34	41	43
4	11	10	10	33
5	9	13	12	24
6	6	15	13	16
7	6	8	7	25
8	4	7	6	20
9	1	9	6	6
Total (N)	(265)	(568)	(833)	32

Source: Personnel records.

will be paid at the same (level 2) basic rate has removed one axis of discrimination, namely that of segregation into different and overlapping job hierarchies associated with different payment structures (IRS, 1991; 1992). However, additions for shift work and overtime will still produce a gender pay gap in actual salaries within each grade. A further dimension also needs to be taken into account, that of vertical segregation between the grades (Table 10.2).

In general, the male manual workers in grades 2 and 3 have borne the cost of integration, for they were the most likely to have been 'losers' when the new salary ranges were set. The simplification of the payment structure, with the reduction of performance related components, has produced some losses for individual men in the higher grades. At the same time, while women operatives in grades 2 and 3 may not have been as likely to be 'losers' as men, women who worked overtime were more likely to be in one of those grades than in any other and will have felt the impact of reduced real rates for overtime working.

The explicit ranking of previous sex-segregated and fragmented grading structures necessitated by the process of integration has tended to benefit women with higher qualification levels, namely female laboratory technicians and clerical employees in the middle level grades. The benefit for women in these middle level graded jobs is in terms of wage increases and in some improvement in the status through gains relative to the more male dominated production jobs which they have been ranked against.

Integration has weakened the bargaining power of male-dominated occupational areas to secure higher wages relative to women segregated into other job areas. But at the same time, it has resulted in significant gains for skilled (male) production workers found to be responsible for expensive capital equipment, who have made significant gains under the job evaluation scheme on the basis that they have managerial responsibility rather than limited supervisory or 'team leader' responsibility.

Looking across the entire vertical distribution of the grades, we can see that integration has been accompanied by a stretching of the wage dispersal. 'Losers' (mostly men) in the unskilled and semi-skilled grades have paid for the wage increases given to workers with formal qualifications, including production workers with managerial responsibilities and those in the male dominated professional grades. Women in the laboratory and clerical grades, however, have also benefited from the integrated evaluation scheme. The wage gains made by these women were significant, but a gender wage gap persists because they remain underrepresented in the higher grades. One illustration of this fact is that the wage increase received on promotion between grades – namely, a move from level 3 in one grade to level 1 in the grade above – is less than 3 per cent when moving between grades 3, 4 and 5 compared with between 7 and 10 per cent for all other moves between the higher grades (except between grades 7 and 8). Thus the financial rewards from promotion are lowest in that part of the hierarchy where women are concentrated.

The grade and wage relativities will continue to change through collective bargaining and new managerial strategies, which will obviously impact on future gender differentials and need to be taken into account in evaluating the impact of the reformed wage and grading structure. The dominant issues on the bargaining agenda are outlined below.

10.3. FUTURE PAY AND GRADING ISSUES

10.3.1 Adjustment of grade differentials

The union has asked for the differentials between the grades to be changed and for a relative improvement in the position of grade 3 employees, who on average received disproportionately low or zero wage increases in the move to the integrated system. Although the impetus for this may derive primarily from concern for the male grade 3 employees who were disproportionately the 'losers' as a result of integration, women account for over half of the grade 3 workers and also stand to benefit from any gains made through collective bargaining. Thus while the unions have tended to place more emphasis on negotiating on issues of pay differentials than on questions of equal pay and equal value (Rubery and Fagan, 1994), in the context of an integrated grading structure the outcome may have positive gender implications since the sexes are no longer segregated for collective bargaining purposes.

However, management's primary concern is with the higher level and more male dominated professional grades. In particular, grades 8 and 9 (accountants, information technology specialists, personnel officers) are falling behind the market rate according to survey data for these professions. Despite the recession, skill shortages remain for people with three to four years' business experience in addition to their professional qualifications. Employees in these grades can in principle claim overtime but in practice do not. Therefore, the plan is to buy out the overtime with a four per cent real wage increase which will make the rate quoted in advertisements for these jobs more competitive. This will increase the wage dispersal between the higher and lower grades.

10.3.2 Grading, flexibility and career ladders

The personnel department also aims to develop further the flexibility between craft and operator areas and between different managerial areas. For example, an accountant has just moved into product management.

Another area of concern is promotion blockages, which obviously undermine attempts to reward staff through training and promotion. A particular problem is found in production areas because the abolition of the old supervisory grades has left a large gap in many functional areas between the top production jobs in grade 4 and craft and production manager jobs in grades 6 and 7. This gap in the career ladder needs to be addressed, and one possibility is to remove specific production jobs in favour of a fully generic scheme so that grade 5 would encompass both skilled and widely experienced production workers.

Promotion blockages are also found within junior management. To some extent these are 'fiddled' in Research and Development sections by creating jobs to match the persons concerned. The problem is that there is an oversupply of junior managers who are not yet sufficiently experienced to become full departmental managers, but at the same time a way of motivating them needs to be more fully developed.

10.3.3 Working-time reform

The future of automatic annual pay awards linked to the cost of living is under review. The personnel department sees more room for negotiation on working-time issues than on wages in the foreseeable future.

The personnel department is against a straight reduction in contractual hours, because the last reduction led to an increase in overtime worked, except in the clerical grades. Instead, the objective is to develop a package which reduces both ad hoc and contractual overtime and leads to a more effective matching of hours to fluctuations in workloads. Currently at certain times there are peaks in overtime and in other periods production is so slack that some employees ask to go home rather than sit and do nothing. This fluctuation is not regular or seasonal (except for holiday cover to some extent) but could be planned on a three-month basis. Therefore, the personnel department would be willing to increase the flexitime reconciliation period from four weeks to three months as an intermediate step towards the greater flexibility offered by annualized hours arrangements.

The unions have a deferred claim for a 35-hour week and three additional days' holiday. They would like to increase the flexibility of the flexitime system by reducing the core time and increasing the number of hours which can be carried as a credit or debit within the four-week settlement period. They are opposing the personnel department's proposed introduction of annualized hours.

10.4. THE INTERNAL LABOUR MARKET, ENTRY POINTS AND VERTICAL SEGREGATION

We have already noted that men hold 65 per cent of the jobs in the company studied – a gender composition of the workforce which has remained fairly stable over time – and that women are concentrated in the lower grades.

There is a higher turnover of female staff, since 30 per cent of the current female workforce started their employment in or after 1990 compared with 16 per cent of the male workforce. This higher turnover of women is probably associated with the 'woman returner' pattern of women quitting the labour market when their children are young and returning once their children enter school. This pattern is more prevalent in the UK than in other European Union countries (Dex and Walters, 1989;

Bulletin on Women and Employment in the EC, 1992), although there is evidence that younger generations of women in the UK are demonstrating more continuous patterns of economic activity during the early years of motherhood (Martin and Roberts, 1984; McRae, 1991).

While this lack of continuity may account for part of the underrepresentation of women in the higher grades, it does not account for all of it. When we look at women with periods of service similar to those of men we still see that they are more concentrated in the lower grades. For example, of those who started at the company before 1980, 37.2 per cent of the men are in grades 9 to 11 whereas 39.6 per cent of women are in grade 4 or below (see Table 10.6). Furthermore, over 20 per cent of men but only one per cent of women who started their period of employment in 1990 or 1991 are in grades 9 to 11.

Hence, continuity of service is not a sufficient strategy for women wishing to progress up the hierarchy via the internal labour market. Part of the reason is segregated entry points, with men more likely to gain entry via those vacancies in higher grades which are filled through the external labour market. For example, 8.5 per cent of men and only 2.1 per cent of women who were appointed in 1992 and 1993 and are still employed by the company are in grade 9 or above (see Table 10.6).

10.5. EDUCATION AND TRAINING POLICY

Training decisions used to be centralized in one personnel department, but in 1990 this activity was decentralized to line manager level. Line managers now have responsibility for their own training budget and training decisions. This devolution was made on the ground that managers were in a better position than a centralized personnel department to decide what was needed.

Training starts with induction tailored to the requirements of the particular post. It is company policy for everyone to have a Personal Development Plan. At least once a year it should be formally discussed with the appropriate line manager in order to review the individual's career aspirations, progress and development. Training needs would usually form part of this discussion in relation both to the current job and to future or prospective responsibilities or promotion. The review should culminate in an agreed action plan for staff development.

There is a commitment to a minimum average of three per cent of contracted hours to be devoted to off-the-job training. The personnel

Table 10.6. Grade attainment by length of service by sex

	% distribution by grade 1–2	3	4	5	6	7	8	9	10	11	n = 100%
Pre-1980											
Male	0.8	12.6	8.0	12.6	11.1	8.8	8.8	16.5	13.4	7.3	261
Female	1.9	30.2	7.5	9.4	17.0	15.1	7.5	7.5	3.8	0.0	53
1980–4											
Male	1.6	22.6	13.1	12.3	13.9	14.3	9.5	7.9	3.6	1.2	252
Female	3.6	53.0	12.7	10.2	8.4	7.8	2.4	1.2	0.6	0.0	166
1985–9											
Male	2.3	17.2	9.4	13.3	30.5	4.7	6.3	10.2	3.1	3.1	128
Female	2.7	30.7	21.3	16.0	12.0	4.0	8.0	5.3	0.0	0.0	75
1990–1											
Male	5.9	29.4	11.8	13.2	7.4	4.4	7.4	10.3	5.9	4.4	68
Female	3.8	50.6	13.9	25.3	0.0	3.8	1.3	1.3	0.0	0.0	79
1992–3											
Male	17.2	39.7	6.9	3.4	15.5	0.0	8.6	3.4	3.4	1.7	58
Female	22.9	47.9	12.5	6.3	2.1	0.0	6.3	2.1	0.0	0.0	48
Total (n)											
Male	22	155	78	92	117	68	65	85	54	30	766
Female	23	190	58	57	33	27	18	12	3	0.0	421

Note: No data available for 1.7 per cent (21) employees
Source: Personnel department, case-study.

department does not envisage a conflict of interest at line management level between the immediate demands of day-to-day cover and long-term training needs. This fact might be connected with the explicit Total Quality Management philosophy and the way in which appraisal and training needs are discussed on a systematic and regular basis. Thus the company can perhaps be considered to have a positive commitment and orientation to training. If staff do not agree with the training needs identified at their appraisal they can appeal through the grievance procedure, but no such action has occurred.

Training is usually organized on a day release basis. The two-year contractual requirement to remain at the end of a period of training has been abolished. The company philosophy is that opportunities and prospects rather than compulsion should be used to retain employees after a period of training.

Because of the recent devolution of training policy there are no centralized records of who is receiving what training, but a computerized company-wide training records system is being developed. Presumably this database could be used to monitor the equal opportunities issues surrounding who gets access to what training.

Receiving company-sponsored training is thus an important means of moving up in the internal labour market. It is theoretically possible to move from General Certificate of Secondary Education level up to degree/PhD level, and more commonly people with passes in the General Certificate of Education at Advanced level have been sponsored through to PhD level. Exceptional operatives have gained promotion to junior laboratory posts and subsequently received sponsorship to obtain the qualifications necessary for further promotion. At the same time, experience remains an important criterion as well, for example, some clerical workers have moved into junior management positions on the basis of their experience and aptitude as well as formal training.

10.6. SUBCONTRACTING

Some activities are contracted out because it is cheaper and more flexible than performing them in-house, and the extent of contracting out has remained stable over time. The type of activities covered range from the usual areas of cleaning, security and catering through to more skilled work on certain engineering projects. In addition, some individuals who have left or retired have returned on a freelance basis, for example in the library and patent office.

10.7. IMPACT OF THE INTEGRATED GRADING AND PAYMENT STRUCTURES ON LABOUR COSTS AND PRODUCTIVITY

Increased flexibility was achieved, primarily in blue-collar areas, because laboratory and clerical staff were already highly flexible. Some costs increased because people now move between a wider range of tasks, and for some tasks they may be less effective or require a longer warm-up time than for others. Other costs have been reduced, for example covering tasks associated with higher grade positions or horizontally graded jobs elsewhere on the site. Furthermore, the wider grades have reduced the likelihood of successful regrading appeals and the associated costs.

Output and productivity increased at the same time as the bonus system was removed, but this fact cannot be disentangled from the concomitant introduction of substantial capital investment. However, the combination of the prior redundancy programme and the new integrated system means that the payroll is now six to eight per cent less than it was in 1990.

Notes

1. Department of Sociology, University of Liverpool.
2. The information in this case study was collected through two interviews with a senior personnel manager. The first interview explored a standard list of issues which formed the basis for the fieldwork in each case study and each country in this book. It lasted two and a half hours. Notes were taken and were written up in conjunction with analysis of various company documents containing detailed information on employment terms and conditions and the new grading and payment structure. A second more structured interview took place with the same member of staff. It lasted one and a half hours and part of it involved a second personnel manager, who had particular knowledge of the job evaluation scheme which had been used. Subsequent contact was made by telephone to clarify or confirm specific points of information.
3. This figure was taken from an internal document which did not contain information for grades 10 and 11.
4. One compensation in terms of net rather than gross pay was that in 1992 the company pension scheme become non-contributory, which amounts to around a 6% pay rise. The scheme will remain non-contributory for the foreseeable future.

References

Bulletin on Women and Employment in the EC. (Manchester: University of Manchester Institute of Science and Technology 1992) No. 1.

S. Dex, and P. Walters, 'Women's occupational status in Britain, France and the USA: Explaining the difference', in *Industrial Relations Journal*, Vol. 20, No. 3 (1989) pp. 203–12.

Industrial Relations Services (IRS) *Pay and gender in Britain*, Report for the Equal Opportunities Commission (London: IRS 1991).
—— *Pay and gender in Britain* 2, Second report for the Equal Opportunities Commission (London: IRS 1992).
S. McRae, *Maternity rights in Britain* (London: Policy Studies Institute 1991).
C. Martin, and J. Roberts *Women and employment survey: A lifetime perspective* (London: Her Majesty's Stationery Office 1984).
Office of Population Censuses and Surveys (OPCS) *Standard occupational classification*, Vol. 1 (London: Her Majesty's Stationery Office 1990).
J. Rubery, *Wage determination and sex segregation in employment: Report for the UK*, Report for the European Commission Network on the Situation of Women in the Labour Market (Manchester: University of Manchester Institute of Science and Technology 1993).
J. Rubery, and C. Fagan, *Occupational segregation of women and men in the European Community, Social Europe Supplement 3/93* (Luxembourg: Official Publications for the European Communities 1993a).
J. Rubery, and C. Fagan, Wage determination and sex segregation in employment in the European Community, Social Europe Supplement 9/94 (Luxembourg: Official Publications for the European Communities, 1994).
J. Rubery, C. Fagan, and J. Humphries, *Occupational segregation in the UK*, Report for the European Commission Network on the Situation of Women in the Labour Market (Manchester: University of Manchester Institute of Science and Technology 1992).

APPENDIX 1: OTHER GENERAL CONDITIONS OF EMPLOYMENT

The standards and procedures applicable to everyone in the company are set out in a staff handbook and summarised below. The handbook is given to employees, but is not automatically given to non-executive directors.

A1.1 Equal opportunities policy

The company has had an equal opportunities policy since 1986 and the staff handbook states that the company is committed to the development of positive policies to provide opportunities in employment. The policy has been updated over time and an action plan has been developed, which includes a formal positive action programme with built-in targets. As yet there are no positive action training programmes to desegregate the workforce through training women and men in non-traditional areas of work.

A1.2 Pensions and other occupational benefits

The normal retirement age for all employees is 65 years, extensions beyond this are approved only in exceptional circumstances. The company has a contracted-out Company Pension Scheme and there are no criteria which must be satisfied, such as an hours or length of service threshold, all employees are entitled to join. The same pension scheme applies to all grades and around 90% of the workforce are members.

The Occupational Health Department is responsible for the health and welfare needs of staff. Sick pay entitlement is related to length of service, ranging from 5 weeks' full pay for staff with less than one year's service up to 26 weeks' full pay and 26 weeks' half pay for those with more than 4 years' service.

An accident insurance policy covers employees worldwide on a 24 hour basis and provides a lump sum benefit equivalent to two years salary. A death in service benefit, equivalent to 3 years' salary, is available to members of the company pension scheme. The main fringe benefit is a company car for managers in grades 10 and 11. There is also a sports and social club for a nominal membership subscription and the Company has a number of privilege customer schemes including one for health care, mortgages and personal loans.

A1.3 Hours of work

The normal working week for all employees is 37.5 hours. Actual hours worked each day may vary depending on job and department. There is a formal flexitime system in operation which permits employees to carry a credit/debt of 7 hours in a four week settlement period and covers 800 employees. There are about 30 part-timers and job sharers (2.5% of the workforce), and these working-time arrangements are increasing. Part-timers are scattered through the grades, including senior management and junior production workers. Most part-timers are women, but some are older men working in the warehouse who were originally recruited as temporary workers to cover a daily 3 hour peak demand connected with courier activities.

A1.4 Maternity leave and other family leave arrangements

Both full- and part-timers are entitled to maternity leave and the right to return if they have completed two years' continuous service by the beginning of the eleventh week before the expected birth date. Holiday entitlement is calculated on a pro-rata basis for each completed month prior to and after maternity leave.

After two years' continuous service up to four days' paid paternity leave may be granted, to be taken within three months of the birth of the child. A period of extended unpaid family responsibility leave may be applied for, either as a short career break or as extended maternity leave. This must be agreed with the appropriate line manager. Employees taking unpaid family responsibility leave are overwhelmingly female.

A1.5 Annual leave

Employees are entitled to 25 working days including three to be taken for the Christmas and New Year break. In addition there are 8 paid public holidays a year. After 10 years' service an extra 8 weeks' extra holiday may be granted in the 12 months preceding the date of retirement and in addition to the annual holiday entitlement. This retirement holiday can be taken in a variety of ways, for example to gradually reduce the working week in the lead up to retirement. This entitlement does not apply to those members of staff retiring before their normal retirement date.

11 Women's Pay in Banking in the United Kingdom: Case Study of XYZ Bank

Marilyn Carroll and Jill Rubery

11.1. INTRODUCTION

The banking industry in the UK has, for many years, been a major employer of women. The Banking, Insurance and Finance Union reports that female employment grew very rapidly during the 1960s and 1970s, so that by 1980 there were three women for every two men in banking. Although the banks, in common with many other organizations, used to be overtly discriminatory with regard to female employment – for example, there were inferior pay structures for women, and it was assumed that they would leave their jobs on marriage – discriminatory practices disappeared in the 1970s. The banks formally adopted practices which were supposed to provide equality of opportunity for all their employees. However, despite some increases in the number of women reaching managerial and supervisory positions, Morris (1986) reported that the banks still displayed the characteristics of a segregated employment structure, with the majority in the lower grades being women and the majority of managers being men. This report examines the current situation.

The first section looks at the industrial relations, labour market and business backgrounds against which the UK's clearing banks have developed their current employment structures. The next section outlines the terms and conditions, including pay and grading structures, which apply to employees of one of the main clearing banks (referred to throughout this report as XYZ Bank). The final section presents data which have been obtained on the relative position of men and women employed in one of the Bank's geographical regions, and two typical branches within that region.

11.2. BACKGROUND

During the 1980s the British banking sector underwent a number of significant changes which have had far reaching effects on the pay and grading systems used in the banks. The relaxation of controls within the financial sector, effected through the Financial Services Act 1986 and the Building Societies Act 1986, enabled the high-street banks to compete for business with other financial institutions to provide mortgages, loans, savings plans, pensions and insurance. As a consequence, the banks' organizational culture has changed to one which is more sales-oriented. Amidst fierce competition for staff in the mid-1980s, the breakdown of industry level bargaining meant that each of the banks, instead of having to adhere to a common set of terms and conditions, was able to negotiate pay and conditions internally, and this afforded them scope to develop their own individual systems. These included systems designed to facilitate and reinforce organizational culture change, including 'flatter' grading structures and performance related pay.

It was this combination of decentralized bargaining, increased competition in the labour market, and competition between a wider range of organizations providing financial services that led the banks to develop and redesign their pay and grading structures. The information below relates to one bank in particular (XYZ Bank).

11.3. GRADING STRUCTURE

As in most UK banks, XYZ Bank staff are divided into 'appointed' grades (managers and assistant managers) and 'unappointed' grades (clerical, secretarial and manual). The Bank operates a typically hierarchical structure, with seven grades of managers (MG to MA), three grades of assistant managers (AK to AH) and five unappointed grades (G1 to G5).

At branch level, managers and assistant managers do not specialize in any particular functional area according to grade, but those with appropriate previous experience may specialize as corporate, small business or personal account executives. The unappointed grades, however, do have broad specialities:

- Grade 5 – lending officers (mortgages, etc.);
- Grade 4 – foreign work, custody (of valuables, etc.);
- Grade 3 – processing work, accounts, standing orders, etc.;

- Grade 2 – as above, but with less responsibility for supervision, or in a smaller branch;
- Grade 1 – office junior level.

All jobs in the Bank, from unappointed to managerial, are evaluated according to the Hay system.

11.4. ENTRY LEVELS

The Bank operates as a typical internal labour market, with entry for all except graduates being at either of the two lowest grades, and career progression depending on promotion from within through the grading structure.

There are four main entry schemes: graduate entry, accelerated management trainees, management trainees and general entry. For graduate entry, candidates spend two days at an assessment centre. Depending on their performance, they are then assigned to Scheme A, B or C. Scheme A entrants start at Grade AK (the lowest appointed grade). For those assigned to Scheme B the entry grade is G5 and for those assigned to Scheme C it is G4. Graduate training is controlled by the Graduate Development Office in London and trainees are supernumerary in the branches. Each scheme lasts two years, after which graduates compete for promotion alongside everyone else.

Candidates with passes in the General Certificate of Education at Advanced level (or equivalent qualifications) may enter as accelerated management trainees at G2. Successful applicants are included in the Bank's Management Development Programme, which provides for promotion through the grades, dependent on satisfactory performance at each stage of the programme.

Entry as a management trainee is at the lowest grade, G1. No specific qualifications are required; candidates complete an application form and are interviewed. (In practice, it would be unusual to select anyone with fewer than four General Certificate of Secondary Education passes.) Entrants are provided with the appropriate training to allow them to progress through the grades, and may be given the opportunity, later in their careers, to apply for accelerated training on the Management Development Programme.

General entry is also at G1, and again no specific academic qualifications are necessary. According to the Bank, this level of entry is aimed at those who do not feel ready to commit themselves to studying for professional qualifications, or to a career in management. However, the Bank's recruitment literature states that those who develop the ambition, and whose performance is at an appropriate level, may later be given the opportunity to advance through the unappointed grades and possibly into junior management.

There is also a secretarial entry scheme, for which prospective applicants need to demonstrate appropriate typing proficiency levels.

The Bank now also uses agency staff, mainly for Grade 1 routine clerical and cashiering jobs. Contracts are negotiated nationally and the Bank pays the agency the same rates as for its own permanent staff in the equivalent grade. It is not known, therefore, how much the agency staff actually receive.

The Bank operates an employment break scheme open to both male and female employees who have family commitments that involve looking after children or elderly relatives. Those applicants accepted for the scheme may leave and resume employment with the Bank at a later date, usually within five years, although there is discretion to extend this period to seven years. The scheme operates at two levels: those individuals who are deemed to have potential, or whose services are highly valued, are guaranteed a return to their jobs. Others may apply to be put on a reserve list: they are given two weeks' employment a year, and are recalled for permanent employment if and when needed.

11.5. PROMOTION

Progression through the grades depends on merit, and officially there are no barriers to promotion (geographical mobility, for example, is not a requirement.) In common with the other banks, XYZ Bank uses a system of 'tiering' to establish each individual's expected career progression early on in his or her employment. The system takes into account actual performance as well as pre- and post-entry qualifications, and although reassessments can take place periodically, it does mean, that a person's likely promotion prospects are to a large extent established by his or her initial aptitude and qualifications.

Vacancies in the lowest junior management grade, AK, are advertised internally, and those in clerical Grade 5 may apply to join the appointed ranks. Other specialist vacancies may also be advertised internally, such as personal account executives and selling jobs at managerial level. Apart from these exceptions, those deemed suitable for promotion are selected without having to apply for specific posts.

Although the banks have traditionally been able to offer some prospects of promotion to most employees with appropriate performance levels and length of service, at XYZ Bank and at the other banks there are currently fewer opportunities for promotion than before. This is due to a number of factors, including automation, branch reorganization and reduced staffing levels generally.

11.6. TRAINING

The Bank provides the appropriate in-house training for its staff, according to grade and type of work, as their careers progress. Training may be provided by colleagues, or by means of computer based training packages which are studied in the branches. Staff at any level may study for the professional qualification of the Chartered Institute of Bankers. This qualification is not a prerequisite for promotion to any of the grades, but those seeking entry into management who have obtained this qualification would be looked upon more favourably than those without it. Staff in specialist functions are also encouraged to study for professional qualifications (for example, Institute of Personnel Management qualifications for personnel staff, insurance qualifications for sales staff). Study may be undertaken at evening class; to qualify for day release a minimum of one year's service with the Bank is required.

11.7. PAY STRUCTURE

For Grade 1 there is a service-based pay scale starting at £5822, with one increment of £177 after six months, increments of £239 after 12 months, two years and three years, and further increments of £120 each year, up to 24 years' service (although in practice it would be very unusual for anyone to remain at this grade for so long). Increments may be withheld if performance is not satisfactory.

For the other grades salary range systems are in operation. The current salary ranges for unappointed staff are shown in Table 11.1.

Progression through the ranges is by means of performance rises dependent on the results of an annual written appraisal The percentage performance rises for 1993 were:

fully satisfactory 3.0–4.5 per cent; good 4.5–6.0 per cent; outstanding 6.0–7.5 per cent.

Table 11.1. XYZ Bank unappointed staff salary ranges, 1993 (£ sterling)

Grade	Min.	Performance maxima		
		Fully satisfactory	Good	Outstanding
2	7 042	9 739	10 693	11 338
3	7 519	10 527	11 529	12 531
4	9 071	12 221	13 271	14 321
5	10 741	14 083	15 037	16 111

Source: Information provided by case study bank.

Table 11.2 sets out the salary ranges for managerial and appointed staff. In common with the unappointed staff ranges, there are performance maxima for each grade, beyond which a person performing at that particular level may not progress. However, the percentage pay rise depends not just on the performance category, but also on the percentile on the salary range in which the current salary lies. The system operates so as to award higher increases to those at the lower ends of the salary ranges, in order to bring them more quickly into the main part of the scale.

Figure 11.1 shows the performance maxima for each grade together with the percentage matrix rises according to percentile and performance category. Currently, the performance increases vary from zero to one per cent for a less than fully satisfactory performer at the lower end of the salary range through to between eight and 10.5 per cent for an outstanding performer at the lower end of the salary scale. Once the position on the matrix has been established, the final choice of percentage increase depends on whether the performance was judged to be at the lower, middle or upper end of the performance category.

11.8. APPRAISAL SYSTEM

Under the Bank's appraisal system, the reporting officer is the next line manager, and the reporting year runs from January to December. The appraisal is based on competencies (strategic awareness, initiative, decisiveness, and so on) and each competency is measured on a behaviourally anchored rating scale from 1–6. The appraisal form for unappointed staff differs from that for managers and appointed staff in that it contains different competencies, divided into indicators of performance and potential.

Table 11.2. Salary ranges for managerial and appointed staff (£ sterling)

%	Performance maximum for	Matrix rises for Full satis-factory (%)	Good (%)	Out-standing (%)	AK	AJ	AH	MG	MF	ME	MD	MC	MB	MA
100	Outstanding			0–3 (0–4.5)	19 094	22 078	24 465	27 105	31 498	38 219	45 861	52 509	61 816	72 524
80	Good		0–3 (0–4)	3–5 (4–6.5)	18 140	20 885	23 272	25 761	29 855	35 672	42 804	49 009	57 696	67 690
60	Fully satisfactory	0–3 (0–3.5)	3–5 (3.5–6)	5–7 (6–8.5)	17 185	19 692	22 079	24 417	28 212	33 124	39 747	45 508	53 575	62 855
20		3–5 (3–5.5)	5–7 (5.5–8)	7–9 (8-10.5)	15 276	17 305	19 693	21 729	24 926	28 028	33 633	38 507	45 333	53 185
Minimum					14 321	16 111	18 499	20 384	23 282	25 480	30 575	35 006	41 212	48 350

Notes: For staff whose salary is exactly on the 20th, 60th or 80th percentile, the percentages in the box below the percentile line should be used according to performance evaluation rating. Matrix rises in brackets apply for 1993 only. MA–MG = managers; AH, AJ, AK = assistant managers.
Source: Information provided by case study bank.

Figure 11.1. Performance-related pay matrix

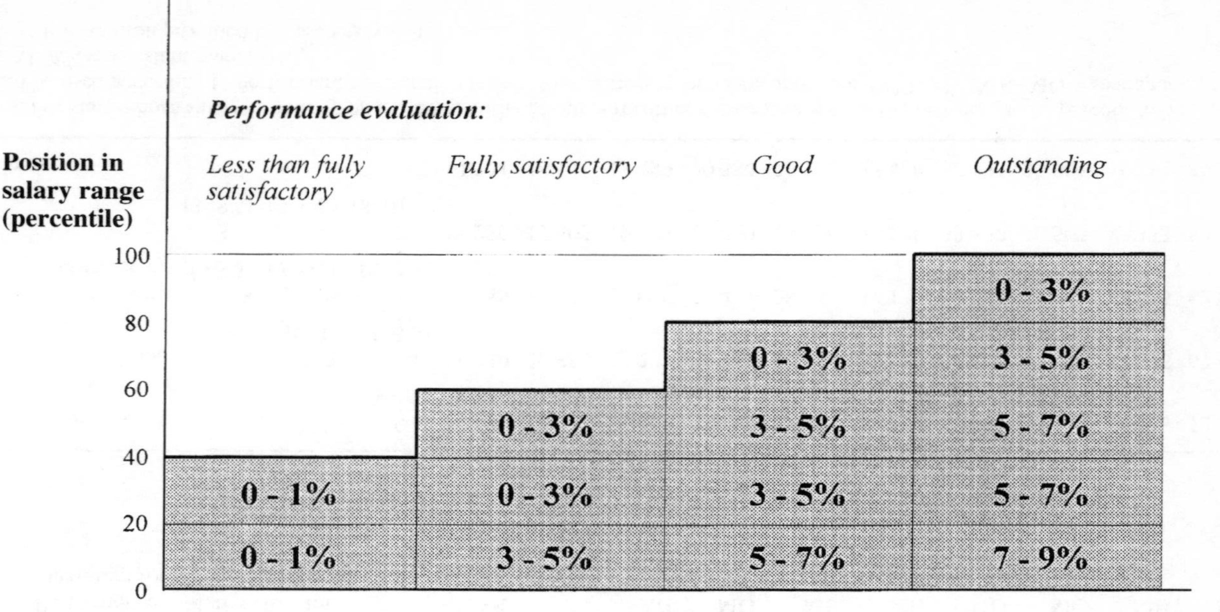

Note: The bold line indicates the maximum salary level according to performance evaluation rating. For example, an outstanding performer can reach the 100 position in the salary range but a less than fully satisfactory performer can only reach the 40th percentile position. The pay increase therefore depends on the evaluation of performance in the current year and on the current position in the salary range.

Source: adapted from personnel records

There are also spaces for general comments, indication of training and development needs, and so forth. On completion, the report is countersigned by a senior manager and handed to the appraisee. He or she keeps the form for 24 hours, after which the appraisal interview takes place. Staff are entitled to appeal against the appraisal and an appeal usually takes the form of a letter from the appraisee which accompanies the report when it is sent to the regional personnel office. Personnel office staff score the report forms as follows: majority of markings 3 and 4 – fully satisfactory; majority of markings 4 and 5 – good; majority of markings 5 and 6 – outstanding. The individual salary increase is then determined by the personnel department according to the above criteria.

11.9. BONUS SCHEME

Staff at the Bank also have the opportunity to earn an annual bonus, which is performance related. Before 1988, there was an annual Christmas bonus scheme covering all staff. It paid out 2.5 per cent of salary each November, and was independent of corporate or individual performance.

The present bonus scheme was introduced in 1988, and originally applied only to senior management grades MC to MA. It involved targets and objectives being set in different areas, such as sales. A year later it was extended to include all management grades. In 1990 a performance related bonus scheme was introduced for all appointed staff. This scheme, however, did not relate to the attainment of individual targets, but provided for a share out from a bonus pool linked to managers' targets.

Problems associated with the recession and a number of weaknesses with the scheme led to a full scale review of the arrangements in 1991. Seven thousand of the 18 000 managers and assistant managers were consulted through questionnaires, interviews and group discussions to identify the strengths and weaknesses of the scheme. The consultations revealed that most managers wished to see the annual performance related bonus retained because it helped to convey overall objectives and shifted the emphasis from 'inputs' to 'outputs'. However, the scheme was criticized for the setting of unrealistic targets, and many thought that the subsequent link with reward did not accurately reflect individual performance. The scheme was also found to be unwieldy and complicated, causing a great deal of administrative paperwork for managers and regional personnel departments. After considering the options, the Bank decided to retain the performance bonus scheme, but with considerable modifications. The key features of the new scheme for managers and appointed staff are as follows:

1) Local managers, together with their appointed staff, constitute management teams or units. Units are not limited to the branches: all the Bank's operations, including head office functions, are divided into units.
2) Each team is allocated a 'bonus pool' the amount of which depends on the level of achievement in relation to unit objectives, as set out in the unit's business plan. Unit objectives are communicated via regular team meetings, and involve both qualitative and quantitative targets.
3) Each member of the unit management team has an individual performance contract, which indicates how he or she will be expected to contribute to the unit's objectives. Performance management provides for regular feedback to assess performance against objectives.
4) The head of each unit has responsibility for distributing the bonus pool in a manner which ensures, by following a common marking key, that those who make the greatest contribution receive the largest awards as a proportion of salary.
5) The bonus year runs from 1 January to 31 December and payments are made in the following March.

Example

Staff participating in the bonus pool salaries:

Manager (MC)	£40,000
Manager (MF)	£25,000
Manager (MG)	£22,000
Assistant manager (AH)	£20,000
Assistant manager (AJ)	£17,000
Assistant manager (AK)	£16,000

The unit is marked by an allocator to determine the overall size of the bonus pool. The mark relates to the unit's achievement of targets, and the scale ranges from A (most targets not achieved and some falling below an acceptable level) to F (all targets substantially exceeded). The overall mark then translates into a percentage of salary, which varies for the different grades. For example, a mark of D applied to the unit in this example would produce a bonus pool of £14 675, calculated as follows:

	Salary	Percentage	Amount
Manager (MC)	£40 000	15.0	£6 000
Manager (MF)	£25 000	10.0	£2 500
Manager (MG)	£22 000	10.0	£2 200
Assistant manager (AH)	£20 000	7.5	£1 500
Assistant manager (AJ)	£17 000	7.5	£1 275
Assistant manager (AK)	£16 000	7.5	£1 200
Total			£14 675

The allocator then awards a mark to the Unit Head, according to individual contribution to results, from A (unacceptable) to F (exceptional). This translates into a percentage of salary which is the bonus awarded to the Unit Head and deducted from the bonus pool. The Unit Head then awards a mark to each of the other members of the team and the bonus is calculated in a similar way. The sum of the individual bonus payments must not exceed the bonus pool; if it does, the Unit Head must reconsider the individual assessments. For the example given above, the following results might be obtained:

	Salary	Assessment	Bonus (%)	Bonus (£)
Manager (MC)	£40 000	C/D	12.5	5 000
Manager (MF)	£25 000	E	15.0	3 750
Manager (MG)	£22 000	D	10.0	2 200
Assistant manager (AH)	£20 000	C	6.25	1 250
Assistant manager (AJ)	£17 000	C	6.25	1 062.50
Assistant manager (AK)	£16 000	E	8.75	1 400
Total				£14 662.50

Source: 'Performance related award: Incentive bonus scheme', XYZ Staff Guidance Note 9, April 1992.

The aims of the scheme are to reduce paperwork, give the Unit Head more discretion to decide on the allocation of bonuses and to promote teamworking.

A merit bonus scheme was introduced for clerical staff in 1992, and also replaces the Christmas bonus which everyone used to receive. In this case, the percentage bonus awarded depends on the performance level indicated by the last recorded appraisal. But where there has been a substantial change in performance since that appraisal, this may be amended at the manager's discretion. The merit bonuses as a percentage of salary are, however, much smaller than those awarded under the scheme for managers and appointed staff, and are currently as follows: fully satisfactory – 2.5 per cent; good – 3.5 per cent; outstanding – 5 per cent. It does seem that the bonus scheme for managers and appointed staff with its potentially higher rewards and greater emphasis on targets has been more specifically designed to act as an incentive than has the scheme for unappointed staff.

11.10. NON-PAY CONDITIONS

Paid holiday entitlement ranges from 21 days to 27 days for unappointed staff (according to length of service), 28 days for assistant managers and 30 days for managers. All staff are entitled to sick pay. Managers and their families are covered by the British United Provident Association, and there is a staff sickness fund for appointed staff.

Subsidised mortgages and loans are available. The amount depends on salary, and assistance with house purchase is available for all except those under 23 on low grades. There is a non-contributory pension scheme for all staff.

The standard working week is 35 hours. Daily starting and finishing times are set by branch management. Starting times may vary between 08.00 and 10.00 and finishing times between 16.00 and 18.00.

Overtime is paid to unappointed grades only. Saturday working is carried out by volunteers on a rota system. The work is carried out under a separate contract and is remunerated by fixed payments depending on job category and seniority.

11.11. BARGAINING ARRANGEMENTS

As indicated above, until the mid-1980s pay and conditions in the clearing banks were determined by industry level bargaining. The arrangements did not merely set out minimum standards for terms and conditions, but specified in detail the salaries, location payments, service payments and so forth for the 200 000 plus employees which they covered. However, the national agreements began to disintegrate in 1986 when the Midland Bank and the Clydesdale Bank withdrew from them. In 1987, citing the need to adapt its pay policies to changing circumstances, the National Westminster Bank, followed by the two other English clearing banks, also withdrew. Recruitment and retention factors were instrumental in this move because at that time the banks were faced with intense competition for staff, particularly in London and the south-east. Pay and conditions have since then been negotiated internally by each of the banks.

The XYZ Bank recognizes the Banking, Insurance and Finance Union, as well as its own Staff Association, for collective bargaining purposes. Other than for the three most senior management grades, the Bank negotiates pay and conditions with these two bodies. Approximately one-third of the staff belongs to each of them, the other third being non-members. In the latest pay round, the unions were unable to negotiate an across-the-board increase, and so all increases depended on performance. The Bank therefore claims to operate an 'all-merit' system of pay increases, in which those who do not reach the required performance level are not guaranteed a pay rise.

11.12. DIFFERENTIALS BETWEEN MEN AND WOMEN

Information on the relative position of male and female employees was obtained from one of XYZ Bank's regional offices. In the region as a whole there are 2285 staff in branches and 350 staff in the regional office, which is outside the branch hierarchy and provides support functions such as personnel management. (There is also a separate sales force, which has its own pay structure and is not included in these figures.) In addition, there are currently 113 agency staff in branches in the region, as well as approximately 20 on fixed-term contracts (three to six months) some of whom are former permanent employees doing similar work in the lowest grade. These are important to the Bank, as there was an embargo on permanent recruitment at the time the case study was conducted.

In total, there are 1155 male employees and 1480 female employees in the region. Table 11.3 shows how they are distributed through the grade structure. It can be seen that women are underrepresented in the highest grades and tend to be concentrated in the lower clerical and secretarial grades. While 50 per cent of men are either managers or assistant managers, the corresponding figure for women is only seven per cent. On the other hand, 81 per cent of women are in the clerical grades (as opposed to the remaining 50 per cent of men).

The concentration of women in the lower grades has more far reaching implications for pay differentials because of the performance related systems which the Bank operates. Since the annual performance related pay rise is calculated as a percentage of salary, those on lower salaries in the clerical grades receive a smaller increase. In addition, the percentage increases for unappointed staff range from 3–7.5 per cent, whereas those

Table 11.3. Distribution of men and women in each grade

	Men		Women	
	Total	%	Total	%
Managers				
MA	1	less than 1	0	0
MB	2	less than 1	0	0
MC	4	less than 1	0	0
MD	22	2	0	0
ME	31	3	0	0
MF	78	7	1	less than 1
MG	93	8	8	less than 1
Total	231	21	9	1
Assistant managers				
AH	87	7	15	1
AJ	152	13	48	3
AK	104	9	32	2
Total	342	29	95	6
Clerical				
G5	229	20	257	17
G4	65	6	171	12
G3	109	9	373	25
G2	142	12	313	21
G1	37	3	86	6
Total	582	50	1 200	81
Secretarial				
All grades	0	0	176	12
Total	1 155	100	1 480	100

Source: Information provided by case study bank.

for appointed staff range from 3–10.5 per cent. The bonus system similarly awards the highest pay outs to the highest grades. For managers and assistant managers, the higher the grade, the higher the possible bonus as a percentage of salary (the bonuses range from five per cent for an acceptable performance in all grades, up to 10 per cent in grades AK–AH, up to 20 per cent in grades MG–MD, and up to 25 per cent in grades MC–MA). Typical examples of the latest bonus payments awarded in two branches are as follows:

Branch No. 1		
Senior manager	10.00 per cent	£4,600
Other managers	8.75 per cent	£1,280
		£2,254
Assistant managers	6.875 per cent	£1,400
		£620
		£500
Branch No. 2		
Senior manager	10.00 per cent	£3,100
Other managers	10.00 per cent	£2,500
		£2,600
Assistant managers	7.50 per cent	£1,400
		£1,700
		£1,500

For clerical staff, on the other hand, on the basis of the overall performance marking awarded on the latest staff appraisal, the possible bonuses range from two and a half per cent for a fully satisfactory performer to five per cent for an outstanding performer in any grade. The bonus schemes thus differentiate not only between appointed and unappointed staff, but also between the grades in the appointed category, the rewards being proportionately greater for those at the higher levels. Consequently, they operate in a way which widens existing pay differentials even further, with the resulting implications for women's pay.

One possible explanation for the concentration of women in the Bank's lower grades may be that they have different career patterns during their working lives and therefore shorter service than men. As already indicated, the Bank's grading structure is very hierarchical and since all except graduates enter at Grade 1 or Grade 2, it can take quite a long time to progress to assistant managerial or managerial level. Information on employees' length of service was obtained from two of the Bank's branches, and is summarized in Table 11.4. (Where an employee had left the Bank, and later re-entered, the length of service was calculated on the later date of entry.)

These results are rather mixed, but show that 22 per cent of the women have less than five years' service compared with only 7 per cent of the men. On the other hand, 24 per cent of the men have 20 or more years' service, while the corresponding figure for women is 12 per cent. Therefore, although the Bank recruits more women than men (or greater

Table 11.4. Length of service of men and women

	Men		Women	
	Total	%	Total	%
Less than 5 years	4	7	27	22
5–9 years	25	43	44	36
10–14 years	10	17	20	16
15–19 years	5	9	17	14
20 or more years	14	24	14	12
Total	58	100	122	100

Source: Information provided by case study bank.

numbers of men leave with less than five years' service), those men who remain tend to stay longer with the Bank.

Furthermore, when these figures are analysed according to grade, the results reveal that even with similar lengths of service men and women have different career paths. For example, of those with less than 10 years' service, 55 per cent of the men are in Grade 3 or above, compared with only 23 per cent of the women. After between 10 and 20 years' service, 47 per cent of the men have achieved managerial or assistant managerial status, compared with only three per cent of the women. On the other hand, in the same service category 33 per cent of the women were still in Grade 3 or below, whereas the corresponding figure for men was only seven per cent.

These differences cannot be explained by performance levels, since despite their being underrepresented in the higher grades, information supplied by the Bank indicates that women tend to earn higher appraisal ratings than men, as shown in Table 11.5. The figures indicate that there was a higher proportion of women in the top two performance categories, and a smaller proportion in the bottom two categories. It could be the case that because of the nature of the work involved, high appraisals are easier to obtain in the lower grades, and these figures may merely reflect the gender segregation in the Bank's hierarchy. However, the evidence does seem to indicate that when it comes to promotion, factors other than staff appraisals are taken into account.

Of the 180 staff at the two branches concerned, 24 (13 per cent) work part-time. All except one of the part-time workers is female, and they are distributed through the grades as follows:

	Nos. part-time
Managers	0
Assistant managers	0
Grade 5	2
Grade 4	0
Grade 3	2
Grade 2	14
Grade 1	6

The figures indicate that part-time working is concentrated in the two lowest clerical grades. However, it is not necessarily associated with short length of service. In a sample of 16 part-timers, six had 10 or more years' service with the Bank. According to the Bank, it is quite common for those who have taken an employment break for family reasons to return to work part-time afterwards.

Table 11.5. Appraisal ratings for men and women

	Men		Women	
	Total	%	Total	%
Outstanding	398	34	873	43.5
Good	685	59	1 086	54
Fully satisfactory	61	5	34	2
Unsatisfactory	13	2	9	0.5
Total	1 157	100	2 002	100

Source: Information provided by case study bank.

11.13. SUMMARY AND CONCLUSIONS

This report has shown that despite the abolition of openly discriminatory employment practices, and apart from some small improvements, which are possibly due to the increase in the numbers of highly qualified female graduates now entering the industry, the career and earnings structure in banking in the UK is still highly differentiated between men and women. Performance-related pay systems could operate in a way which will widen pay differences even further. Banking is a typical 'career industry' and once one is on the career path, there are valuable financial inducements to stay with the organization, such as subsidised home loans and non-contributory pensions. Promotion prospects are also seen as a way of offsetting low starting salaries. However, Morris (1986) argues that to enable this career path to function in a strong internal labour market, high fall out rates are required from the lower grades and that males over 25 who remain with the banks have a good chance of achieving managerial status. This seems to be borne out by the evidence in this report. The banks have explained the differences in career achievements in terms of differing ambitions and attitudes (Morris 1986, p. 92). However, according to the Banking, Insurance and Finance Union, men and women do not have equal access to the career path, and it is only the presence of large numbers of women in the lower clerical grades which has enabled the career path of men to be maintained.

References

Banking, Insurance and Finance Union. *Jobs for the girls?* (BIFU Research Department).

T. Morris, *Innovations in banking* (London: Croom Helm 1986).

12 The Health Sector in the United Kingdom: A Case Study

Damian Grimshaw

12.1. INTRODUCTION

During the last decade, the UK National Health Service (NHS) has been the subject of radical economic and organizational reform. At the macro-economic level, the UK Government has pursued a commitment to curb the growth of public expenditure, both to meet the conditions of convergence criteria laid down in the Maastricht Treaty and in response to Conservative economic doctrine, which predicts an inverse correlation between the size of the public sector and a nation's rate of economic growth. At the organizational level, the Government has implemented a number of reforms in the public services designed to replace national level pay bargaining, in which a multi-employer group meets with a multi-union group, with local pay determination characterized by single-employer bargaining. In the health sector, this agenda of pay devolution has been encouraged by transforming hospitals into self-governing NHS Trusts, which have autonomy to manage their own terms and conditions of employment. These economic objectives coincide with two political aims of the present Government: first, to reduce the incidence of trade-union participation at the national level; and second, to give greater power to the local employer to determine pay and conditions of employment unilaterally and thus to devolve the accountability and responsibility for public services provision to the local level.

The transformations taking place in the NHS illustrate very well the general direction of institutional change in the labour market in the UK: from national level collective bargaining to decentralized pay determination; and from the active role of the State in generating employment to the role of implanting market forces in an attempt to generate efficiency. Given the importance of the UK Government and the NHS as an employer of women, it is necessary to address the extent to which the radical departure from past practices has had a negative impact upon the traditional role of the public sector as a 'good employer', both in terms of stable employment opportunities and 'fair' earnings.

This chapter seeks to address this question by analysing the impact of the various strategies of rationalization and changes in pay determination being undertaken in the NHS on the position of women employed in the health sector compared with that of men, with particular attention to differences in experiences for occupational groups.

The first section briefly consider these issues from a national perspective. Analysis of the future impact of changes in pay determination on different groups in the NHS begins with an assessment of the differences in wage gains made over the last 15 years between professional and less skilled groups of workers. These differences are driven largely by changes in government public sector pay policy and the different traditions of wage bargaining adopted by occupational and professional groups in the NHS.

The second section contains a case study analysis of a Trust in north-west England. Women's relative earnings in the Trust vary widely between occupational groups from low skilled ancillary work to qualified nursing duties. Compared with men in similar grades, women are less likely to benefit from additional payments in the form of shift premiums or overtime. The purpose of recent initiatives in local pay determination is to reduce the pay bill and satisfy new performance targets. Although these initiatives are primarily aimed at groups with relatively weak bargaining power, they represent potential pilot strategies for the future wholesale replacement of the national wage bargaining structure by local pay for all employees, and are therefore a significant threat to the past relative wage gains made by women in the NHS.

12.2. EMPLOYMENT COMPOSITION

In September 1992, the NHS employed 1,049,690 staff in England alone and was thus the largest single employer in the UK. Eight per cent of employees were employed as general practitioners, nurses and other staff in the general medical services (GMS) and the remaining 92 per cent worked in hospital and community health services (HCHS). In 1992, women represented 75 per cent of all HCHS staff in whole-time equivalent (wte) employment,[1] a proportion confirming the NHS as an important employer of women (see Table 12.1). However, although the NHS is a sector where women are clearly overrepresented, it is also a sector that has been subject to repeated demands from policy-makers to cut employment expenditure.

Table 12.1. Employment composition of NHS staff directly employed in HCHS, by main staff group and sex in whole-time equivalents, 1982–92

Main staff group and selected grades	1982 All staff	% of women	1986 All staff	% of women	1992 All staff	% of women
Hospital medical and dental staff	35 650	21.3	37 4706[5]	24.9	43 530	27.5
Consultant	11 980	11.0	13 280	13.1	15 290	15.8
Senior registrar	2 670	19.9	2 960	25.0	3 590	28.1
Registrar	5 630	20.8	5 810	22.9	6 160	24.7
Senior house officer	9 610	27.3	9 580	35.1	11 690	38.1
House officer	2 850	37.2	2 900	43.1	3 140	45.9
Nurses, midwives and health visitors[1]	394 040	89.9	397 240	89.6	378 790	88.5
General nursing	155 400	95.4	158 000	95.3	161 450	94.1
Qualified	107 360	94.7	114 730	94.8	119 930	93.7
Unqualified	48 040	97.1	43 270	96.7	40 510	95.2
Paediatrics, midwifery, maternity	35 270	99.7	36 570	99.3	39 910	98.9
mental health/learning	73 180	69.9	80 960	70.8	82 340	70.5
Qualified	42 780	60.3	46 910	62.5	47 050	63.9
Unqualified	30 400	83.4	34 040	82.4	35 000	79.4
Education and training	86 960	89.9	75 500	89.6	42 730	87.3
Primary health care	38 860	97.9	40 730	98.1	41 760	98.0
Professions allied to medicine[2]	28 200	87.6	33 590	86.8	39 200	86.4
Scientific and professional[3]	10 310	50.0	10 250	62.3	13 680	66.4
Other professional and technical	28 550	62.7	32 250	60.2	36 940	61.9
Administrative and clerical	108 800	81.2	110 840	81.7	135 010	84.2
Ancillary	170 520	67.0	124 270	63.9	79 000	60.7

Table 12.1. (continued)

Main staff group and selected grades	1982 All staff	% of women	1986 All staff	% of women	1992 All staff	% of women
Other support staff (mainly health-care assistants)	–	–	–	–	6 300	68.6
General and senior managers	–	–	510	15.7	17 700	41.9
Maintenance and works	27 130	0.8	24 980	0.8	17 910	0.9
Ambulance staff	18 320	10.7	18 960	13.6	17 720	22.0
Total staff[4]	821 520	74.8	790 360	75.0	785 780	75.1

Notes: [1]Figures exclude agency nursing. Figures for 1992 also exclude Project 2000 students (approximately 18300). [2]Figures for 1982 are estimates since data are missing for 'Others', which ranges between 870 and 1530 for the period 1987–92. [3]Figures for 1982 are an estimation since data are missing for 'Other scientific and professional staff', which varies between 180 and 920 for the period 1987–92. [4]Total figures exclude locum medical and dental staff, as no information on gender is provided. [5]1987 figures are given for hospital medical and dental staff because 1986 figures are unavailable
Source: Department of Health NHS Executive (1993).

During the period 1982–92, total wte employment in the NHS fell by four per cent. These cuts appear to have affected men and women equally, with the share of women in wte employment remaining at 75 per cent throughout the period. However, in terms of actual numbers of full-time and part-time staff employed, aggregate data show a drop of only 1.8 per cent in the same period: this suggests that savings were made by employing a greater ratio of part-time to full-time employees, which in turn implies a greater reliance on lower paid female staff.

Nurses, midwives and health visitors represent by far the largest group of staff in the NHS and this group is highly female dominated. Women's share in nursing varies, however, from 98.9 per cent in paediatrics, midwifery and maternity to 63.9 per cent among qualified mental health nursing personnel (1992 data). In contrast, medical and dental staff are highly male dominated. Women's share in this group increased, however, from 21 to 28 per cent between 1982 and 1992, which suggests that the trend of male overrepresentation is slowly reversing. The fall in the recorded number of wte nursing staff is the result of a new training system. Nurses undertaking the traditional system of training, which involves responsibility for duties on the hospital ward, are included in the data in Table 12.1, whereas learners in the new Project 2000 training scheme are not assigned duties and are therefore not included in the data.[2] Although the number of wte nursing staff employed has fallen by four per cent, the actual number employed has increased by two per cent (see Table 12.2). This reflects an overall decrease in the proportion of nursing staff employed as full-timers.

Major structural changes have occurred for some occupational groups. The number of ancillary staff employed has been drastically cut primarily as a result of the imposition of compulsory competitive tendering (CCT) of ancillary services (see below). By 1992, ancillary wte employment represented just 10 per cent of total employment compared with 21 per cent in 1982. This massive reduction (54 per cent) was accompanied by a fall in the share of women employed, which suggests that women have disproportionately suffered from policies that contracted out ancillary services to the private sector or that cut the number of staff hours contracted by the NHS. The other major group of employees subject to CCT is maintenance and works staff, 99 per cent of whom are men. This group of staff experienced a reduction of about 9000 wte positions (or 34 per cent) between 1982 and 1992. Both these reductions in wte positions are reflected in figures for actual numbers employed (see Table 10.2), which implies that the reduction in wte employment is predominantly accounted for by redundancies or transfers to the private sector, rather than by reductions in

Table 12.2. Percentage change in directly employed staff by main staff groups, 1982–92

Staff group	All staff Whole-time equivalents (%)	All staff Numbers employed (%)
Hospital medical and dental staff	22.1	18.8
Nurses, midwives and health visitors	–3.9	1.9
Professional and technical[1]	33.6	35.6[3]
Administrative, clerical and managerial staff[2]	40.4	43.1
Ancillary staff	–53.7	–49.8
Maintenance/works	–34.0	–33.8
Ambulance staff	–3.3	1.4
Total staff	–4.2	–1.8

Notes: [1]This group comprises professions allied to medicine, scientific and professional staff, and other professional and technical staff. [2]Since 1984, general and senior managers have been categorized separately, but are shown together here for the purposes of comparison. [3]Owing to incomplete data, this is an estimated figure
Source: Department of Health NHS Executive (1993).

hours worked. Indeed, the reduction in the number of maintenance and ancillary staff directly employed by the NHS is the primary factor underpinning the overall drop in NHS employment. Most other groups have experienced either an increase or relatively little change in the numbers employed. Where occupational groups have increased in wte employment, for example in administrative and clerical, managerial or medical and dental staff groups, women have also increased their share of employment in these groups. Therefore, where a large number of women may have experienced redundancies or reduced working time within low-skilled occupational groups, this has been offset by an expansion of opportunities at the higher end of the labour market.

Health care assistants (HCAs) were introduced in 1989 with the aim of introducing a new level of support for qualified and unqualified nursing staff and providing a well defined structure of training opportunities for this new grade. The introduction of HCAs has met with significant resistance from trade unions representing nurses' interests, which are concerned that HCAs threaten to undermine the professional status of job tasks undertaken by nurses.

As Table 12.2 shows, there was a dramatic increase in the number of managers in the period 1982–92, which reflects the gradual introduction of a new management class that began in 1984. The figures overstate the increase, however, since from 1989 many of the less senior management posts represent a relabelling of jobs formerly classified as administrative and clerical work. Nevertheless, bringing the two categories together in Table 12.2 clearly shows that the level of employment of these staff groups has increased by a greater proportion than that of any other group of employees. It is widely held that this is the result of the imposition of government reforms devised for implementation by a new class of managerial staff and managerial techniques.

12.3. PAY DETERMINATION IN THE NHS

The relative level of pay earned by employees in the NHS and the changing wage differentials between occupational groups are largely influenced by two major factors: first, the Government's public sector pay policy; and second, the bargaining strategies of different occupational groups. During the 1960s and 1970s, public sector pay policies were driven by conflicting strategies. There was a great deal of oscillation between applying some form of comparability in pay recommendations (as recommended in the reports of the Priestley Commission in 1957, the Houghton and Halsbury Committees of Inquiry in the mid-1970s and the Clegg Standing Commission on Pay Comparability in 1980), advocating greater links between pay and productivity (as with the implementation of the Government's 1965 White Paper by the National Board for Prices and Incomes), and applying strict incomes policies (such as the pay restraint of the late 1970s). On the one hand, pay comparisons were seen to ensure fair treatment and reward for public services, yet on the other hand they were viewed as 'engines of inflation', extending pay rises to groups regardless of productivity improvements (Clegg, 1980, p. 6). Since 1979, the Government's public sector pay policy has rejected comparability in favour of a focus on public finance and affordability. There have been two major developments: a renewed commitment to restrictive incomes policies (or 'cash limits') for the public sector, first introduced in 1979 and strengthened by the imposition in 1987 of a statutory duty not to exceed them (Seifert, 1992); and an effort to replace national level bargaining by decentralized pay determination. Rather than linking public sector to private sector pay through comparability at the national level, the Government aims to inject methods of private sector pay determination into the public sector.

As indicated above, the second main factor underpinning the pay system in the NHS concerns the different wage bargaining strategies of professional and non-professional staff groups. These differences and the different relations with government have led many commentators to describe NHS pay determination as a two-tier system. Since the creation of the NHS in 1948, pay and conditions of employment have been set by the General Whitley Council (GWC), which was already established in the civil service and in local authorities. Under the umbrella of the GWC are ten functional councils. The different bargaining groups involve a management side composed of civil servants from the Department of Health and NHS managers, and a staff side composed of representatives from the trade unions and professional associations recognized by the NHS. These groups are separated according to broad occupational groups. Only maintenance staff and craftsmen negotiate pay directly with the Department of Health, which is advised by NHS management.

Traditionally, bargaining strategies on the staff side were split between representatives of employees covered by professional associations and representatives of those covered by trade unions. Currently, about two-thirds of NHS staff are represented by professional associations, namely the Royal College of Nursing, the British Medical Association and those professional associations representing the professions allied to medicine. The remaining third is represented by a wide array of trade unions, most of which are registered with the Trades Union Congress. Professional associations have traditionally sought to defend pay, professional status and job task demarcations through legal procedures, encouraging limitations on the numbers of persons qualifying, long training periods, demarcation disputes and defence of customary pay differentials (Seifert, 1992, p. 46).

In the 1970s, however, many of these associations registered as trade unions, and owing to the increasingly restrictive public sector pay policies of the 1980s were forced to consider trade union strategies of collective bargaining in order to defend a living wage as the professions became increasingly subject to supply and demand rather than state protection by legal enactment (Seifert, 1992, pp. 46–50). This situation exploded in the early 1980s, resulting in the setting up of a Pay Review Body for nurses, midwives, health visitors and professions allied to medicine. (The pay of doctors and dentists has been decided by the Review Body on Doctors' and Dentists' Remuneration since 1963 following recommendations by the Pilkington Commission.) The Pay Review Body deals primarily with basic pay increases. Other terms and conditions are negotiated within the respective functional councils. The Government appoints the members of the Pay Review Body; it presents the management evidence according to government objectives; and it retains the right not to implement its recommendations.

The greater bargaining strength of staff covered by pay review bodies is illustrated by the Government's application of the policy of 'cash limits'. For groups not covered by pay review bodies, annual pay negotiations at the national level are tightly constrained by cash limits, and this results in very similar annual pay increases awarded across different functional Whitley Council groups. In contrast, in making its recommendations for the majority of NHS employees, the Pay Review Body has often stated that affordability is not the primary consideration; and partly to avoid public disputes and in response to the stronger bargaining position, the Government has always made funds available where pay increases have exceeded the limits imposed (Seifert, 1992).

12.4. RELATIVE PAY IN THE NHS

The differences between groups are highlighted by an analysis of relative pay. Table 12.3 shows relative pay differentials from 1971 to 1994 for women working full time in selected NHS occupational groups: qualified nurses and midwives, unqualified nurses, administrative and clerical workers, and ancillary staff. Occupational pay levels are compared with average earnings of men and women in manual and non-manual employment in order to indicate general trends in pay equity. Although there are limitations and problems of measurement with the New Earnings Survey (NES) data, they do provide the most useful source for longitudinal comparisons of relative pay in the United Kingdom.[3]

The relatively high pay of employees covered by pay review bodies is evident from Table 12.3. Average earnings of qualified nurses and midwives increased over the whole period relative to all four groups used as standards of comparison. High points occurred in 1975 and 1991. Figures for 1975 reflect the national industrial action of 1974, which led the Halsbury Committee of Inquiry to recommend an average increase of 30 per cent in nurses' pay (Seifert, 1992). High relative pay in 1991 represents the sustained level achieved as a result of the large one-off increase that accompanied the clinical grading review of 1988.[4] Throughout the late 1970s and the 1980s, qualified nurses did not improve their position from approximately 60 per cent of male non-manual pay, but in recent years this fraction has increased to about 70 per cent. The average pay gap between qualified nurses and male manual workers converged until the

Table 12.3. Relative pay of women working full time in the NHS: 1971–94, selected years

Occupational groups	1971	1975	1978	1982	1984	1987	1991	1994
Pay as % of all female non-manual employees								
Qualified nurses and midwives	97	108	91	97	95	96	114	110
Unqualified nurses	80	89	81	80	77	76	74	70
Administrative and clerical staff	103	–	95	85	85	82	80	82
Ancillary staff	81	97	88	77	73	69	–	66
Pay as % of all female manual employees								
Qualified nurses and midwives	126	133	109	127	127	131	170	174
Unqualified nurses	104	110	97	105	103	103	109	111
Administrative and clerical staff	133	–	114	111	113	111	119	126
Ancillary staff	105	120	105	101	96	94	–	105
Pay as % of all male non-manual employees								
Qualified nurses and midwives	49	63	54	57	57	57	72	71
Unqualified nurses	41	52	48	47	46	45	46	45
Administrative and clerical staff	52	–	56	50	51	48	51	54
Ancillary staff	41	56	52	45	43	41	–	43

Table 12.3. (continued)

Occupational groups	1971	1975	1978	1982	1984	1987	1991	1994
Pay as % of all male manual employees								
Qualified nurses and midwives	66	77	67	76	78	81	107	108
Unqualified nurses	54	64	59	63	63	64	69	69
Administrative and clerical staff	69	–	70	66	69	69	75	82
Ancillary staff	54	69	64	60	59	58	–	65

Notes: Pay differentials are calculated using data for average gross weekly earnings, which include overtime pay for each occupational group and exclude those whose pay was affected by absence. 'Qualified nurses' refers to registered and enrolled nurses. For 1991 and 1993, figures do not include midwives and thus underrepresent the actual differential. 'Unqualified nurses' refers to assistant nurses and auxiliary nurses. Earnings information for administrative and clerical workers and ancillary staff is taken from information in the NES Analysis by Agreement.

– = missing data, or data that are recorded in a manner inconsistent with the rest of the series.

Source: *New Earnings Survey.*

late 1980s; thereafter, qualified nurses' earnings exceeded the average wages of male manual workers.

Although qualified nurses and midwives have made significant gains, the relative position of unqualified nurses and ancillary workers has generally declined from the 1975 levels. For women employed in non-manual full-time occupations, the health sector represented a 'good employer' throughout the period in question, especially for qualified nursing employees (relative pay fluctuating around the average pay level of all non-manual female workers). However, pay for unqualified nurses in the NHS seriously deteriorated throughout the 1980s and 1990s and remains attractive only in comparison with the average earnings of female manual workers.

In the case of female ancillary staff in full-time employment, the high relative pay levels of 1975 represent the gains achieved from the 1972–3 national strike over low pay. Since 1975, ancillary workers' earnings have declined considerably. In relation to all non-manual women workers, their comparative pay fell from almost 100 per cent in 1975 to about two-thirds in 1993. Also, during the late 1980s the pecuniary benefits in the health sector for women seeking manual employment were negative, a fact which suggests a reversal of the traditional notion of the public sector as a 'good employer' for this group of workers. Furthermore, although the gains achieved by ancillary workers in the early 1970s exceeded those by unqualified nurses, since then employment as an unqualified nurse has offered relatively greater levels of pay. This reversal in relative pay is partly the result of the report of the Clegg Standing Commission on Pay Comparability in 1979, which recommended increases for NHS ancillary staff in a range of 3.8 per cent to 16.9 per cent, and an average increase of 19.6 per cent for nurses (Seifert, 1992). Nevertheless, relative pay levels for ancillary workers did experience an upsurge in the early 1990s. To some extent, however, the data overstate ancillary workers' earnings because some of the least well paid have lost their jobs or been transferred to the private sector as a result of subcontracting and privatization (Elliot and Murphy, 1987; Brown and Rowthorn, 1990).

Table 12.4 substantiates the changes in relative pay for NHS occupational groups in full-time employment across three different periods of time. The periods were chosen to reflect changes before and after 1980 – the last year when significant positive recommendations were made to improve public sector pay in relation to pay in the private sector. In the NHS, the period of change from 1979 and from 1982 shows that women's earnings have diverged more widely than in the private sector. For the period 1979–94, the relative average pay of female qualified nursing staff

Table 12.4. Percentage change in occupational pay relative to all employees' earnings

	1974–94	1982–94	1989–94
Medical practitioners (M)	22	4	–1
Registered and enrolled nurses* (F)	40	29	7
Nurses auxiliaries/assistants (F)	0	–3	–3
Administrative and clerical (F)	0	9	15
Hospital porters (M)	–23	–16	–5
Ambulance staff (M)	0	–8	0
Ancillary staff (F)	–4	–2	9
Private sector non-manual (M)	6	–	–4
Private sector non-manual (F)	23	–	4
Private sector manual (M)	–16	–	–5
Private sector manual (F)	–10	–	–1
All male employees	–1	–1	–1
All female employees	15	12	5
All employees	0	0	0

Notes: *Before 1991, NES data classified occupations according to Key Occupations for Statistical Purposes (KOS), under which the definition of registered and enrolled nurses included midwives who earn a higher average wage. Hence, comparison of data for 1979, 1982 or 1989 with the Standard Occupational Classification data of 1994 will underestimate the relative percentage change in pay. M = male full-time employees; F = female full-time employees; – = missing data
Source: *New Earnings Survey.*

improved dramatically, whereas the pay of female ancillary staff fell by four per cent. In the private sector, the divergence in relative pay between female manual and female non-manual employees was less, although the wage floor to female manual earnings is higher in the NHS. The bad experience of female ancillary staff is overshadowed by the massive drop in the relative pay of male hospital porters, which, unlike that of female ancillary staff, has not reversed in the last five years. Since 1982 there has been a nine per cent relative increase in the pay of women employed as administrative and clerical staff, and since 1989 their gains have exceeded those of qualified nursing staff. In general, it is difficult to identify a long-lasting pattern of customary pay differentials between occupations in the NHS. Women employed as full-time qualified nursing or clerical staff have improved their relatively favourable position, whereas unqualified staff have seen their earnings deteriorate.

It would appear, therefore, that evidence for a two-tier pay structure is substantiated by analysis of pay trends from 1979 to 1994. There is also recent evidence of the adverse impact of separate occupational pay bargaining for the NHS workforce on the degree of pay inequality between male and female employees of similar skills. In a well known equal value case, a speech therapist claimed that her work was equal in value to the work done by a clinical psychologist and a pharmacist, yet these jobs were awarded higher pay – 25% and 40% more respectively. The initial industrial tribunal rejected the claim. Key to the rejection was the argument that the pay differentials were the result of separate bargaining structures which were seen to constitute a non discriminatory 'material factor' in pay determination (Committees A and B of the Professional and Technical Staff Whitley Council group A) (IRLR 1993). This result was later overruled by the European Court of Justice which held that the existence of separate bargaining groups for male-dominated and female-dominated professions did not amount to an objective justification. The Court stated that: 'If the employer could rely on the absence of discrimination within each of the collective bargaining processes taken separately as sufficient justification for the difference in pay, he could easily circumvent the principle of equal pay by using separate bargaining processes.' (op. cit.). This ruling highlights the dangers of separate occupational pay bargaining units in sectors such as the NHS which is characterised by strong horizontal sex segregation.

12.5. NHS REFORMS

In recent years, the UK government has attempted to replace national pay determination with decentralized public sector pay determination. Since the late 1980s, many of the national Whitley agreements for the NHS workforce have contained provisions to allow local employers a degree of flexibility in adjusting the terms and conditions of employment according to local labour market conditions. These enable local employers to adjust the wage rate in a variety of ways:

1) to recruit or promote staff onto a pay scale above the minimum for a particular grade in response to difficulties with recruitment and retention;
2) to enhance an employee's pay by a specified percentage amount;
3) to redefine and upgrade a particular post if it is proved to have a greater job content than that specified in the national description; and

4) to determine incentive bonus schemes, now referred to as local performance agreements.[5]

For some commentators, the provision of local flexible employment practices within national agreements was representative of 'watershed agreements' towards the full transition to local employment practice beyond the confines of national regulation (Glasscott and Bowden, 1993). Others, however, doubt the widespread implementation of flexibility arrangements beyond the south-eastern regions of England (Fillingham, 1991).

Publication in 1989 of the White Paper on NHS reform, *Working for Patients,* represented a more ambitious attempt by the Government to consolidate local pay bargaining. This established the right of hospitals and community health services to apply for self-governing NHS Trust status beginning in 1991. NHS Trusts have independent power to develop their own local pay structures, although incumbent employees have the right to maintain their existing national terms and conditions if they choose. Although hospitals have been quick to apply for Trust status (by April 1995, 492 Trusts representing 98 per cent of all hospitals had been established), only a small proportion of Trusts have implemented local pay structures. There are various explanations for the slow emergence of local pay. Bach and Winchester (1994) argue, for example, that the presence of professional groups such as nurses will hinder the development of local pay because of their particular occupational characteristics, in terms of their professional aspirations, high trade union density and high political profile. Others point to the high costs involved in establishing local pay in terms of time, resources and developing the necessary expertise among personnel managers and trade union leaders (Corby, 1992; IRS, 1993). In addition, personnel directors may fear the replacement of the 'comfort factor' of national level industrial relations practices with a less well known and perhaps more unstable local environment characterized by a higher trade union membership. These fears have been exacerbated by recent ballots in several of the largest health sector unions, which reveal that members support the threat of industrial action to prevent the Government from imposing local pay determination.

Perhaps in response to the slow emergence of local pay structures in the NHS, Whitley Council agreements have encouraged further flexibility at the local level in the form of 'enabling provisions'. These were introduced in the 1994 agreements for most groups whose pay is covered under the Whitley Council, including ancillary staff, administrative and clerical workers and professional and technical staff. The relevant clause in the contract states: 'Employing authorities may make payments to employees under locally agreed schemes based on the performance of the organization in relation to its objectives for the provision of high quality patient care.' The conditions for implementation include agreement with staff representatives; an unbiased, transparent and unambiguous link between pay and performance that clearly relates to the needs and objectives of the trust; and the resolution of grievances and disputes at local level (IDS, 1994). Importantly, the emphasis is on the performance of the organization rather than that of the individual; this represents a reversal in government policy recommendations, which now recognize the overwhelming difficulties of individual appraisal of public services workers.

12.6. CASE STUDY OF AN NHS TRUST

The case study Trust was established in April 1994, and is currently one of the 10 largest in the UK. It consists of two hospitals located within five miles of each other. For the year 1994–95, the trust employed approximately 5500 staff (4700 wte) with a pay bill of £87 million and a turnover of £150 million. Funding is allocated by the Department of Health according to 'Finished Consultant Episodes' (FCEs), which represent a productivity measurement or performance index. The target activity levels set for each Trust are in terms of FCEs and represent an attempt to impose financial performance targets comparable to those in the private sector.

For many Trusts, Trust status involves substantial reorganization and restructuring of existing services as well as pressure to cut costs in order to balance the organizational budget. This case study Trust is no exception. Considerable time and resources have been required to manage the transfer of in-patient acute services to a single, expanded hospital site and to institute a new, reduced role for the other hospital site. The Trust management predict a reduction of approximately 16 000 FCEs (20 per cent) and 370 beds (27 per cent) by 1999, which will have a major impact on staffing levels, affecting perceived job security and the ability of management to recruit. The Trust management expect to cut the number of wte staff by 900, some of whom will be transferred to a neighbouring Trust 10 miles away.

In common with the national picture, women are overrepresented among the Trust's workforce: 77 per cent of all employees are women (the figure for the NHS as a whole is 75 per cent of all wte staff). About 42 per cent of staff employed at the Trust are part-time employees, 90 per cent of whom are women, concentrated in the three main occupational groups – nursing and midwifery, administrative and clerical, and ancillary staff (see Table 12.5). Table 12.6 gives more detailed information according to the pay grade structure for three occupational groups. Ancillary staff – cleaners, caterers, porters, gardeners, drivers and laundry workers – are collected together under broad pay bands, apparently to encourage the principle of staff flexibility regarding job tasks. Ancillary staff are the only occupational group in the trust where a clear majority of workers are employed part-time. When one compares full-time and part-time ancillary staff it is clear that men and women are segregated into each category. There is also sex segregation between different ancillary job tasks. Portering and security are dominated by male full-time staff, whereas catering, cleaning and laundry staff are generally female and part-time.[6] Within the two categories of full-time and part-time ancillaries, women's share of employment across the grade hierarchy is evenly spread: women are just as likely to be employed at the supervisory level as at the entry level of grade A. Overall, however, women's employment opportunities are not as good as those of men since the ratio of the number of higher grade to lower grade staff is greater for full-time employees than it is for part-time employees. This suggests that male dominated groups have secured greater opportunities for promotion into higher grades than groups such as cleaning and catering. This is reflected in figures for the total number of ancillary staff employed: women make up 70 per cent of grade A staff compared with only 54 per cent of supervisory staff.

Administrative and clerical staff and nursing and midwifery are both strongly female dominated, especially among part-time employees. The grading definition for administrative and clerical staff follows broad guidelines which distinguish a range of jobs – from those involving repetitive tasks and close supervision, to those involving complex duties and accountability. Few clerical staff are employed at the more senior grades (7–9) because of the regrading of staff onto managerial scales, and grade 1 is practically not used, a fact which reflects the problems of attracting new staff from the local labour market. Part-time employees are clustered around grades 2 and 3. Among full-time staff, the relatively few male clerical staff are more likely to be employed in the higher grades of 5 and 6 than grades 1 to 4.

For nursing and midwifery, unqualified nursing auxiliary staff are employed in grades A and B. Newly qualified nursing staff are employed in grade C, and then move from grade D to grade E according to experience. Grades F and G are assigned to the post of ward sister, and grades H and I are managerial grades for senior nurses with responsibility for managing more than one ward. Most nursing auxiliaries are female part-timers and

Table 12.5. Employment structure in the case study trust by full-time and part-time and by sex, at 31 May 1995

Occupation	No. of part-time	% women	No. of full-time	% women	Total employment	% women	% of total
Medical and dental	184	22.3	299	32.4	483	28.6	8.9
Nurses and midwives	959	98.1	1 324	87.5	2283	91.9	42.0
Professions allied to medicine	88	95.5	136	84.6	224	88.9	4.1
Scientific and professional	11	100.0	55	50.9	66	59.1	1.2
Other professional and technical staff	60	93.3	247	53.8	307	61.6	5.7
Administrative and clerical	476	98.3	521	82.9	997	90.3	18.4
Senior managers	1	100.0	120	44.2	121	44.6	2.2
Ancillary staff	495	92.1	371	33.4	866	67.0	15.9
Maintenance and works	2	0.0	84	0.0	86	0.0	1.6
Total employment	2 276	90.4	3 157	67.8	5433	77.3	100.0

Source: Information provided by the case study trust.

Table 12.6. Employment composition of three occupational groups by full-time and part-time and by sex

Occupation/grade	No. of part-time	% women	No. of full-time	% women	Total employment	% women	% of total
Nurses + midwives							
Grade A	293	96.9	185	87.6	478	93.3	20.9
Grade B	18	100.0	5	100.0	23	100.0	1.0
Grade C	21	100.0	14	78.6	35	91.4	1.5
Grade D	129	95.3	355	85.1	484	87.8	21.2
Grade E	297	99.3	395	87.8	692	92.8	30.3
Grade F	93	100.0	124	85.5	217	91.7	9.5
Grade G	102	99.0	199	92.0	301	94.4	13.2
Grade H/I	5	100.0	28	85.7	33	87.9	1.4
Other	1	100.0	19	94.7	20	95.0	0.9
Total	959	98.1	1324	87.5	2283	91.9	100.0
Administrative + clerical							
Grade 1	1	100.0	1	100.0	2	100.0	0.2
Grade 2	288	98.3	111	83.8	399	94.2	40.0
Grade 3	116	99.1	157	88.5	273	93.0	27.4
Grade 4	53	100.0	142	90.8	195	93.3	19.6
Grade 5	10	100.0	61	70.5	71	74.6	7.1
Grade 6	4	100.0	41	53.7	45	57.8	4.5
Grade 7	1	100.0	6	83.3	7	85.7	0.7
Grade 8/9	2	50.0	2	0.0	4	25.0	0.4
Other	1	0.0	0	0.0	1	0.0	0.1
Total	476	98.3	521	82.9	997	90.3	100.0

Table 12.6. (continued)

Occupation/grade	No. of part-time	% women	No. of full-time	% women	Total employment	% women	% of total
Ancillary staff							
Grade A	465	91.8	271	32.5	736	70.0	85.0
Grade B	9	88.9	44	25.0	53	35.8	6.1
Grade C	4	100.0	8	87.5	12	91.7	1.4
Grade D	0	–	0	–	0	–	0.0
Supervisor	17	100.0	48	37.5	65	53.8	7.5
Total	495	92.1	371	33.4	866	67.0	100.0

Source: Information provided by the case study trust.

this group constitutes 13 per cent of all nursing and midwifery staff. In all other grades except grade C, which is rarely used, most staff are employed full-time. Compared with clerical staff, however, there is a surprisingly high proportion of part-time staff among the senior grades E, F and G; but we cannot necessarily interpret this as meaning that part-time nursing staff are more likely to be promoted. There are a number of other factors which may be relevant, such as a greater reliance on temporary agency staff to fill senior positions, or a higher number of ports of entry into the internal nursing labour market for those women wishing to re-enter a senior part-time position after maternity leave.

Table 12.7 shows the average gross annual earnings for male and female, full-time and part-time employees in nursing, administrative and clerical, and ancillary work. Gross earnings include the basic salary, enhanced pay such as shift premiums, on-call payments and productivity bonuses, and overtime payments. The basic rate of pay for part-time employees is calculated on a pro-rata basis according to the full-time hourly rate. Focusing on the overall spread of earnings for full-time employees across all three occupational groups, Table 12.7 shows that the main reason for the divergence is occupational differences rather than a variation between male and female earnings. Women in managerial nursing positions share the top of the wage hierarchy with their male counterparts, and women are also located at the bottom where the least well-paid categories are dominated by female ancillary staff; the even lower level of pay for women employed full-time as grade 1 clerical staff probably explains why this grade is used very little. The range of average occupational wages for women in full-time work – from £9439 for ancillary work to £15 713 for nursing – reflects not only the different rates of pay between groups but also the distribution of staff across grades within each group. The relatively high average earnings of female full-time nurses and, to a lesser extent, clerical staff reflect their ability to benefit from training and promotion opportunities compared with women in ancillary work, 89 per cent of whom are concentrated in the lowest paid grade A positions.

Female ancillary staff are further penalized by the greater gender pay gap that exists among ancillary workers compared with that existing among nursing staff (see Table 12.8). Among clerical staff, the difference in pay is largely due to an overrepresentation of men among higher grades. Among ancillary staff, this factor is complicated by the fact that, unlike the annual earnings of nursing and clerical staff, those of male and female ancillary staff differ markedly within the same grade. For example, men and women entering full-time employment in nursing or clerical work

Table 12.7. Average gross annual earnings for three occupational groups (in £ sterling)

	Female full-time	Female part-time	Male full-time	Male part-time	Number in sample
Nursing staff					
Student nurse	8 296	–	8 409	–	74
Grade A	10 398	7 200	11 020	9 191	395
Grade B	9 314	8 311	–	–	15
Grade C	12 874	7 838	11 961	–	38
Grade D	13 555	9 562	13 742	9 037	369
Grade E	16 583	11 803	16 740	10 267	592
Grade F	19 189	13 684	20 462	–	195
Grade G	21 407	16 198	22 289	7 550	266
Grade H/I	24 370	18 140	22 692	–	30
Senior nurse	26 364	–	34 351	–	4
Total	15 713	10 693	15 904	9 642	1 978
Administrative and clerical					
Grade 1	7 489	–	–	–	1
Grade 2	9 047	6 083	9 282	–	278
Grade 3	10 402	6 910	9 702	5 419	188
Grade 4	12 103	9 148	11 894	–	162
Grade 5	14 166	9 197	14 207	–	58
Grade 6	17 452	12 523	17 674	–	37
Grade 7	21 630	–	19 378	–	5
Grade 8/9	–	24 294	25 175	10 731	3
Total	11 569	6 859	13 011	8 075	732
Ancillary staff					
Grade A	8 669	5 202	10 133	7 727	518
Grade B	10 044	6 397	11 354	4 109	50
Grade C	10 865	4 163	14 711	–	12
Supervisor	11 747	7 815	14 698	–	60
Total	9 439	5 350	10 866	7 555	640

Note: The information is derived from data on annual earnings for 1994–95 provided by the trust personnel department. The sample size is lower than actual numbers employed as shown in Table 12.6 because it does not include those employees who held an employment contract in a particular job description for less than the full year. Excluded categories consist of temporary staff, employees newly recruited, promoted, retired or made redundant, as well as workers who were absent or sick for a significant period.
Source: Information provided by the case study trust.

Table 12.8. Gender pay gap in three occupational groups for whole-time equivalent employment

	Full time %	Part-time %	Total %	Number of wte in total sample
Nursing	99	112	101	506
Administrative and clerical	89	66	72	616
Ancillary staff	87	91	86	1 703

Source: Information provided by the case study trust.

receive similar gross annual salaries on average, whereas among ancillary staff there is a difference of about £1500.

Gender pay inequality within the same grade of ancillary staff occurs largely as a result of the differential capability of men and women to earn additional payments on top of the basic wage rate. Table 12.9 disaggregates average gross annual earnings for each occupational group in terms of basic pay, enhanced pay and overtime payments. Basic pay represents receipt of the basic salary rate. Enhanced pay refers mainly to premium pay awarded for shift work and unsocial hours, but also includes other allowances which vary by occupational group, such as lead rates paid to psychiatric and geriatric nurses, stand-by and on-call allowances which are available to all nursing and clerical staff, and productivity bonuses paid to ancillary staff. Overtime payment refers to pay received for work done in addition to full-time contracted hours.

For the UK labour market as a whole, additional payments in the form of overtime, payment by results, and shift premiums make up a larger fraction of gross earnings for manual workers than for non-manual workers, and for men than for women (Rubery, 1994). Table 12.9 reveals that these trends are true for the case study Trust. Male ancillary workers, whether full-time or part-time, staff or supervisors, receive a greater addition to their basic salary than do female ancillaries. Almost a third of male ancillaries' earnings is made up of enhancements and overtime compared with only a fifth for female ancillaries. It is this factor which fuels gender pay inequality among ancillary staff. Among clerical staff overall earnings are almost entirely made up of the basic salary for both men and women. The only exception concerns part-time female clerical staff, who earn nine per cent of average earnings in the form of enhanced payments. For nursing staff, where women dominate the occupation, men in both full-time and part-time employment are slightly more likely to earn shift premiums than are women.

Table 12.9. Composition of average gross annual earnings for three occupational groups

(a) Full-time employees

	Sex	Total average pay	Make up of average annual pay			Number in sample
		£	Basic	Enhanced	Overtime	
Nursing staff						
Unqualified	M	10 610	85	14	1	29
	F	9 899	90	10	0	225
Qualified	M	17 163	87	12	1	122
	F	17 320	90	10	1	814
Total	M	15 713	87	12	1	151
	F	15 904	90	10	1	1039
Administrative and clerical	M	13 011	96	2	2	71
	F	11 569	96	2	1	345
Ancillary staff						
Staff	M	10 368	70	16	14	186
	F	8 999	80	11	8	84
Supervisors	M	14 172	60	24	17	28
	F	11 746	70	16	14	16
Total	M	10 866	68	17	14	214
	F	9 439	79	12	9	100

Table 12.9. (continued)

(b) Part-time employees

	Sex	Total average pay	Make up of average annual pay			Number in sample
		£	Basic	Enhanced	Overtime	
Nursing staff						
Unqualified	M	9 191	67	33	0	8
	F	7 305	84	16	0	260
Qualified	M	10 243	86	14	0	6
	F	12 403	83	17	0	514
Total	M	9 642	75	25	0	14
	F	10 690	83	17	0	774
Administrative and clerical	M	8 075	100	0	0	2
	F	6 859	91	9	0	314
Ancillary staff						
Staff	M	7 555	72	19	9	21
	F	5 212	78	19	4	287
Supervisors	M	–	–	–	–	0
	F	7 815	70	25	5	16
Total	M	7 555	72	19	9	21
	F	5 350	77	19	4	303

Source: Information provided by the case study trust.

The rate of overtime pay and the ability to work overtime are an important issue for ancillary staff. For this group, overtime is defined for full-time and part-time employees as hours in excess of the full working week of 39 hours and is paid at a rate of time and a half for weekdays and Saturdays, and double time for Sundays and public holidays. Where overtime pay is received by part-time ancillaries, it is paid at the basic rate. For clerical staff, overtime payments usually take the form of time-off in lieu. Although time-off is also the general form of payment for nursing staff, different arrangements are available to the Trust management. Regrading of some senior nurses onto managerial scales means that these nurses are often required to work unpaid overtime. Also, the Trust can avoid the payment of overtime (and shift) premiums by employing nurses on a temporary basis from a 'nursing bank'. The bank is a means by which part-time nurses supplement their weekly income or re-enter the labour market after a period of absence. Nursing bank staff are not entitled to any form of enhanced payments.

Differences in conditions for the payment of overtime represent just one example of the complexity of the national Whitley Council agreements on general terms and conditions for the NHS workforce. The standard working week varies from 39 hours for ancillary staff to 35 hours for radiographers and even within the same Whitley functional council, differences exist. For example, among professions allied to medicine, helpers and technical instructors are entitled to four weeks of annual leave, whereas all other grades of staff receive five weeks. Both the complexity of the Whitley system of terms and conditions of employment, and the costs of additional elements of the gross pay bill imposed by those terms and conditions are elements of the national system which local pay initiatives are designed to address. The following section will discuss some of these new practices and analyse the gender impact of the new pay systems.

12.7. LOCAL PAY INITIATIVES

The overriding strategy of the Trust management is to negotiate a local pay structure for the whole workforce that sets pay and general terms and conditions of employment. At present, this objective is far from being achieved. This is due in part to the difficulties in reorganizing patient care services between the two hospital sites, but is also a direct result of the current concern of the Department of Health to avoid aggravating major industrial disputes with the NHS professional groups. However, some of the foundations for local pay bargaining have been laid. Pilot local pay bargaining has been implemented for ancillary staff and a new trust contract has been drafted which will transform the nationally agreed Whitley Council terms and conditions of employment. Although these developments have long-term implications, one personnel manager interpreted them as short-term measures to cut costs either by reducing staff or through the abolition of some terms and conditions of employment.

The new Trust contract will reduce all employees' entitlement to sick pay. Under the national agreement, all staff receive graduated payments while on sick leave which vary according to length of service from one month's full pay and two months' half pay to a maximum of six months' full pay and six months' half pay. The new system will not make payments for the first two days of sickness absence, nor will it pay weekend enhancements during the period of absence. Also, in response to a regional study conducted by a management consultancy firm that highlighted the high costs of overtime and shift working compared with the private sector, the trust is seeking to consolidate all pay enhancements as part of the basic rate. This will enable the Trust to raise the basic rate of pay for all employees and to achieve a reduction in the overall pay bill. Although the precise form of the new pay structure is not available, the effect on total earnings for different groups of staff will depend on the prior importance of pay enhancements as a fraction of an employee's total earnings. Therefore, the main losers are likely to be part-time nursing staff and ancillary workers, whose earnings depend heavily on shift premiums and overtime. Among ancillaries there may even be some reduction in the wage differential between men and women (unless male dominated ancillary staff in portering and security secure greater basic wage rates in negotiations between trade unions and management). However, reduction in the gender pay gap will be at the cost of a general levelling down of earnings. Consequently, women's relatively low earnings position among ancillary staff compared with their position in other occupational groups is almost certain to deteriorate further, thus encouraging a wider income dispersion between groups of women employed in the Trust.

Introduction of the Trust contract is being delayed until after the current period of reorganization of patient services, as management are aware that staff are less likely to accept a new local contract in the midst of considerable threats to job security and career prospects. However, the choice of contract lies only with incumbent employees: as in all other NHS Trusts, this Trust contract applies automatically to new recruits or re-entrants into the organization, employees who have been promoted or demoted to a new grade, and staff who have changed their contractual working time.

The Trust has also introduced a pilot local pay structure for some ancillary staff. This mirrors developments in most NHS Trusts. In general, where tentative steps have been taken towards local pay bargaining these involve first the local transformation of terms and conditions for ancillary staff in response to CCT; and second, the introduction of the new grade of HCA. The potential for management success in implementing a pilot local pay structure is stronger for less skilled groups in the NHS. The Department of Health has warned against further development of local pay structures for the professional groups, and the ability of nursing staff, doctors and dentists to resist change is great because of strong bargaining power and popular support. On the other hand, the ability of less skilled staff to protect their nationally agreed terms and conditions of employment is not as great, and this fact has to some extent already been exploited by Trust managers, backed by government policies. The following discussion will elaborate upon the two common forms of pilot local pay bargaining.

Since 1983, the Department of Health has required a range of ancillary jobs in the NHS to be subject to competitive tendering by firms in the private sector in five-year periods. This was first applied to domestic cleaning, catering and laundry services, and later extended to include portering, estate services and security. Regional Health Authorities are required to award contracts to the lowest bidder, which could include on 'in-house' bid from the Trust itself. In Trusts across the region, competitive tendering may be said to have four different possible outcomes: no change in employment conditions as a result of the tendering process; the contract is won 'in-house' through a reduction in pay and conditions; the contract is won by a private contractor; or the threat of competition is exploited by the Trust management to reorganize job tasks around a model which encourages flexible deployment of labour and a smaller workforce.[7] The last of these outcomes applies to the case study Trust. Job tasks have been reorganized so that ancillary staff are now able to provide services across a number of traditional operations such as catering, cleaning and basic nursing tasks. In negotiations, management encouraged the staff representatives to accept the new contracts on the basis that they would provide better protection against future competitive tendering, clearly exploiting the backdrop of 'market-testing' as a source of employer bargaining strength. The new positions are also linked to opportunities to expand vocational qualifications through a national training system and as a result to provide a better defined job ladder. No changes in the pay structure were made; rather, the Trust met new financial targets through making a number of staff redundant.

The second form of pilot local pay bargaining commonly used throughout the NHS involves the new support grade of HCA. The Government enabled Trusts to recruit HCAs on local conditions of employment in 1989 – before Trust status was granted to hospitals – and most Trusts in the UK employ them to support the work of nurses, paramedics and clerical staff (*Health Service Report*, 1993). National terms and conditions have never applied to HCAs, although trade unions argue that they perform the work of nursing auxiliaries and should therefore be covered by Pay Review Body terms and conditions for grade A nursing staff. For many Trusts employment of HCAs emerged as an attractive strategy to meet the need for unqualified nursing staff caused by changes in the system of nursing education. Under the new Project 2000 system, student nurses spend much less time on the ward, thus leaving a considerable gap to be filled. However, this does not explain why Trusts choose to recruit HCAs rather than nursing auxiliaries. The answer may lie in the ability of Trusts to determine, often unilaterally, less costly terms and conditions of employment for HCAs. As the case study Trust has not yet recruited HCAs, information has been collected for two other Trusts in the same region of England. It is worth considering the experience of other Trusts, since the employment of HCAs is a common strategy for the NHS as a whole and has significant implications for the standards of employment conditions for women undertaking the work of nursing auxiliaries.

If patterns of recruitment for the post of HCA conform with those for nursing auxiliaries, women are likely to constitute at least 90 per cent of employment. Table 12.10 highlights the potential disadvantages this poses for women's employment in the NHS. Information is given for two Trusts representing polar forms of local pay structures for HCAs. In Trust A, the grading structure mirrors the three grades found in the national agreement for nursing auxiliaries, whereas in Trust B, HCAs are employed only at one level. The minimum basic rates of pay are comparable between national and local systems. However, entitlements to annual increments in pay under national terms and conditions have been abolished in both Trusts' systems. This reflects the unwillingness of many local Trust managers to reward seniority *per se*, unless it is supported by a clear link with improvements in performance. In Trust A, the aim is to link the attainment of national vocational qualification training levels with grade promotion. However, in Trust B increments have been abolished altogether. The ability to top up the basic wage with enhancements and overtime payments is also severely curtailed under both local pay systems. Under national terms and conditions, shift premiums constitute a considerable fraction of earnings paid to unqualified nursing staff. For women working

Table 12.10. Local pay structures for health-care assistants compared with the national agreement for nursing auxiliaries

Employment conditions	National agreement	Trust A	Trust B
Basic wage rate	Grade A: £7,325-8,960 Grade B: £8,675-9,875 Grade C: £9,875-11,700	Grade 1: £7,500 Grade 2: £9,000 Grade 3: £11,000	£7,325-7,845
Hours per week	37.5	38	37.5
Shift premiums (for continuous 24-hour, 7-day rotation)	1 night in 4 shifts: 20% 1 night in 8 shifts: 15 % Other 10%	10% of salary for all staff	None
Enhanced weekend/public holiday rates	Grades A & B: 33% for Saturday; 66% for Sunday and public holidays Grade C: 30% and 60%	None	None
Overtime rates	Time off in lieu. If not possible: 50% premium for Mon.-Sat.; 100% for Sun. Time off and 100% premium for public holidays	Time off in lieu. If not possible, payable at basic rate only	10% premium

Note: The terms and conditions of the national agreement refer to the basic pay rates recommended by the Pay Review Body for nurses and midwives and the agreements negotiated by the Whitley Council as at 1 April 1994 (IDS, 1995).
Source: Information provided by Trusts A and B.

full-time and part-time in the case study trust, for example, shift premiums constitute 10 and 16 per cent of annual earnings respectively. The information provided from Trusts A and B suggests that HCAs will not be able to count on receiving such a large amount of additional income, and this will cut their overall earnings to below those of nursing auxiliary staff employed under national terms and conditions.

It remains to be seen the extent to which these Trust contracts for HCA staff are isolated opportunistic management exercises, or pilot cases which will set a framework for future local pay bargaining for all nursing staff. In policy documents outlining the proposed HCA contract in Trust A, the management state that 'with the introduction of HCAs, the trust will signal its long-term intention to move towards a shift allowance of 10 per cent for all nursing staff'. These aims are likely to meet with considerable resistance by nurses' trade unions. Recently the Royal College of Nursing, which represents most nursing staff, abandoned its long-standing no-strike policy to allow for the possibility of industrial action.

The case study Trust has also invested in a job evaluation programme which will evaluate and rank job tasks and thus facilitate the local reorganization of occupational groups, establish new job descriptions and provide the basis for a future local pay structure for the whole workforce. Again, this is emerging as a popular strategy for many trusts in the region. Importantly, as reported at other trusts (IRS, 1992), the case study Trust acknowledges the need to provide a 'gender sensitive' ranking of jobs in order to minimize future equal pay for equal value litigation, after the experience of nursing staff's dissatisfaction with the national regrading that took place in 1988. Efforts to evaluate jobs against harmonized criteria may represent an improvement on past efforts of the fragmented system of pay determination at the national level. However, the potential for negative effects on gender pay inequality inherent in job evaluation techniques is well documented (Acker, 1989; Blum, 1991). Subjective assessment is involved in the choice of factors and the assignment of points to job factors, thus opening the door for management to exercise discretionary bias against women. Also, transformation of jobs ranked by points into jobs ranked by wage rates depends on the matching of job families with equivalent comparator jobs in the external labour market. The gender neutrality of this process is easily impaired if gender pay inequality exists in the external labour market.

In general, initiatives to develop local pay in the Trust impact on women's employment position in a number of contradictory ways. There are several reasons why the development of local pay structures may be advantageous for women employed in the NHS. First, it allows the Trust to establish a single pay spine for the whole organization enabling, for example, the harmonization of premiums for shift working and unsocial hours. Second, a more detailed investigation of job skills is planned through the use of 'gender sensitive' job evaluation techniques. Finally, the possibility of greater representation of the workforce at the local level gives rank-and-file members a greater voice in pay negotiations, as well as opening up the possibility of greater female participation in pay negotiations.

As might be expected, however, the move towards a local pay structure does not necessarily match with the aims of greater gender equality. Compared with the information available from the national system of pay bargaining, the development of local pay structures may entail a certain loss of transparency. This will reduce the ease with which pay differentials can be monitored for the health sector, and create an asymmetry of information that reduces the bargaining power of employees at the local level. Corby (1992) finds evidence of a shift towards unilateral pay determination, and in many documents outlining the benefits of local pay strategies, the delivery of power to the local management is an explicit part of the package. Also, the sensitivity of a local pay structure to the economic conditions of the local labour market increases the risk of uncoupling economically deprived areas from more prosperous areas, and thus widens pay inequality in general. Furthermore, it is not clear whether job evaluation systems protect women's pay from deteriorating conditions in the external labour market, or institutionalize and rigidify internal wage differentials.

12.8. CONCLUSIONS

The Government's reformist objectives of increasing productivity and cutting public expenditure have paved the way for greater flexibility of working, different payment systems and skill-mix strategies. The above discussion has attempted to document the impact of these changes on women's employment position in NHS Trusts, drawing on the experience of one Trust in north-west England. It appears that early initiatives in local pay bargaining are motivated primarily by cost-cutting pressures and the desire to design jobs according to the needs of the local organization. On the one hand, the analysis of new pay structures for ancillary staff and health care assistants and the introduction of a job evaluation programme highlight the fragile basis of women's relative gains in the NHS – the security of a minimum wage floor for ancillary staff employed under national terms and conditions, and the ability shown by qualified nursing staff to establish significant increases in earnings relative to non-manual women employees in the private sector. Although pilot strategies have initially aimed at less skilled groups of staff, they may represent potential blueprints for the future wholesale replacement of the national wage bargaining structure.

On the other hand, however, future comprehensive development of local pay determination is by no means inevitable. First, recent industrial relations disputes will substantially discourage further 'innovative' management employment practice. Second, in the light of the professional status and bargaining power of certain groups, the Department of Health may well recommend the maintenance of national pay arrangements, while strengthening its resolve to establish local pay for less skilled groups that have less political influence. Third, in order to prevent pay spirals and to ensure predictable levels of public sector pay expenditure, the Government may argue that national pay review bodies remain necessary for those groups for which the NHS Trust is virtually a monopsony employer, but unnecessary for those employees for whom the Trust faces competition with private sector firms which exert downward pressure on the price of labour.

Notes

1. Disaggregated data by sex for actual numbers employed in the NHS are not available. Complete information has been collected for HCHS staff in terms of wte data, which are calculated by aggregating the contractual hours worked by staff and dividing by the standard hours for a full-time employee in that grade. Data for HCHS do not include staff contracted out to the private sector. No further information about employees in the GMS exists and therefore these staff will not be referred to in the following analysis.
2. The introduction of Project 2000 was welcomed by the nursing profession as a strategy which would promote the professionalization of nursing, increasing the proportion of the trained workforce to about 70 per cent. However, the Government's cost focus which accompanies the implementation of the new training scheme aims to achieve a smaller fraction of trained nurses supported by a larger army of unqualified staff (Lloyd and Seifert, 1995).
3. Elliot and Murphy (1987) argue that the results of studies of NES data that compare public and private sector pay levels on the basis of average weekly earnings are bound to misrepresent improvements and deteriorations in relative average pay for four main reasons: the number of hours worked each week may differ over time between sectors; a change in occupational composition within each group will affect the average earnings level; the different rates of ageing of the workforce in each sector will affect average

wages; and different holiday entitlements affect the 'effective' hourly earnings for hours worked in the year. Corrected figures demonstrate that results based upon NES average weekly earnings will tend to bias public sector pay upwards. This is the result of many factors. For example, the relative increase in the proportion of workers employed in the lowest grades in private sector manual occupations between 1973–83 explains much of the relative improvement in relative pay for manual workers of both sexes in the public sector. Also, an increasing proportion of older female employees in non-manual occupations in central and local government obscured the decline in their pay relative to pay in the private sector.

4. In the 1980s, critics of the national grade structure for nurses argued that for some posts acquired skills were matched with career development, while for other posts there was little opportunity for advancement. The national-level clinical regrading in 1988 aimed to improve this situation by linking pay to skills and responsibility rather than job position. Although the nursing and midwifery functional council jointly agreed to the new grade structure, in practice the implementation of new grades for job posts was determined more by financial criteria than by job task (Seifert, 1992; Thornley and Winchester, 1994). This led to thousands of nurses claiming unfair practice through equal pay litigation.
5. New agreements which included local pay supplements were introduced in 1986 for ancillary staff, 1986 for ambulance staff, 1988 for speech therapists and 1989 for clerical staff.
6. Unfortunately, detailed information on employment composition is not available for the separate job tasks undertaken by ancillary staff.
7. In recent years the legitimacy of transferring employees onto worse terms and conditions has been thrown into dispute by application of the Transfer of Understakings (Protection of Employment) Regulations, 1981. Although for several years contractors were uncertain as to its applicability, a Court of Appeal decision in 1994 appears to provide confirmation that the TUPE Regulations will normally apply, thus protecting employees from dismissals or reduced wage rates when transferred from one contracted to another (IRLR 1994). Although this provides a foundation of protection, it is still not clear whether employees are protected in successive rounds of tendering.

Acknowledgements

The author would like to thank Paul Sprung – a personnel manager at the case study Trust – for his cooperation and Jill Rubery for comments on an earlier draft of this chapter.

References

J. Acker *Doing comparable work: Gender, class and pay equity.* (Philadelphia: Temple University Press 1989).

S. Bach and D. Winchester 'Opting out of pay devolution? The prospects for local pay bargaining in UK public services', in *British Journal of Industrial Relations*, Vol. 32 (1994), pp. 263-282

L. M. Blum *Between feminism and labour: The significance of the comparable worth movement* (Berkeley: University of California Press 1991)

W. Brown and R. Rowthorn *A public services pay policy*. Fabian Tract 542 (London: Fabian Society 1990)

H. A. Clegg, *Standing Commission on Pay Comparability: Report No. 9, General Report* London: HMSO 1980.

S. Corby, 'Industrial relations developments in NHS trusts', in *Employee Relations*, No. 14 (1992) pp. 133–44.

Department of Health, *Working for patients* (London: Her Majesty's Stationery Office 1989).

Department of Health NHS Executive, *NHS workforce in England: 1982–1992* (London: Government Statistical Service 1993).

R. F. Elliott, and P. D. Murphy, 'The relative pay of public and private sector employees, 1970–1984', in *Cambridge Journal Economics*, Vol. 11, No. 2 (1987) pp. 107–32.

D. Fillingham, 'When bargaining is a life or death issue', in *Personnel Management*, March 1991.

F. Glasscot, and N. Bowden, 'The development of pay flexibility in the English National Health Service', in D. Marsden (ed.): *Pay flexibility in the public sector*, Public Management Studies (Paris: Organization for Economic Cooperation and Development 1993).

Health Service Report. No. 1. (London: Industrial Relations Services 1993).

Incomes Data Services (IDS) *Report 677* (London: IDS 1994).

—— *Pay in the public services: Review of 1994, Prospects for 1995* (London: IDS 1995).

Industrial Relations Law Report (IRLR) Vol. 22, No. 11, November (London: IRLR 1993).

—— Vol. 23, No. 7, July (London: IRLR 1994)

Industrial Relations Services (IRS) 'Single-table bargaining and job evaluation at Manchester hospitals trust', in *IRS Employment Trends* (London 1992), No. 518.

IRS Employment Trends No. 537, (London 1993).

C. Lloyd, and R. Seifert, 'Restructuring in the NHS: The impact of the 1990 reforms on the management of labour', in *Work, Employment and Society*, Vol. 9, No. 2 (1995) pp. 359–78.

J. Rubery, *Changing patterns of work and working-time: Towards the integration or the segmentation of the labour market in the UK*, Report for the European Commission's Network of Experts on the Situation of Women in the Labour Market (Manchester: University of Manchester Institute of Science and Technology 1994).

R. Seifert, *Industrial relations in the NHS* (London: Chapman and Hall 1992).

C. Thornley, and D. Winchester, 'The remuneration of nursing personnel in the UK', in D. Marsden (ed.): *The remuneration of nursing personnel: An international perspective* (Geneva: ILO 1994).

Appendix

Table A.1. Average monthly gross earnings, full-time manual workers in West Germany (DM)

Industry	Leistungs gruppe[1]	Men		Women		Women/Men (%)	
		1980	1991	1980	1991	1980	1991
Chemical industry	1	2853	4538	2282	3668	80.0	80.8
	2	2602	4070	2031	3200	78.0	78.6
	3	2204	3421	1797	2879	81.5	84.2
	Total	2706	4265	1944	3061	71.8	71.8
Production/processing of metals	1	2957	4300	2152	3330	72.8	77.4
	2	2537	3698	1905	3213	75.1	86.9
	3	2226	3499	1806	2832	81.1	80.9
	Total	2827	4148	1879	3057	66.5	73.7
Mechanical engineering	1	2784	4062	2204	3260	79.2	80.3
	2	2420	3512	1944	2931	80.3	83.5
	3	2200	3286	1853	2802	84.3	85.2
	Total	2650	3906	1901	2888	71.7	73.9
Motor vehicles	1	2853	4521	2217	3784	77.7	83.7
	2	2650	4126	2304	3507	86.9	85.0
	3	2382	3702	2039	3139	85.6	84.8
	Total	2745	4308	2208	3395	80.4	78.8

Table A.1. (continued)

Industry	Leistungs gruppe[1]	Men		Women		Women/Men (%)	
		1980	1991	1980	1991	1980	1991
Electrical engineering	1	2611	3953	2035	3278	77.9	82.9
	2	2269	3438	1849	2832	81.5	82.4
	3	2165	3312	1836	2877	84.8	85.4
	Total	2464	3741	1845	2845	74.9	76.0
Precision instruments engineering	1	2520	3776	2078	3248	82.5	86.0
	2	2191	3330	1819	2823	83.0	84.8
	3	2031	3183	1810	2845	89.1	89.4
	Total	2390	3620	2148	2858	89.9	78.9
Metal products	1	2637	3927	2026	3196	76.8	81.4
	2	2382	3538	1806	2832	75.8	80.0
	3	2156	3235	1762	2715	81.7	83.9
	Total	2451	3663	1780	2758	72.6	75.3
Office equipment	1	2620	3966	2810	4243	107.3	107.0
	2	2269	3447	1961	2901	86.5	84.2
	3	2048	3118	1845	2888	90.1	92.6
	Total	2442	3698	1923	3057	78.7	82.7
Textile industry	1	2369	3559	1858	2810	78.4	79.0
	2	2152	3248	1728	2607	80.3	80.3
	3	1979	2966	1589	2481	80.3	83.6
	Total	2230	3351	1702	2594	76.3	77.4

Table A.1. (continued)

Industry	Leistungs gruppe[1]	Men		Women		Women/Men (%)	
		1980	1991	1980	1991	1980	1991
Clothing industry	1	2429	3321	1745	2563	71.8	77.2
	2	2200	3027	1632	2382	74.2	78.7
	3	2065	2741	1468	2217	71.1	80.9
	Total	2299	3118	1624	2390	70.6	76.7
Food processing	1	2780	4109	1910	3144	68.7	76.5
	2	2494	3624	1788	2802	71.7	77.3
	3	2252	3209	1615	2394	71.7	74.6
	Total	2607	3815	1658	2516	63.6	65.9
Construction industry (including crafts)	1	2793	4066	–			
	2	2490	3715	(1762)			
	3	2204	3317	1793			
	Total	2637	3893	1793			
Manufacturing industry (excluding construction industry)	1	2754	4152	1940	3109	70.4	74.9
	2	2468	3719	1814	2797	73.5	75.2
	3	2213	3369	1749	2706	79.1	80.3
	Total	2594	3923	1788	2776	68.9	70.8

[1] 'Leistungsgruppen' are categories used in German official statistics which summarize several wage groups of collective agreements.

Source: Statistisches Bundesamt, Fachserie 16, Reihe 2.1 and 2.2. © F. Maier and S. Quack 1993

Table A.2. Average monthly gross earnings, full-time non-manual workers in West Germany (DM)

Industry	Leistungs gruppe[1]	Men		Women		Women/Men (%)	
		1980	1991	1980	1991	1980	1991
Chemical industry	II	4591	7479	3883	6357	84.6	85.0
	III	3445	5397	2917	4646	84.7	86.1
	IV	2720	4177	2173	3470	79.9	83.1
	V	2181	3698	1811	2797	83.0	80.6
	Total	3752	6046	2689	4412	71.7	73.0
Production/processing of metals	II	4170	6596	3422	5229	82.1	79.3
	III	3327	5123	2587	4001	77.8	78.1
	IV	2534	3805	2027	3084	80.0	81.1
	V	1914	3063	1677	2539	87.6	82.9
	Total	3687	5882	2409	3785	65.3	64.3
Mechanical engineering	II	4202	6677	3550	5525	84.5	82.7
	III	3270	5128	2654	4108	81.2	80.1
	IV	2502	3958	2065	3198	82.5	80.8
	V	2130	3102	1690	2666	79.3	85.9
	Total	3627	5774	2362	3748	65.1	64.9
Motor vehicles	II	4778	7396	4022	6309	84.2	85.3
	III	3578	5479	2969	4552	83.0	83.1
	IV	2625	4142	2276	3510	86.7	84.7
	V	2175	3166	1768	2946	81.3	93.1
	Total	4060	6404	2661	4312	65.5	67.3

Table A.2. (continued)

Industry	Leistungs gruppe[1]	Men		Women		Women/Men (%)	
		1980	1991	1980	1991	1980	1991
Electrical engineering	II	4305	6889	3693	5845	85.8	84.8
	III	3207	5038	2708	4253	84.4	84.4
	IV	2494	3841	2113	3262	84.7	84.9
	V	2288	3038	1709	2711	74.7	89.2
	Total	3725	5995	2483	4039	66.7	67.4
Precision instruments engineering	II	4224	6541	3530	5523	83.6	84.4
	III	3194	5060	2641	4247	82.7	83.9
	IV	2586	3969	2092	3284	80.9	82.7
	V	2257	3423	1683	2705	74.6	79.0
	Total	3448	5477	2330	3791	67.6	69.2
Metal products	II	4061	6398	3412	5344	84.0	83.5
	III	3231	4959	2577	3941	79.8	79.5
	IV	2564	3891	2015	3123	78.6	80.3
	V	2109	3213	1692	2619	80.2	81.5
	Total	3449	5398	2271	3570	65.8	66.1
Office equipment	II	4861	7487	4224	6537	86.9	87.3
	III	3454	5564	2887	4582	83.6	82.4
	IV	3017	4079	2133	3413	70.7	83.7
	V	1638	2987	1655	2733	101.0	91.5
	Total	4177	6603	2669	4655	63.9	70.5

Table A.2. (continued)

Industry	Leistungs gruppe[1]	Men		Women		Women/Men (%)	
		1980	1991	1980	1991	1980	1991
Textile industry	II	3974	6203	3312	5283	83.3	85.2
	III	3027	4630	2477	3861	81.8	83.4
	IV	2443	3823	1914	3071	78.3	80.3
	V	2022	3042	1656	2744	81.9	90.2
	Total	3172	4903	2170	3454	68.4	70.4
Clothing industry	II	3891	5953	3200	5096	82.2	85.6
	III	2932	4292	2396	3609	81.7	84.1
	IV	2334	3378	1945	2930	83.3	86.7
	V	2052	2763	1605	2553	78.2	92.4
	Total	3143	4756	2191	3429	69.7	72.1
Food processing	II	4130	6536	3399	5476	82.3	83.8
	III	3126	4772	2535	3939	81.1	82.5
	IV	2604	3822	2005	3070	77.0	80.3
	V	2146	3104	1701	2760	79.3	88.9
	Total	3312	5187	2286	3650	69.0	70.4
Construction industry (including crafts)	II	4359	6917	3271	5094	75.0	73.6
	III	3569	5288	2625	3935	73.6	74.4
	IV	2593	3901	1914	2875	73.8	73.7
	V	1917	3373	1442	2276	75.2	67.5
	Total	3799	5807	2350	3563	61.9	61.4

Table A.2. (continued)

Industry	Leistungs gruppe[1]	Men		Women		Women/Men (%)	
		1980	1991	1980	1991	1980	1991
Manufacturing industry (excluding construction industry)	II	4300	6860	3570	5732	83.0	83.6
	III	3284	5116	2688	4208	81.9	82.3
	IV	2570	3930	2064	3219	80.3	81.9
	V	2133	3153	1697	2694	79.6	85.4
	Total	3634	5805	2413	3899	66.4	67.2
Retail trade	II	3568	5278	2909	4386	81.5	83.1
	III	2758	4066	2059	3153	74.7	77.5
	IV	2078	3151	1600	2541	77.0	80.6
	IV	2078	3151	1600	2541	77.0	80.6
	V	1577	2485	1379	2262	87.4	91.0
	Total	2760	3974	1787	2765	64.7	69.6
Banking[2]	II	3872	6041	3353	5316	86.6	88.0
	III	2749	4129	3529	3809	128.4	92.2
	IV	2247	3258	2100	3091	93.5	94.9
	V	2250	3239	1877	2852	83.4	88.1
	Total	3047	4825	2360	3705	77.5	76.8

[1] 'Leistungsgruppen' are categories used in German official statistics which summarize several wage groups of collective agreements. [2] Including related financial services

Source: Statistisches Bundesamt, Fachserie 16, Reihe 2.1 and 2.2. © F. Maier and S. Quack 1993.

Table A.3. Total employment by sector in Italy, 1980–90 (number of job positions in 000)[1]

	1980	1990	% change
All sectors	16 324.3	17 315.3	5.72
Communications	253.9	310.1	18.12
Banking and insurance	347.3	420.3	17.37
Health services			
Private	132.9	167.9	20.85
Public	598.1	669.0	10.60

[1]Job positions as defined by ISTAT, national accounting data
Sources: ISTAT, *Redditi e Occupazione,* 1992; Osservatorio del Pubblico Impiego, *Relazione 1992.*

Table A.4. Gross annual earnings per standard labour unit in Italy, 1980–90[1]

	1980		1990	
	(000 lire)	Index	(000 lire)	Index
All sectors	8 741	100	26 336	100
Communications	11 754	134	29 864	113
Banking and insurance	17 224	197	50 421	191
Public administration (including health service)	9 926	114	32 980	125
Health services				
Private	9 055	104	27 953	106
Public[2]	10 173	116	35 507	135

[1]Labour units as defined by ISTAT, national accounting data. [2]The 1990 figure is our estimate
Sources: ISTAT, *Redditi e Occupazione*, 1992; Osservatorio del Pubblico Impiego, *Relazione* 1992.

Index